Antje Majewski
My Very Gestures

Sternberg Press

**SALZBURGER
KUNSTVEREIN**

Table of Contents

"In song and in dance I express myself as a member of a higher community. I have forgotten how to walk and speak. I am on the way toward flying into the air... dancing. My very gestures express enchantment. I feel myself a god. Supernatural sounds emanate from me. I walk about enchanted, in ecstasy, like the gods I saw walking in my dreams. I am no longer an artist, I have become a work of art."

Frankie goes to Hollywood, *Welcome to the Pleasuredome (Real Altered)*, 1984

"Die Mannigfaltigkeiten, die sich mannigfaltig drehen in den Mannigfaltigkeiten des einen Augenblicks, in dem wir leben. Und noch immer ist der Augenblick nicht zuende, sieh nur!

Fern, fern geht die Weltgeschichte vor sich, die Weltgeschichte Deiner Seele."

Franz Kafka, *Unveröffentlichte Manuskripte*, 1922-24 (II, 21)

L'INVITATION AU VOYAGE

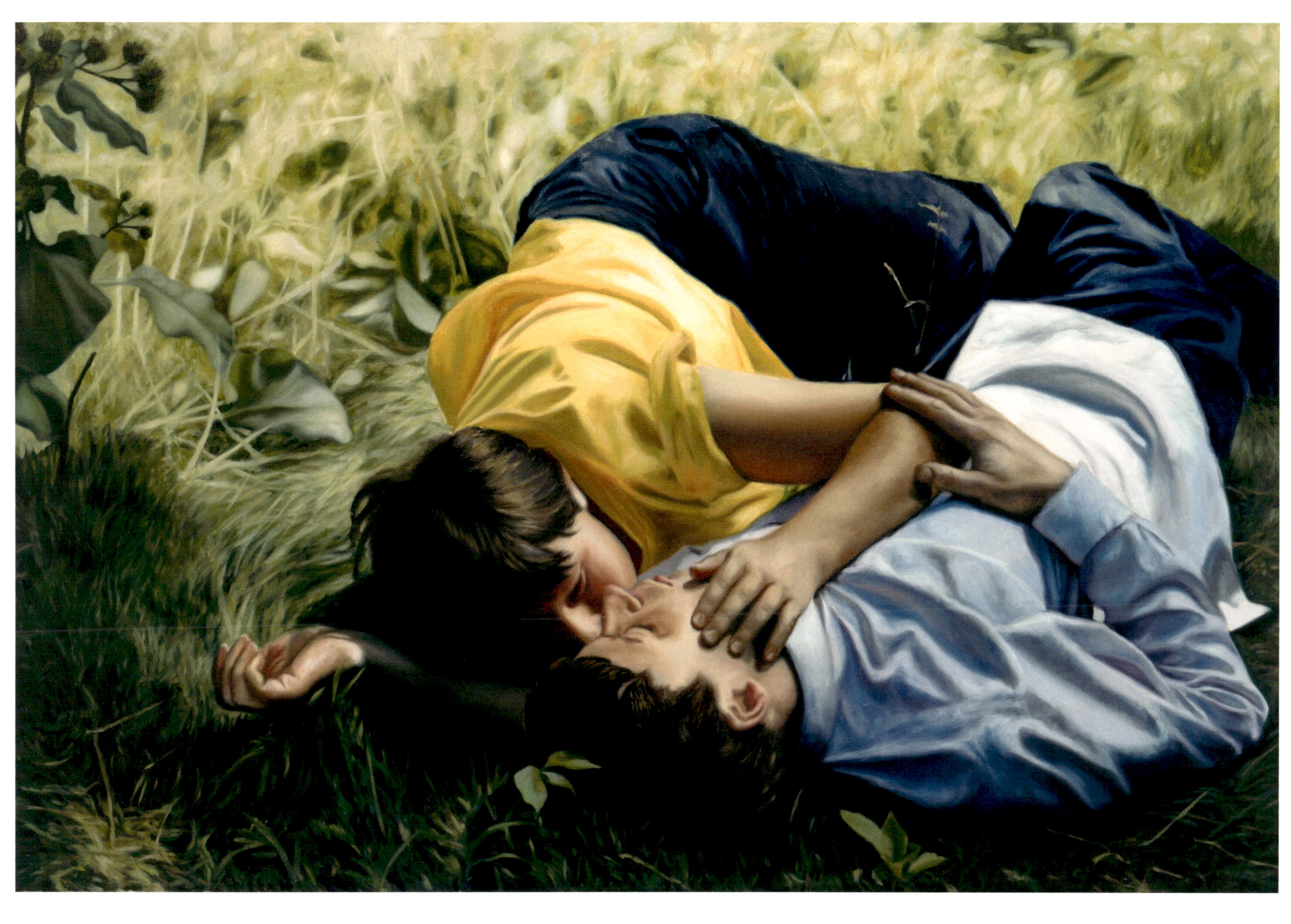

Ingo und Antje
Oil and tempera on canvas
110 x 140 cm, 1999

Liebling
Oil and tempera on canvas
160 x 160 cm, 2000

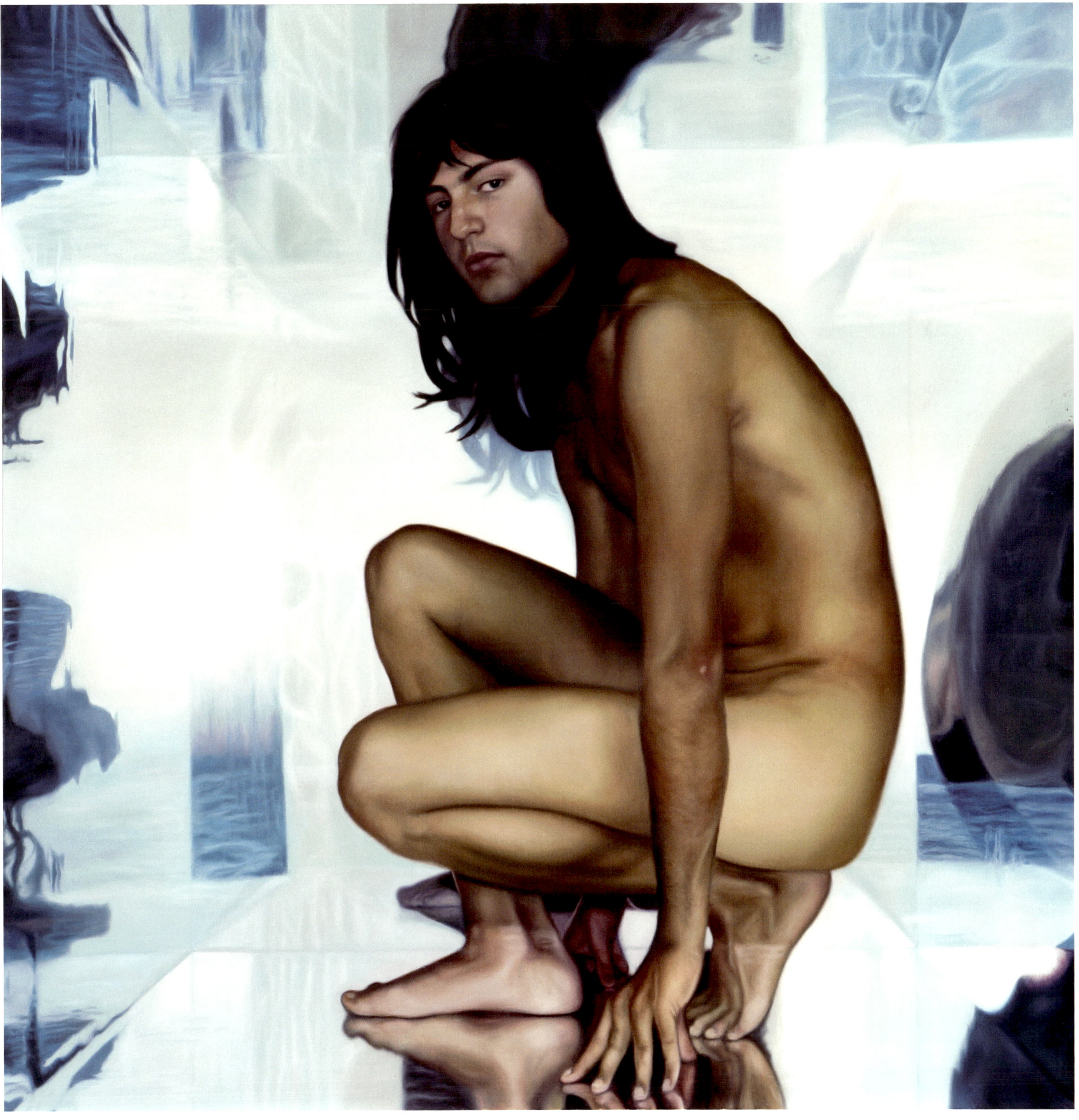

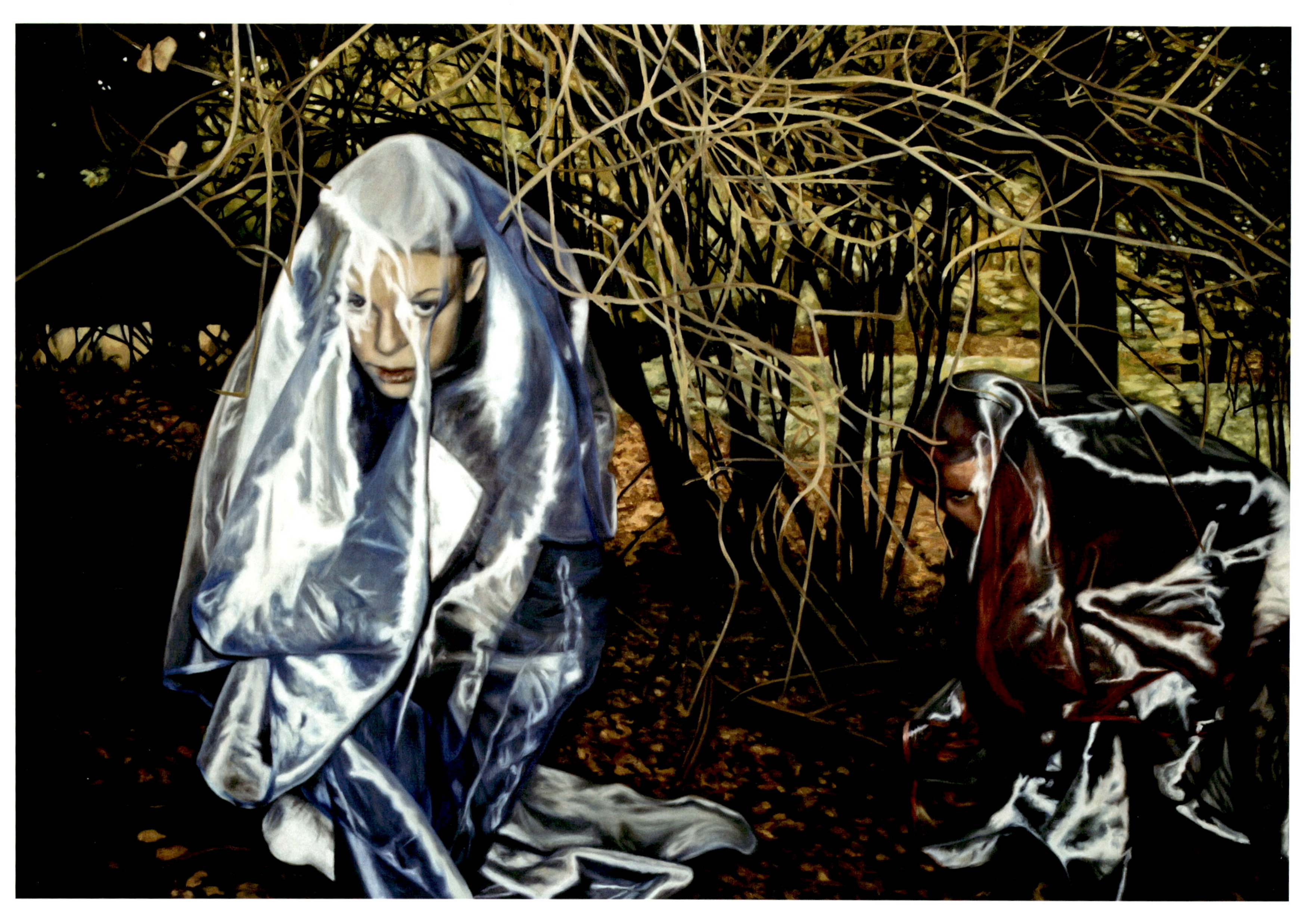

Geister
Oil and tempera on canvas
183 x 274 cm, 2001

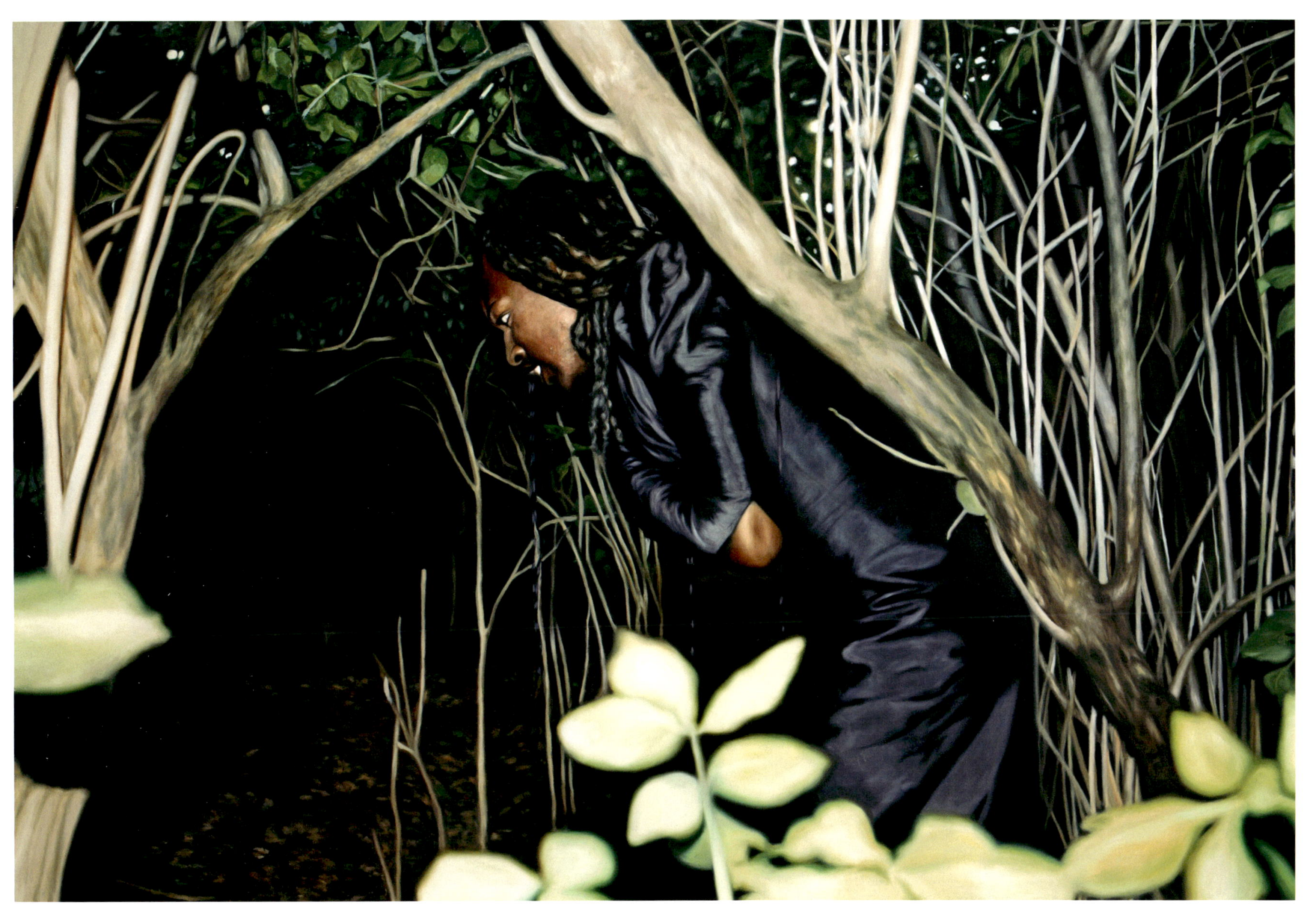

Schreck
Oil and tempera on canvas
183 x 274 cm, 2000

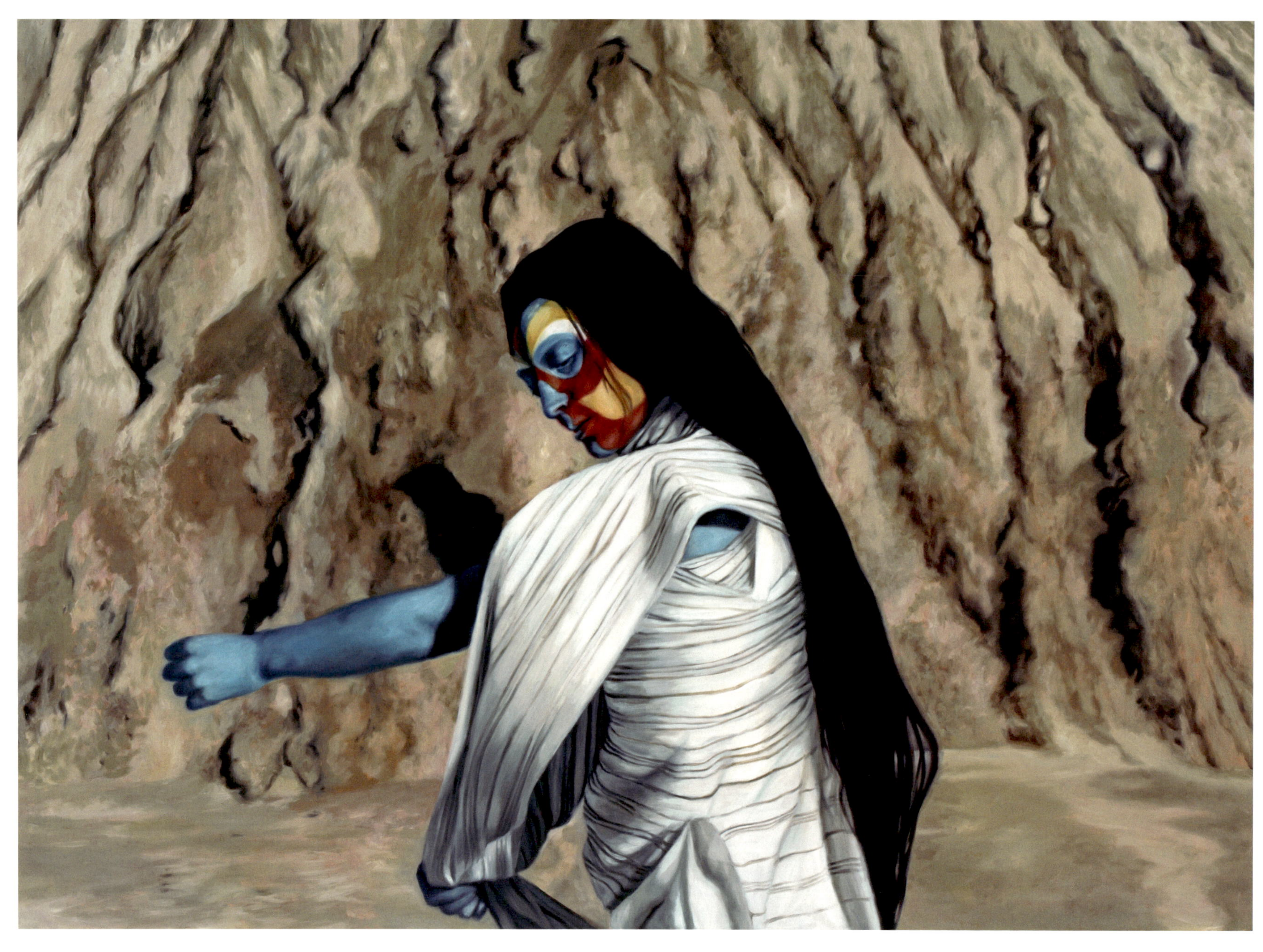

Vorbereitung
Oil and tempera on canvas
152 x 214 cm, 2001

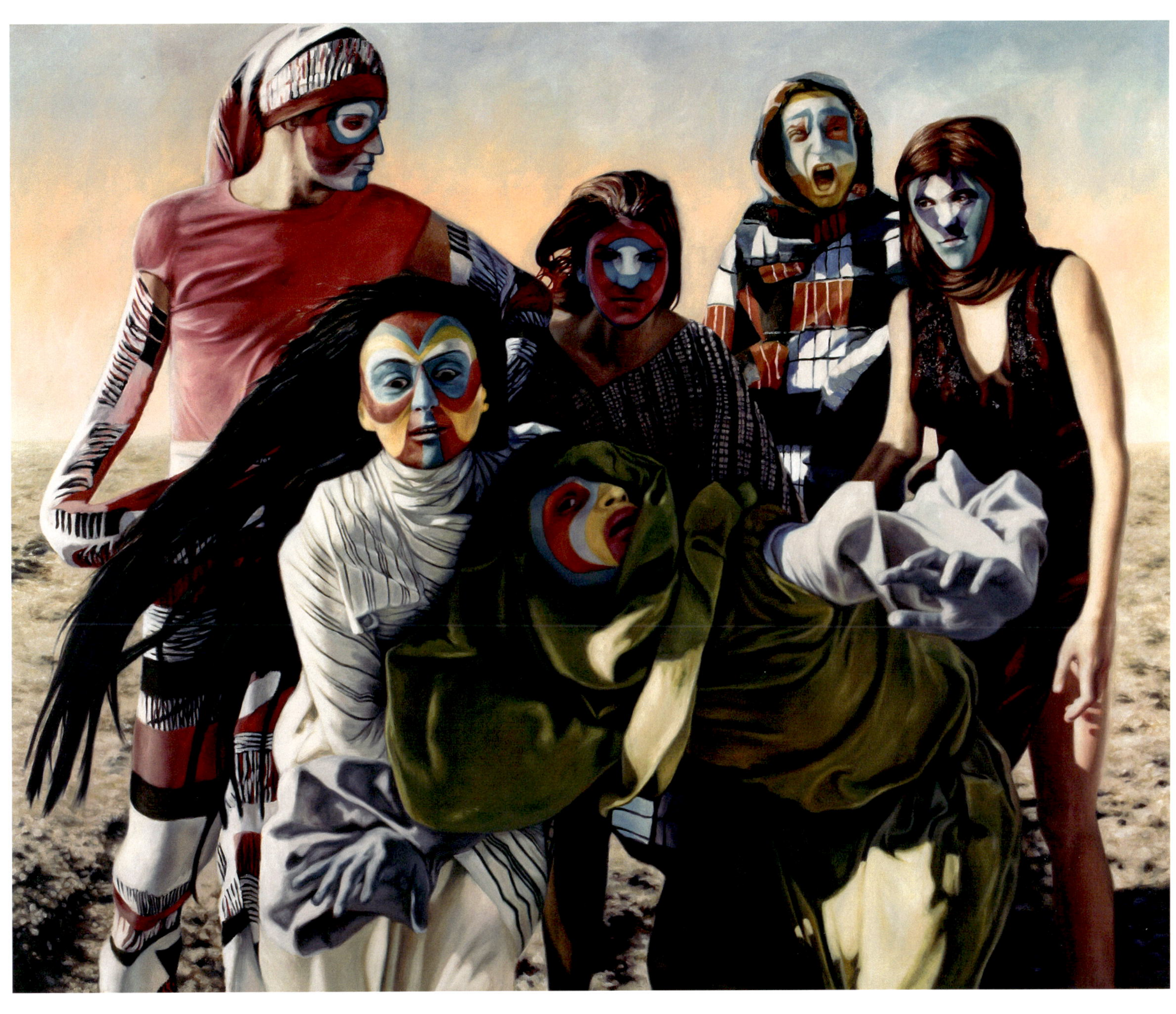

Masken
Oil and tempera on canvas
259 x 320 cm, 2001

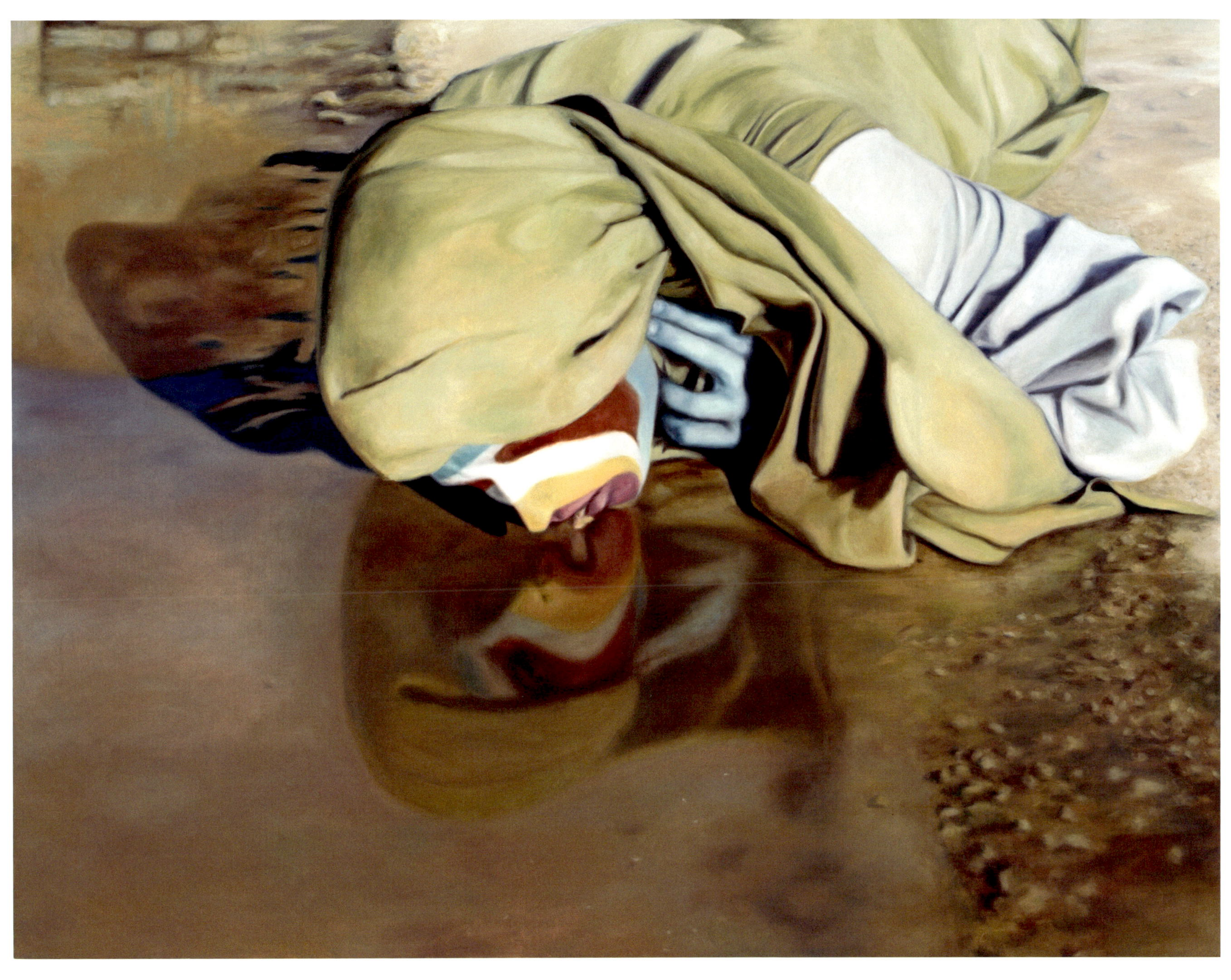

Im Schlamm
Oil and tempera on canvas
122 x 163 cm, 2000

L.A.S.T., L.E.A.K

Sebastian Cichocki

The time is the 1940s. The place is Glasgow. The house of Allan H. Duncan, an enthusiast of things paranormal, renowned in the inner circle as a sophisticated ectoplasm hunter. He not only enjoys the reputation of being an outstanding expert on the ethereal substance, the thrilling *materia prima* of the spirit world, but is also famous as a talented medium, an intermediary in ectoplasm's visits to the mundane world. On every last Friday of the month, Mr. Duncan's living room fills with guests, a carefully selected group of the initiated, craving for contact with the Unknown.

The narrow and winding staircase in an anonymous stone building leads to a massive door in the attic, equipped with iron bolts and numerous locks. On the door there is a silver plaque with an engraved inscription: *Les Magiciens de la Terre*. The door opens directly into the living room, the only space in the apartment guests have access to. Stored in the other rooms, protected from inquisitive glances, is the host's collection of *things*.

Allan H. Duncan loves objects. It is a love as greedy as it is possessive and disciplined. It takes a lot of time and deliberation for Mr. Duncan to decide which object and in what circumstances to bring to light and expose to strangers' eyes. He is capricious and perverse in these decisions. His choices are impossible to predict.

The young woman standing besides Mr. Duncan and welcoming the guests is Stanisława P. She comes from Eastern Europe, is shy, speaks little, blushes and cries often, and never reveals her full name. She has been Mr. Duncan's assistant for three years. She always carries with herself a notebook, in which she writes down interesting aphorisms, puns, grammatical exceptions, and proverbs. Mr. Duncan says the girl has an unusual gift, and the sentences she writes down in her notebook are not from this world. He calls them "whispers from the future."

Before each séance, objects are laid out in the living room: natural curiosities, works of art, precious tableware, medical prostheses, or specimens of various substances. The objects are hung directly on the walls or displayed on special glass shelves or in cabinets. Coming chiefly from the host's vast collection, as well as being leased from his collector friends, the objects are constantly rotated. It is hard to say whether the compositions are to help create a proper atmosphere for the "hunt" for ectoplasm, or are supposed to testify to Mr. Duncan's special capabilities. He himself sometimes speaks of "intuitions," never revealing why this or that object has been put on display in the living room. Most of the objects are accompanied by small caption plaques, containing a laconic description, date of acquisition, and the owner's name.

It is the same this time, though relatively few have been displayed.

A flower vase with a bunch of poppies on a glass shelf on the wall.

A tray with some semi-liquid fat on the windowsill, exuding an unpleasant smell.

A glass of water, hung high, the text on the small piece of paper accompanying it is illegible.

An hourglass filled with Peruvian sand, standing on top of the bookcase.

A small box with a lid, with the inscription "Duncan, A. H., Mr., The Society for Psychic Research, 1939," standing on the floor under the coat tree. The lid is partly open, a piece of white cloth sticks out.

And finally a painting. Placed in the middle of the room, right in front of the entrance door. Quite large, the base is over five feet long. It is not wrapped, but has been propped tightly against the wall with its back facing the viewer, so it is impossible to see what it represents.

It is nine o'clock in the evening. A cool, early spring evening. The invited guests enter one by one, precisely on time. The group is disciplined; the greetings are limited to perfunctory nods. They seat themselves on crude wooden chairs arranged around a table standing in the middle of the room.

The séance begins without any preliminaries. Mr. Duncan stretches widely, cranes his neck, and cracks his knuckles loudly. Stanisława P. pulls out her notebook, which she always carries in the ample pockets of her apron. She browses through her notes for a moment, then comes up to a blackboard hanging on the wall and writes with a piece of chalk: BOURGEOIS ART FREELY.

Mr. Duncan closes his eyes, lifts his leg in the air, and freezes. His body, immobilized in the grotesque pose, soon begins to shake dangerously. His face reddens. Finally, he leans over the table, chokes, and bangs his forehead hard on the table several times. His effort-reddened face now turns blue, and his stiff neck bends unnaturally to the left. A few moments later, his mouth opens, revealing the end of something that looks like a thick hemp rope. The thing shakes slightly, sticking out by several inches. Unmoved, Mr. Duncan takes the rope between his thumb and index finger, wraps it around his wrist and pulls hard. After several pulls the object reveals itself fully—a saliva-covered, sticky, moving oblong amoeba. The guests are delighted. Ectoplasm! Applause. Mr. Duncan deftly catches the slimy thing with silver tongs and places in a sugar bowl on the table.

A short break, during which the guests chat and examine the objects displayed in the room, casting glances from time to time at the supernatural spit resting in the bowl. The atmosphere is solemn.

The second part of the session is unexpectedly brief.

The girl opens her notebook to a randomly chosen page and quickly writes on the blackboard: RADICALLY, DIALECTICALLY.

Before the guests have seated themselves, Mr. Duncan opens his mouth wide, pushes his right hand down his throat, and, with a sweeping gesture, pulls out a bundle of crumpled cloth. The bundle moves and bends, letting out soft squeals. Smiling lightly, Mr. Duncan hands it over to his assistant. She unwraps the cloth and presents the find to the audience.

Inside the bundle is a squeaking baby rat. The creature looks around, if this is how the nervous movements of a tiny head with two black spots still covered with skin can be interpreted, then jumps down on the floor and, to the viewers' surprise, darts under the kitchen cupboard. Applause. The trick prompts laughter and cries of delight. Amid the commotion, no one notices a slimy streak left by the suckling. From the table to the cupboard runs a line of slightly phosphorescent liquid.

Mr. Duncan puts his finger to his mouth to silence the audience. He takes the crumpled piece of cloth from his assistant, straightens it out on the table, rubs it with the edge of his hand, and strikes a match to see better. With a triumphant grunt, he points to a blurry, worn inscription embroidered with red thread on the cloth. He clears his throat and reads out aloud, "Disturbed places. Unstable places. Windows disturbed by what happens behind them. Doors disturbed by those who open them. Corridors disturbed by those who walk along them."

At this point, someone in the back row bursts out laughing hysterically, faints, and collapses on the floor. It turns out that the unfortunate is Mr. Sazonov, a Russian art collector, the owner of the painting propped against the wall. The man lies on the floor for the next hour, undisturbed by anyone. When he will get up on his feet again, rested, his head full of exotic visions, everyone will have already left.

The third part of the session takes a violent course, though it inevitably leads toward a disappointment. Stanisława P. carefully rubs out the previous inscriptions, looks into her notebook, muses, and sucks on a piece of chalk before finally calligraphing the following words on the board: DESTRUCTION, EXISTENCE, FRAGMENT.

Mr. Duncan's mouth shakes. He sits in an unnatural pose, his torso pressed against the edge of the table, his arms stretched out wide, as if he was preparing to fly. He mumbles something under his breath. Before long, a sticky substance, a slightly luminous semi-saliva starts emerging from his mouth. As it trickles down his chin, his body is shaken by convulsions. Mr. Duncan cries out, waggles his legs, and finally collapses on the floor with a loud thud. He immediately gets up again, brushes himself down and moves closer to the table. Holding his right hand by his mouth, he leans over the sugar bowl. With a disgusted expression on his face, grimacing, he spits out a small sticky ball into the sugar. The ball rolls up the sugary slope and out of the bowl, leaving a slimy, snail-like trail with crystals of sugar on the tabletop. After spiraling chaotically for a dozen or so seconds, it clings to a water-filled plate standing on the table. It is only at this point that the guests notice that the water in the dish has a funny, salmon-pink hue and that letters are visible on the bottom: L.A.S.T., L.E.A.K.

Silence hangs in the air. For some time, nothing worth mentioning happens. A small bit of spit rests on the table, a crumpled piece of paper covered with sticky human saliva. Mr. Duncan massages his throat, grabs a glass of water, empties it, and rinses out his mouth, gurgling loudly. He spits out the last fragments of wet paper on the floor. He grabs the paper ball delicately and starts unfolding it. A moment later, it becomes clear for everyone that there is no message inside. The piece of paper is completely empty. Stanisława P. presses her notebook to her chest, letting out a long, drawn-out piercing shriek. This is a sign that the séance is over.

Tea is served. The fragments of the previously collected ectoplasm lying at the bottom of a large cut-glass bowl pulsate slightly. The guests watch those peculiar remnants with attention, in silence—comments would be inappropriate—nibbling sweet biscuits. Ashtrays are brought in. The room fills with cigarette smoke and shuffling noises. The pulsations of the fleshy matter are weaker and weaker.

When the guests are getting ready to leave, Mr. Duncan points to the painting propped against the wall, which throughout the session stood with its front facing the wall. He turns it around carefully, then kneels down and delicately, feeling with his fingertips, examines its surface. The picture is large, colorful, illusive. From the upper right corner leans out a figure filling over a quarter of the canvas surface. The figure, it is hard to say whether it is a man or a woman, lies on the ground, its face touching a muddy puddle of water, which fills much of the bottom part of the painting. The figure is clad in cloth from under which only the face and one hand are visible, both of an uncanny bluish skin color. The face is covered with stripes of color—red, white, and yellow. The lips remain pink. The figure laps up the muddy water, while its blurry countenance is reflected in the surface of the puddle. From the mouth sticks out a tongue that, upon a closer examination, very much resembles a fragment of the substance that only fifteen minutes earlier emerged from inside Mr. Duncan. The coincidence does not however make the expected impression on the viewers. The painting is covered with a blanket. The guests leave in silence.

The new entry in Stanisława P.'s notebook reads: THE HISTORY STILL TO BE MADE SHOWS ITSELF.

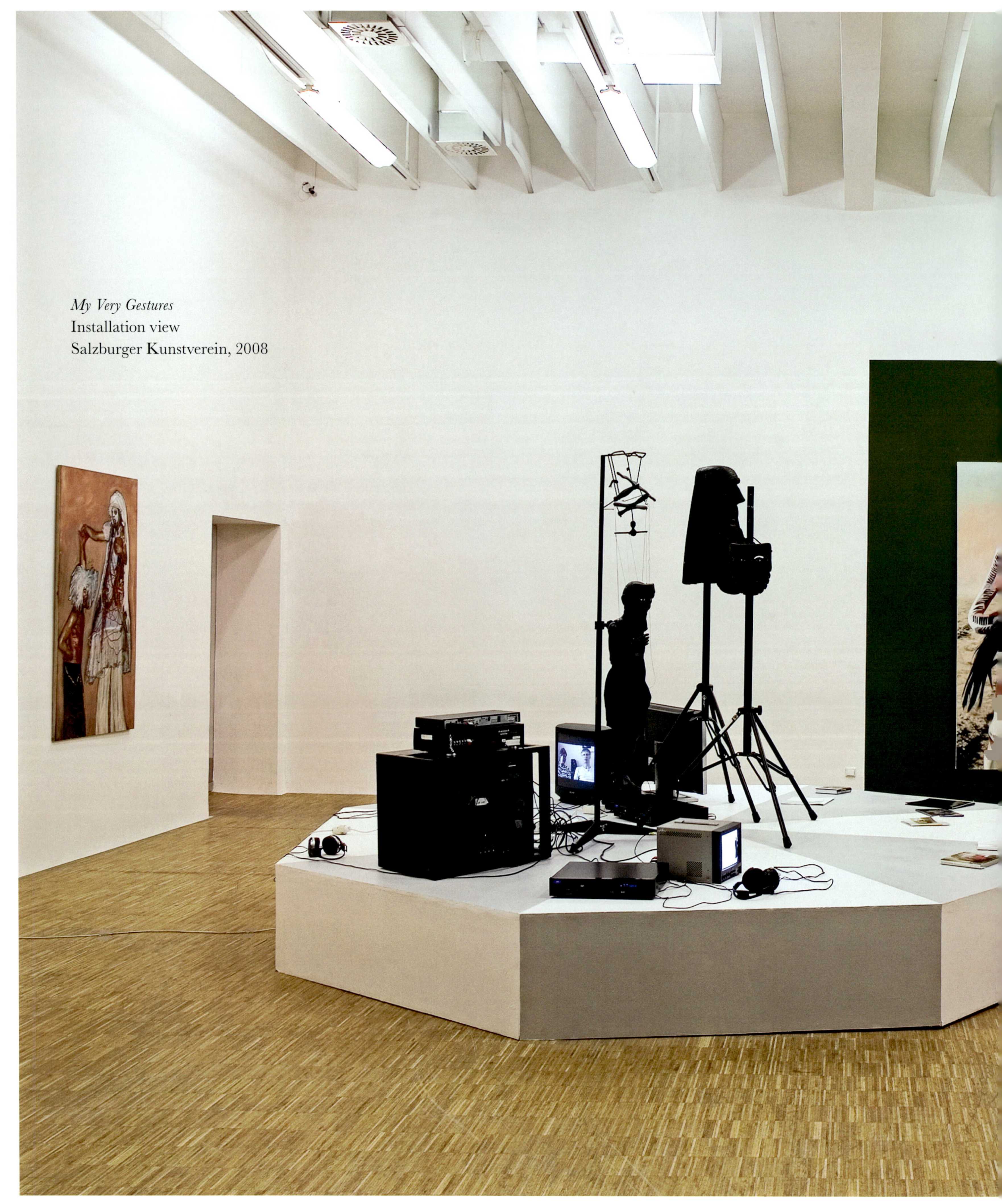

My Very Gestures
Installation view
Salzburger Kunstverein, 2008

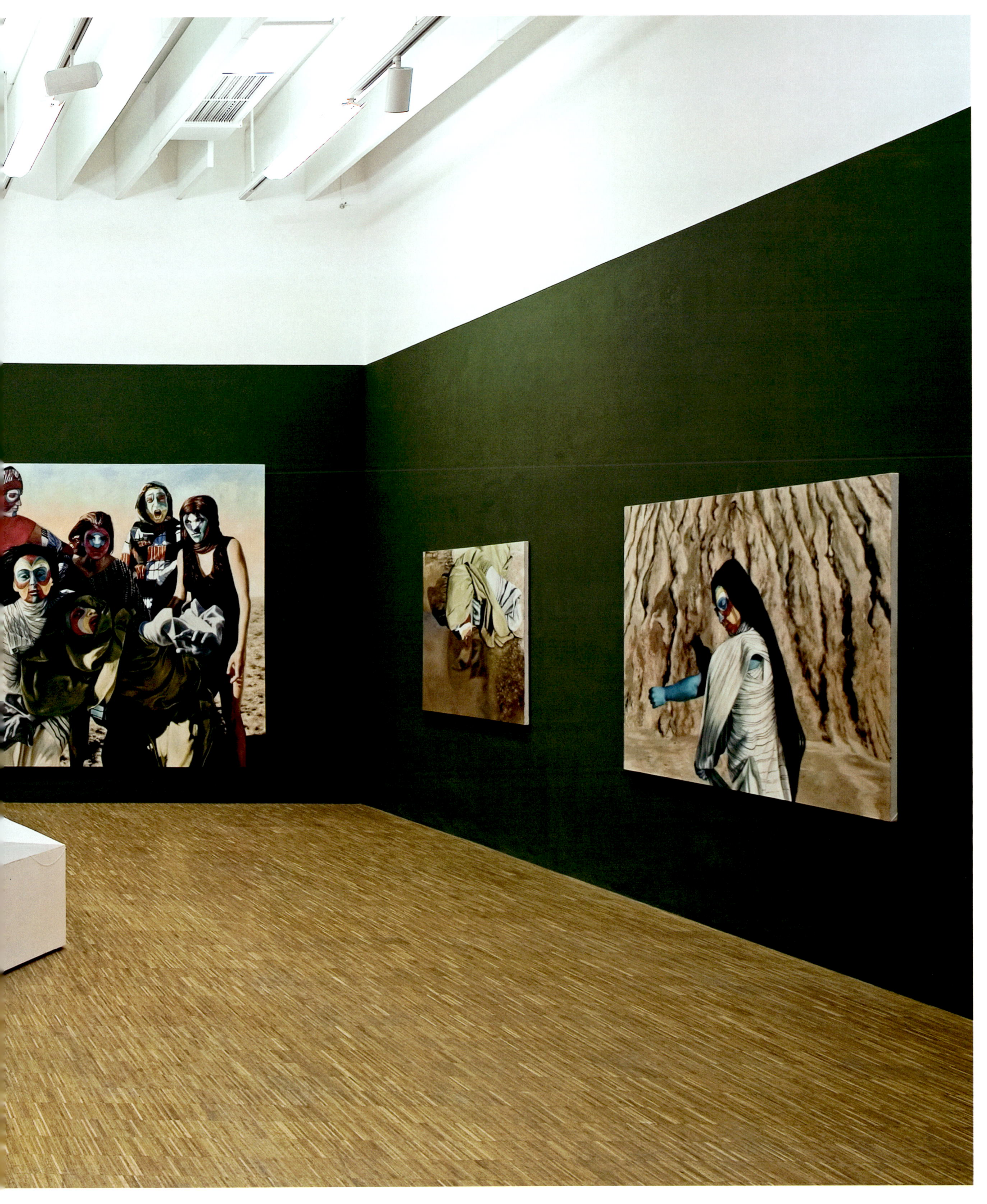

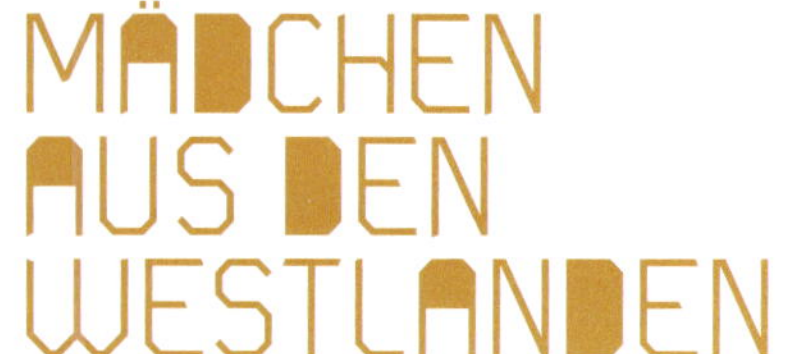

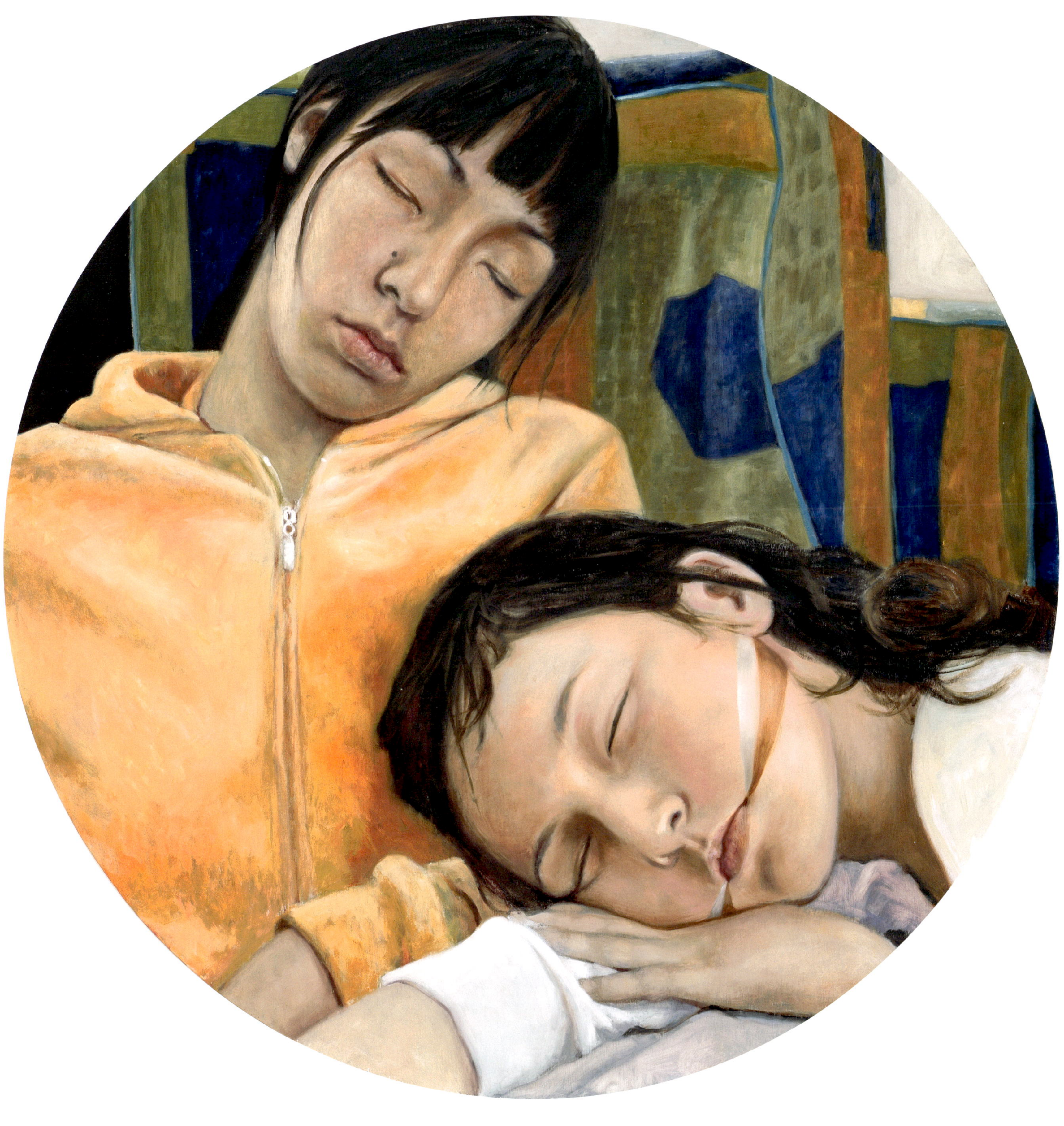

Mädchen aus den Westlanden
Oil on wood, 100 cm in diameter, 2005

GOODS

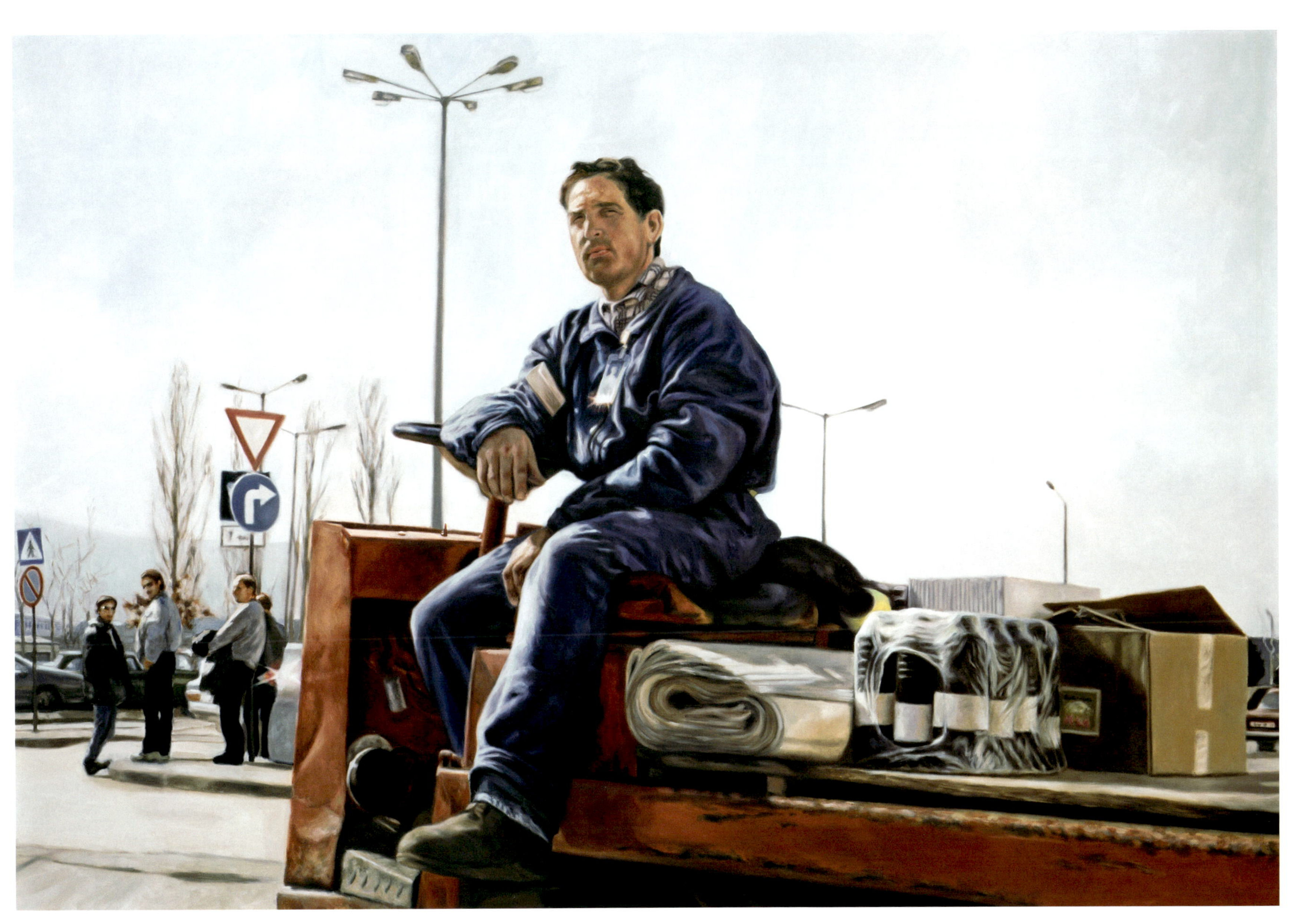

Goods 1: Flughafen Sofia
Oil and tempera on canvas
184 x 274 cm, 2002

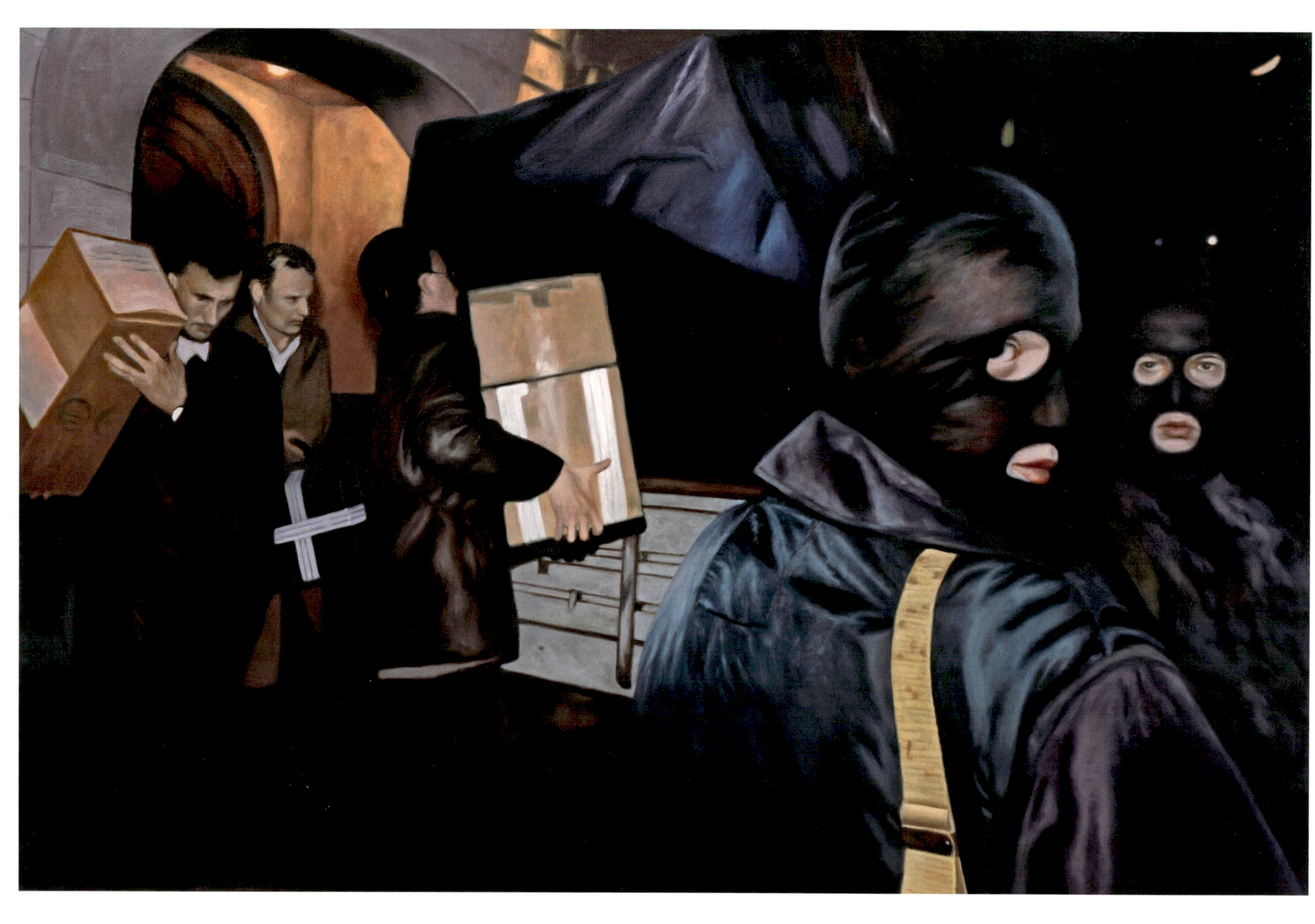

Goods 2: Durchsuchung des Gusinsky-Konzerns
Oil and tempera on canvas
125 x 200 cm, 2003

24

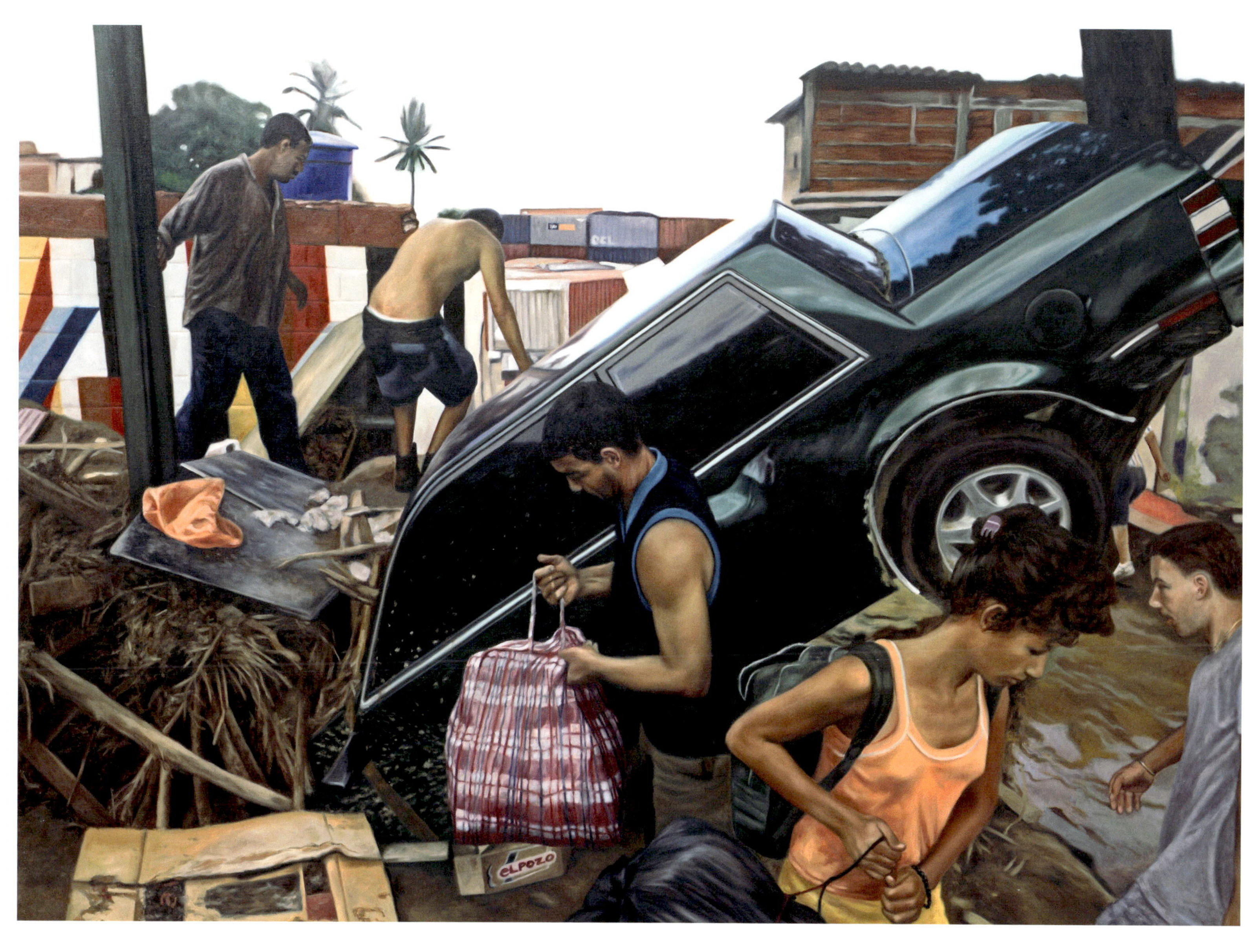

Goods 3: Flut in Venezuela
Oil and tempera on canvas
200 x 290 cm, 2003

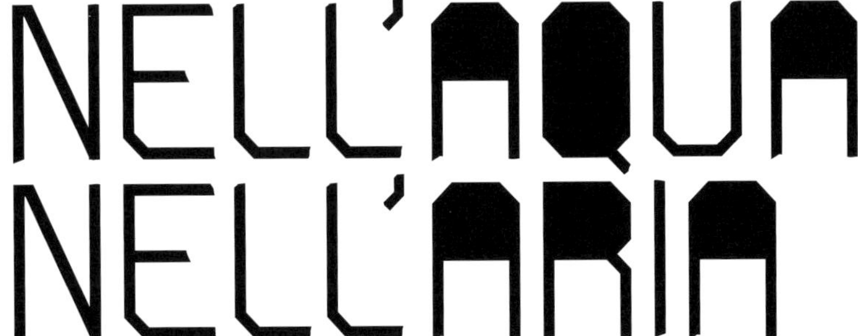
NELL'AQUA
NELL'ARIA

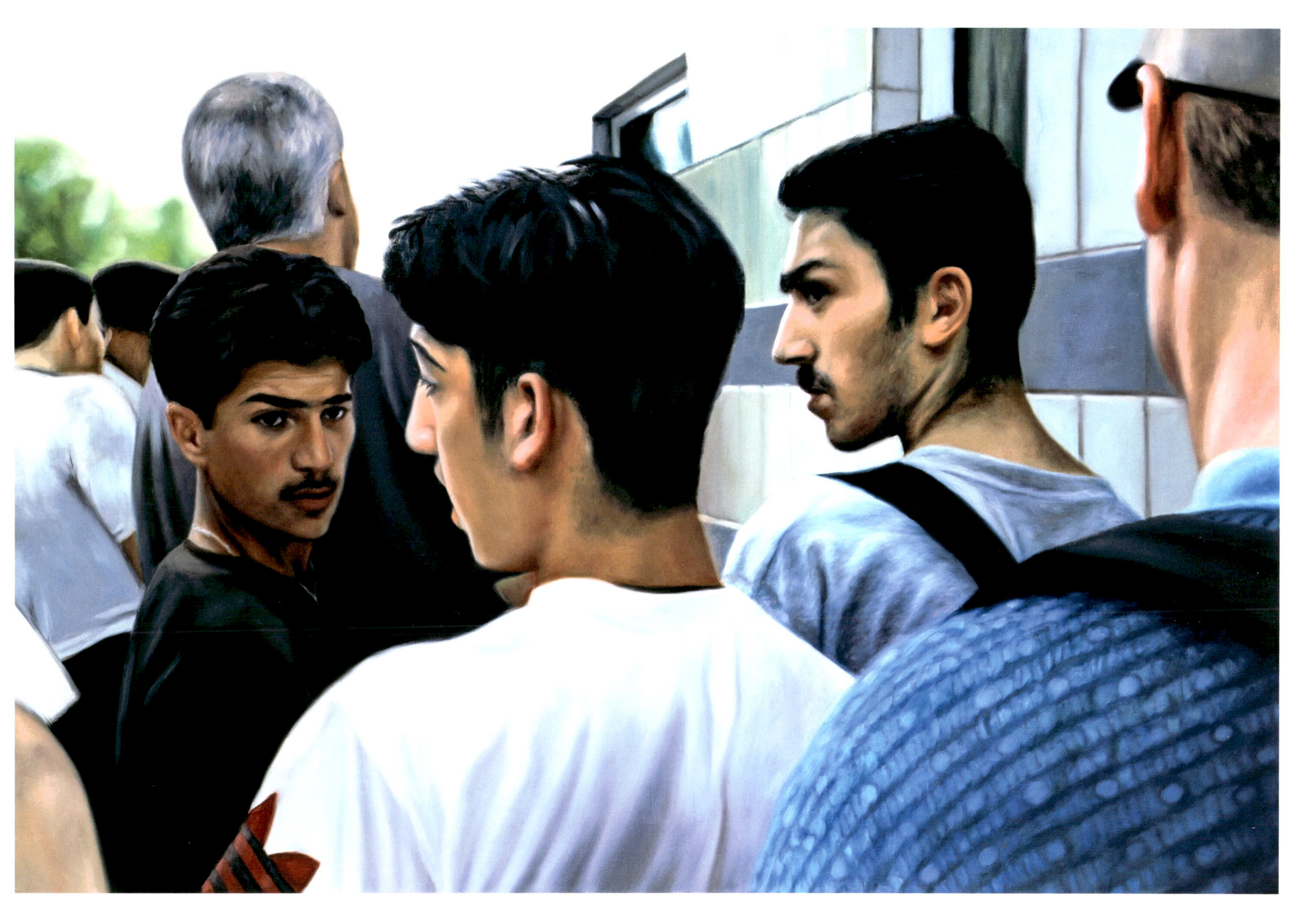

Eingang zum Schwimmbad
Oil on canvas
90 x 135 cm, 2003

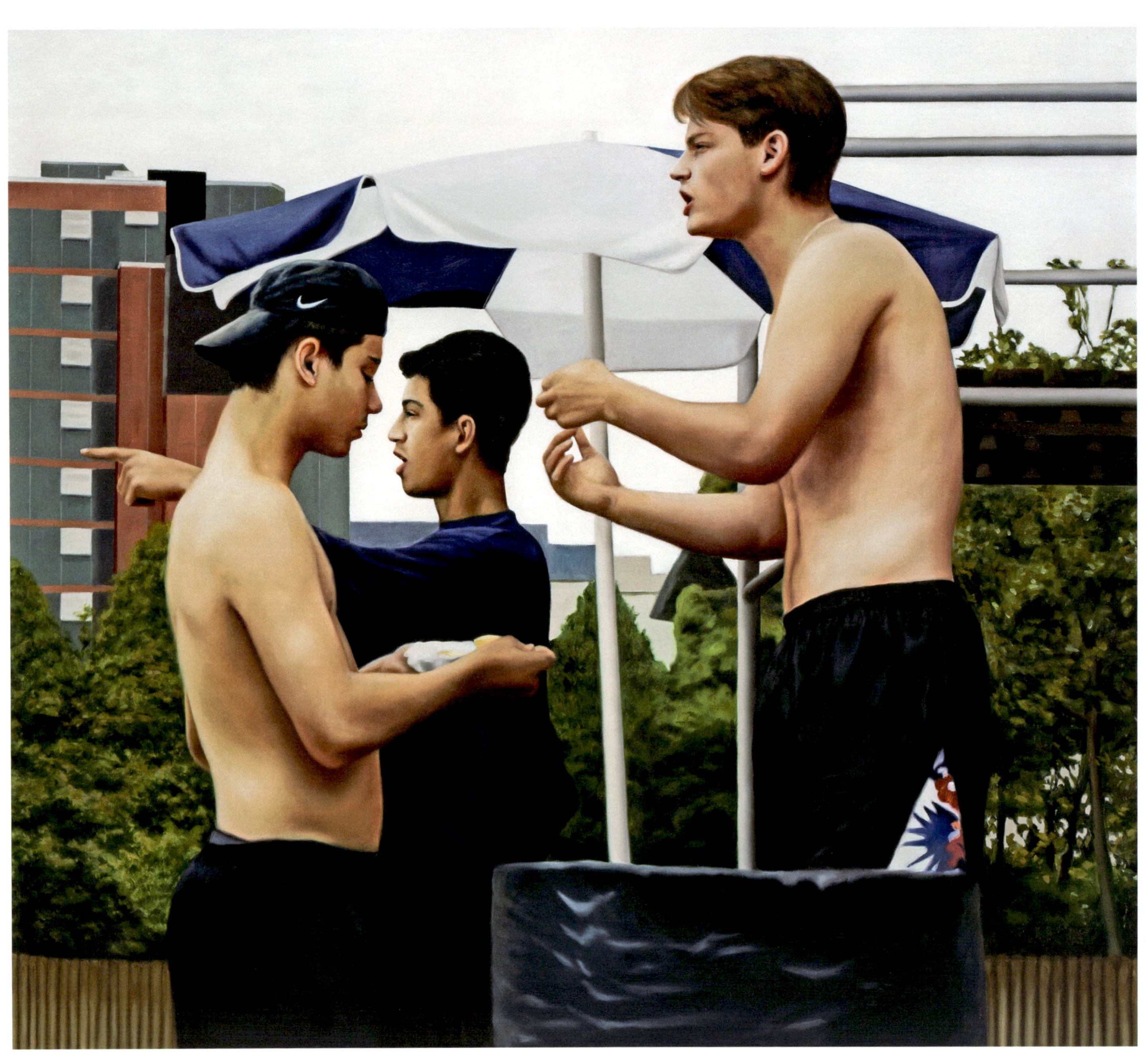

Im Schwimmbad
Oil on canvas
140 x 160 cm, 2003

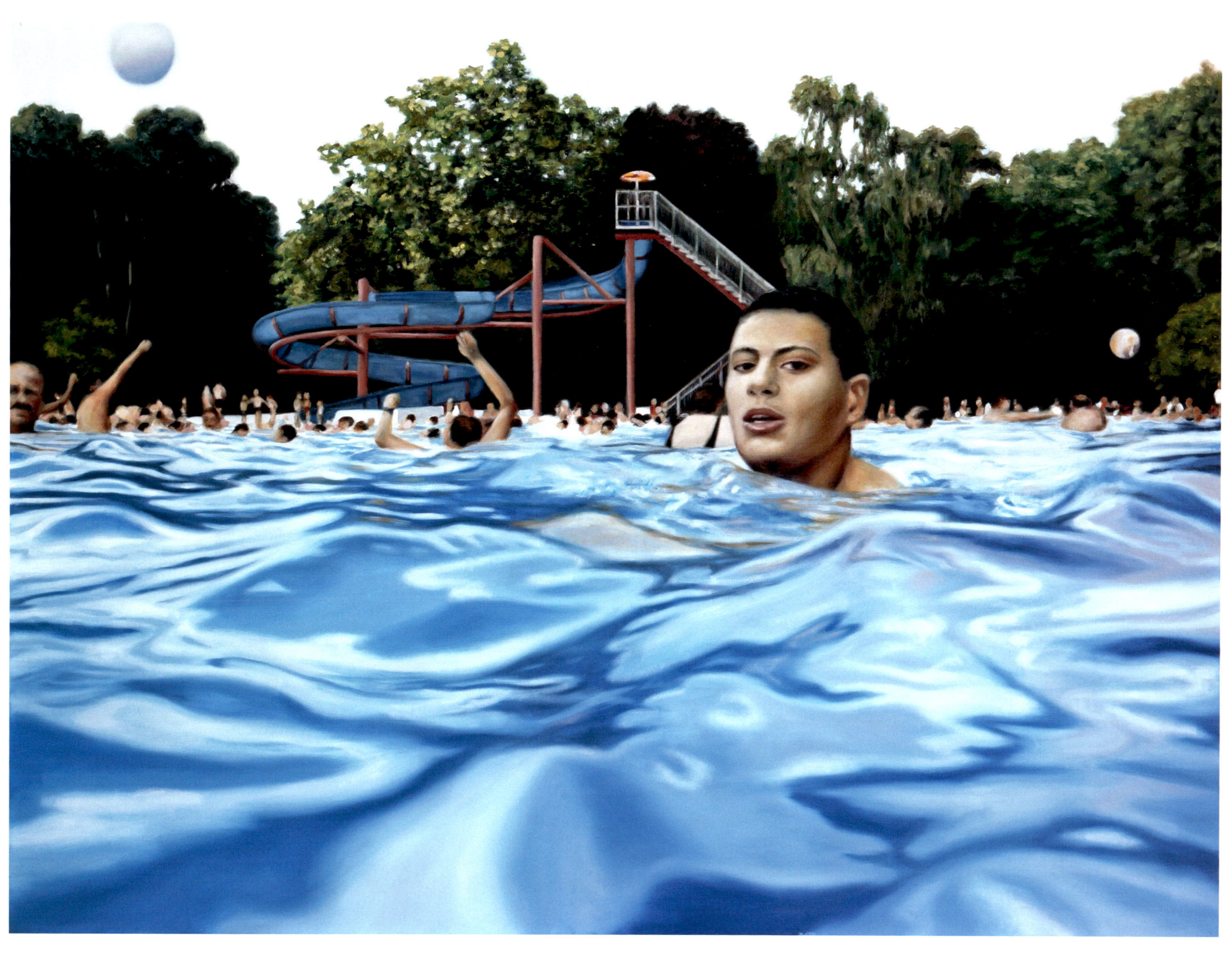

Im Wasser
Oil on canvas
110 x 160 cm, 2003

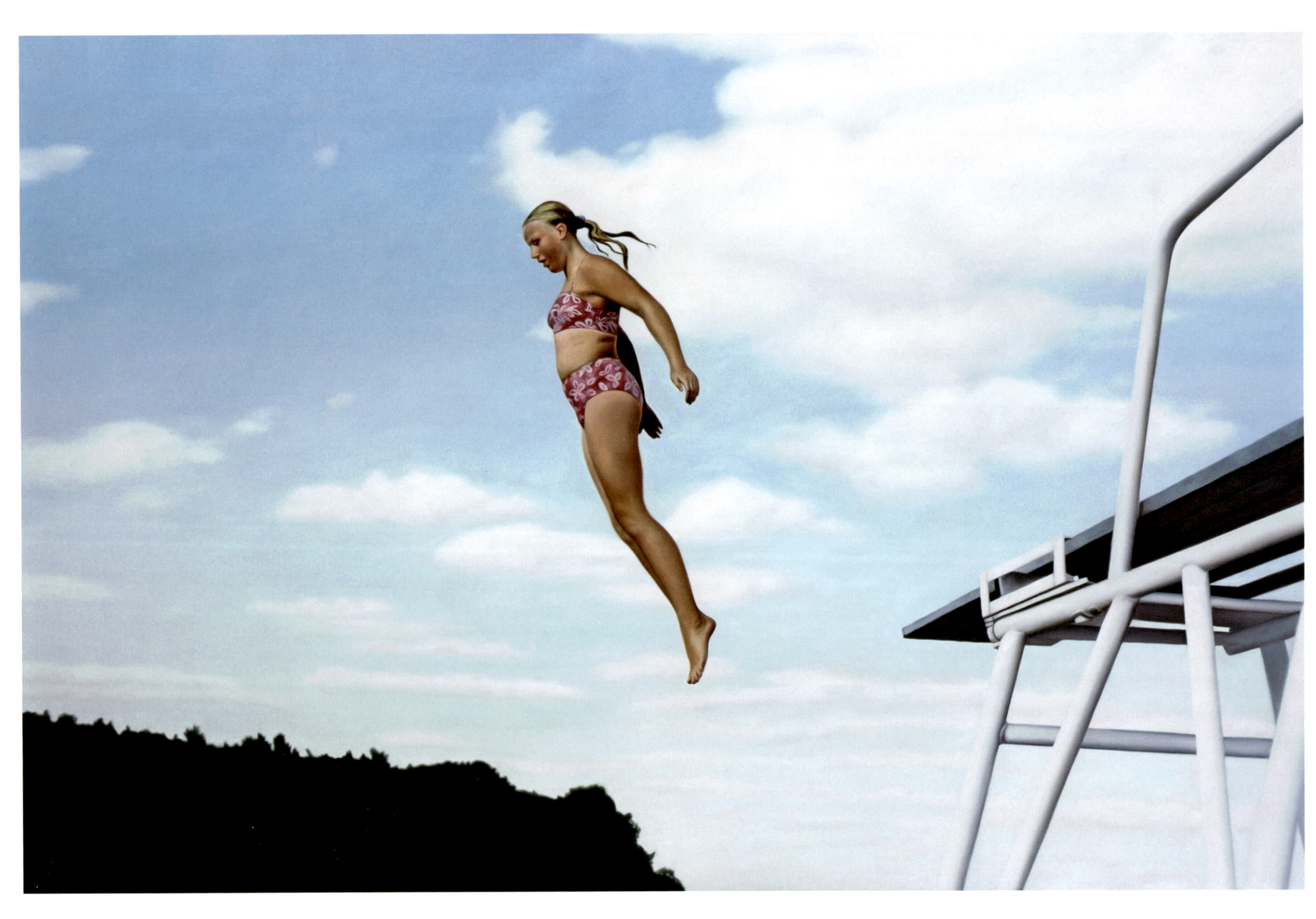

In der Luft 1
Oil on canvas
220 x 340 cm, 2003

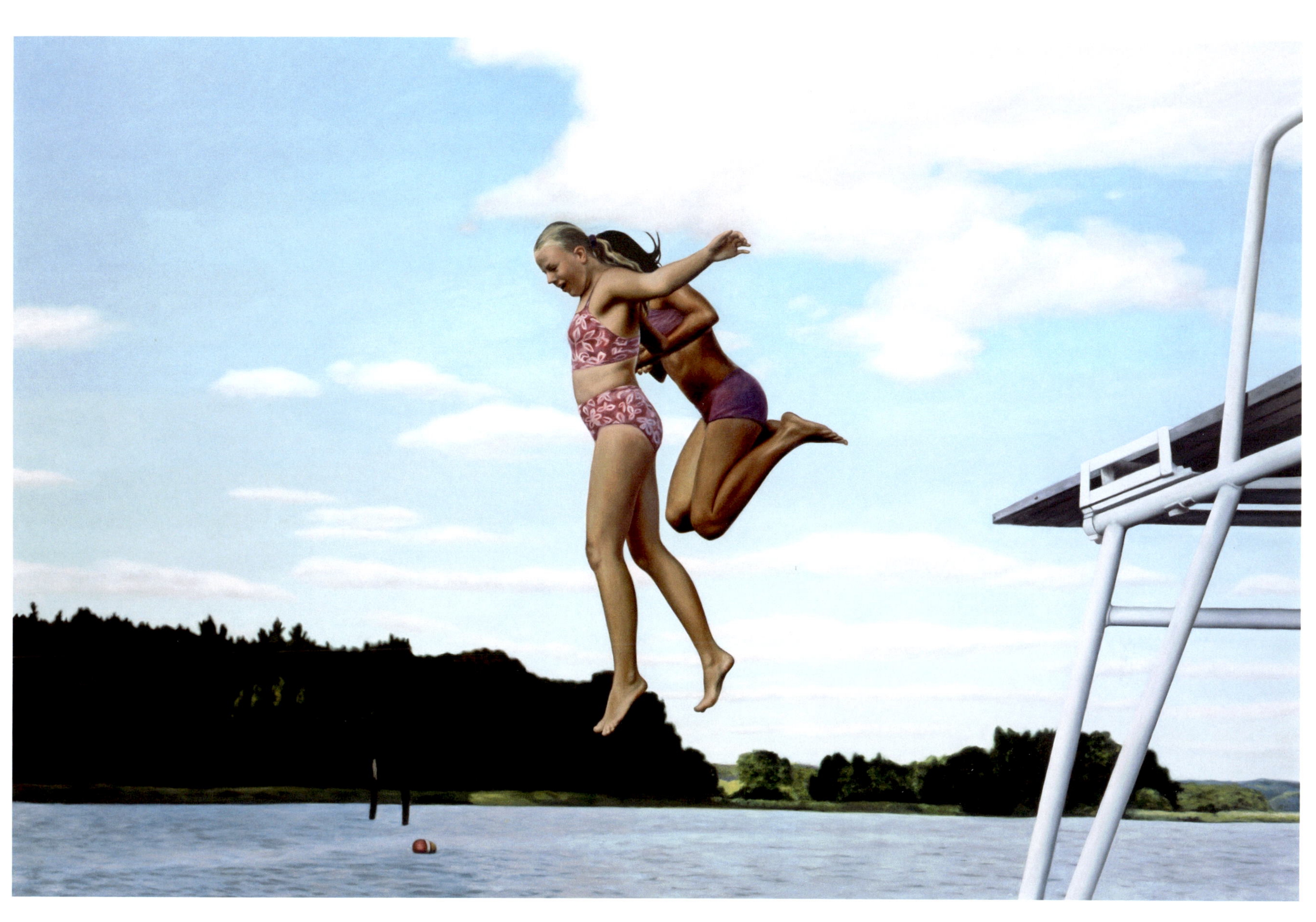

In der Luft 2
Oil on canvas
220 x 340 cm, 2003

CRYSTAL PALACE AND THE DINOSAURS

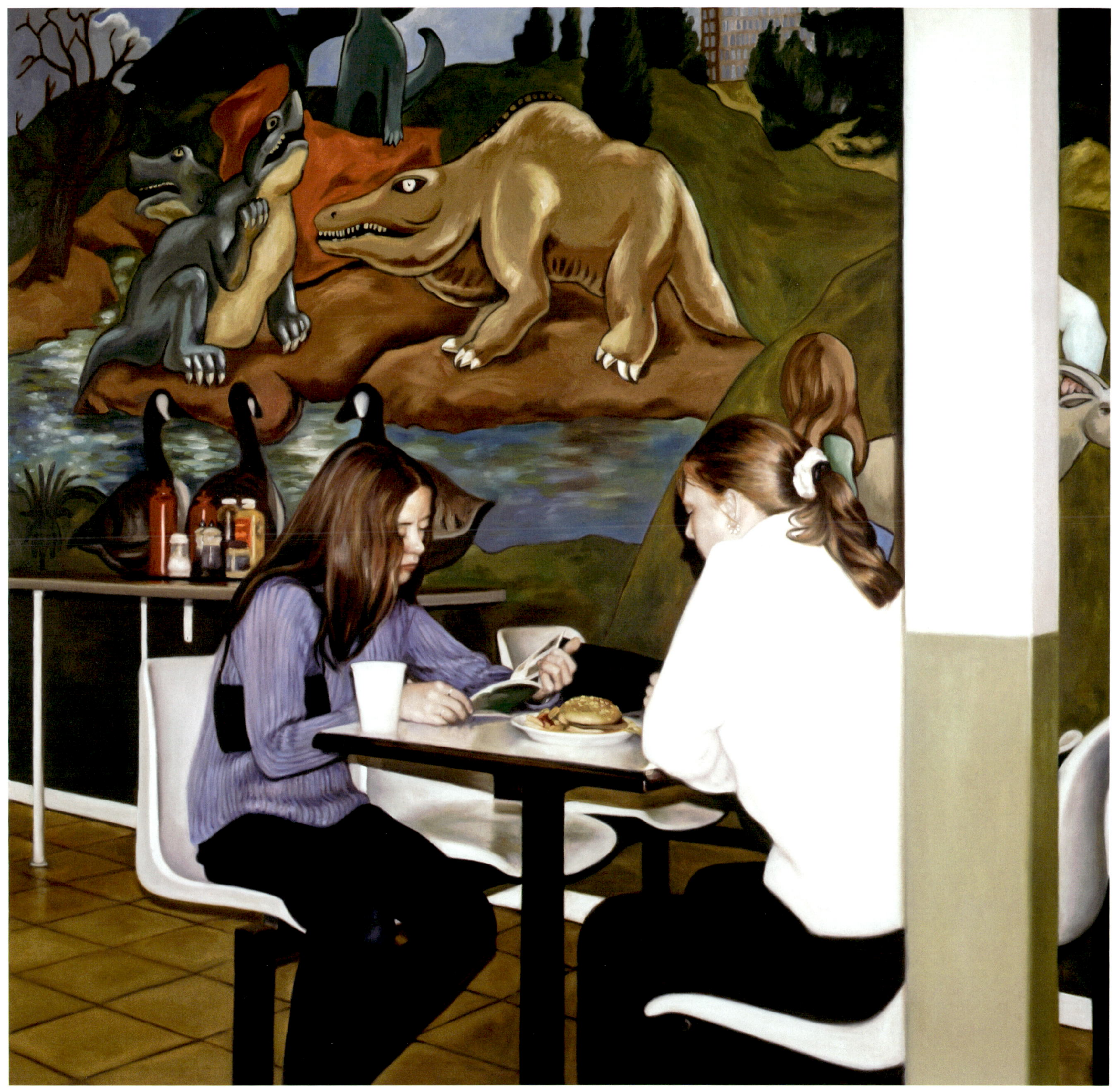

Dinosaurs
Oil on canvas
190 x 200 cm, 2002

Today, the Crystal Palace grounds are a nice, somewhat run-down park visited mainly by lower and middle income families. The gigantic building is long gone, its former position marked only by the fake Egyptian sphinxes guarding its now non-existent entrance. Landscape designer Sir Joseph Paxton built the Crystal Palace, essentially an oversized glass-and-iron greenhouse, to house the Great Exhibition held in London's Hyde Park. Prince Albert planned the exhibition as an impressive demonstration of power at the height of British colonialism and the country's successful industrialization. When the Great Exhibition closed, Paxton had the idea of moving it to Penge Place Estate, Sydenham, as a winter park and garden under glass.

The palace and the grounds became the world's first theme park, offering education, entertainment, a roller coaster, cricket matches, and even hosted twenty FA Cup Finals between 1895 and 1914. Although the palace saw many successful years and welcomed millions of visitors, it was plagued by financial problems. Sheer size alone made it financially unsustainable, and it declared bankruptcy in 1911. A foundation was set up, hiring Henry James Buckland as the Crystal Palace manager. Walking their dog on the night of November 30, 1936, Buckland and his daughter Crystal—named after his beloved Crystal Palace—noticed a small fire. By morning, most of the Palace was destroyed.

The dinosaurs were part of the Dinosaur Park, another Sir Joseph Paxton concept that opened in 1854. With the help of some experts on anatomy and prehistory, Benjamin Waterhouse Hawkins created the life-size sculptures—one of the very first attempts at palaeontological reconstruction. The Dinosaur Park was built six years before Darwin published his *On the Origin of Species* and thirty years after the first dinosaur bones were discovered, an event that was to shake the belief in man as the center of the universe—and a contradiction of sorts to the monument to (white, British, masculine) mankind standing next to it. What the little English girls on their outing will make of all this is not yet known; they appear almost oblivious to their surroundings, still at an age when the self consumes all of their attention. *A.M.*

Postcards: *1* C. 1895. View from the Glass Tower adjacent to the lower level (L.B.S.C.R.) station showing upper grounds, Italian terrace and Palace.
2 The Crystal Palace fire showing the Centre Transept from Crystal Palace Parade at about 8.30 pm on the night of Monday 30th November 1936.
3 C. 1860. These life-size model dinosaurs, the World's first, were constructed in 1854 by Benjamin Waterhouse Hawkins from brick on a frame of iron and finished with cement. They are listed Grade II.
4 Sir Henry Buckland in the ruins of the Crystal Palace on the morning of 1 December 1936. He is standing by the entrance to the Centre Transept. Crystal Palace Parade is to the left.

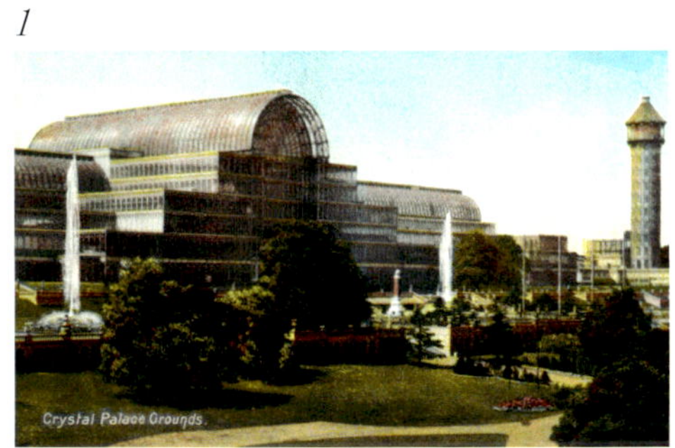
Crystal Palace Grounds.

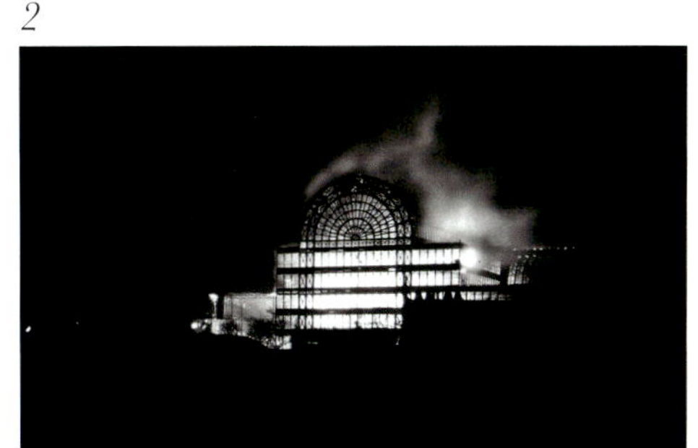

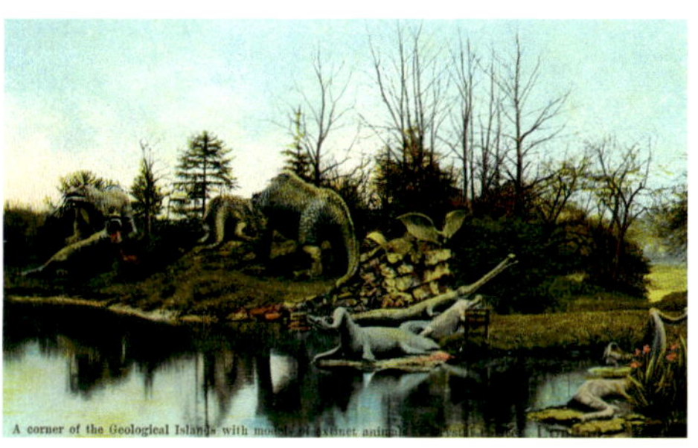

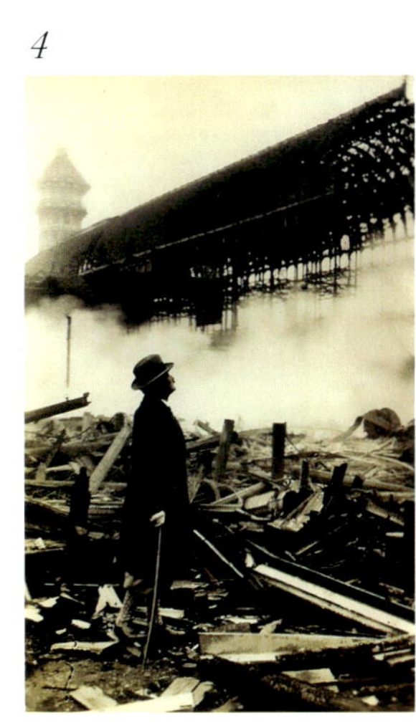
A corner of the Geological Islands with models of extinct animals

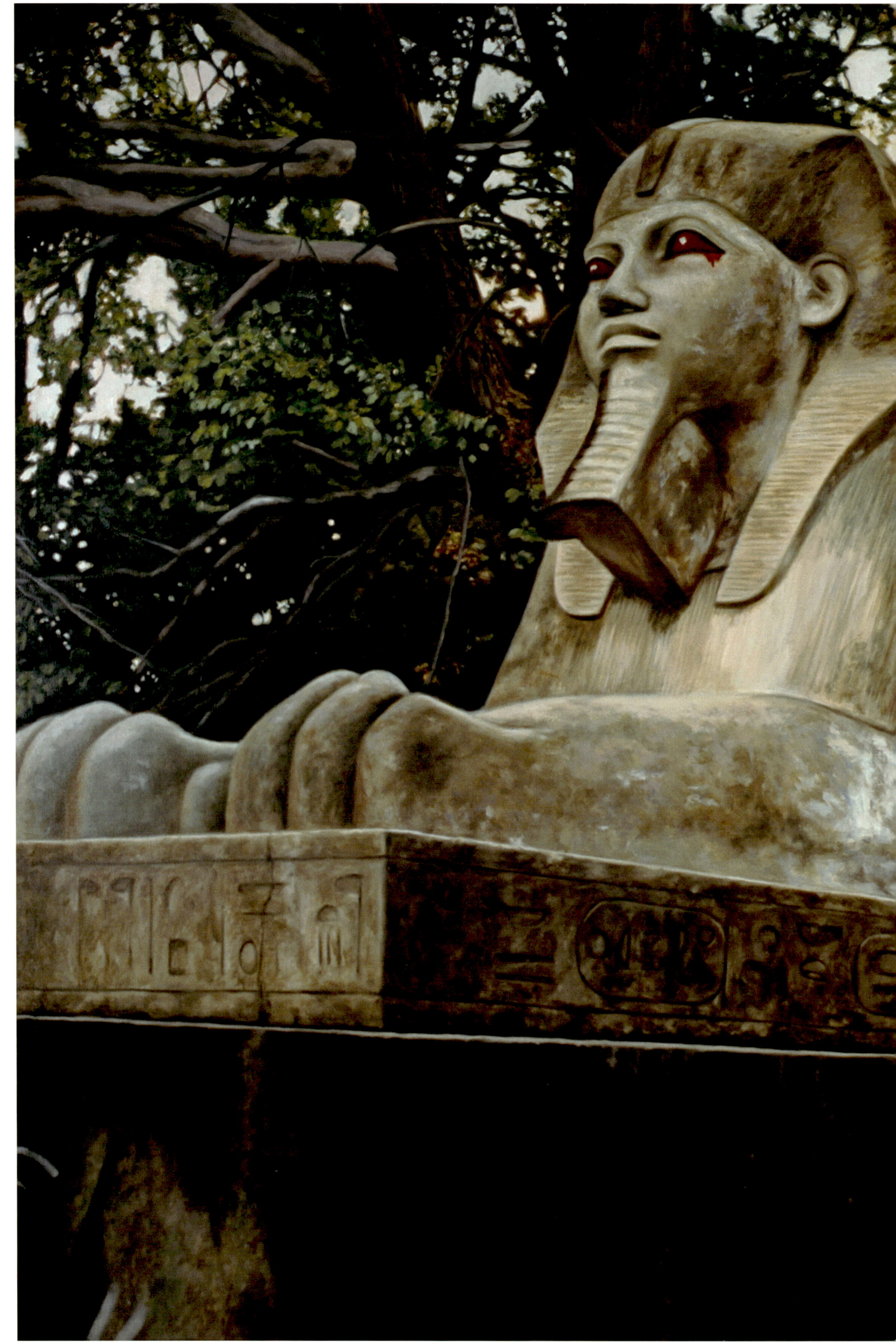

Entrance to
Crystal Palace
Oil on canvas
240 x 380 cm
2002

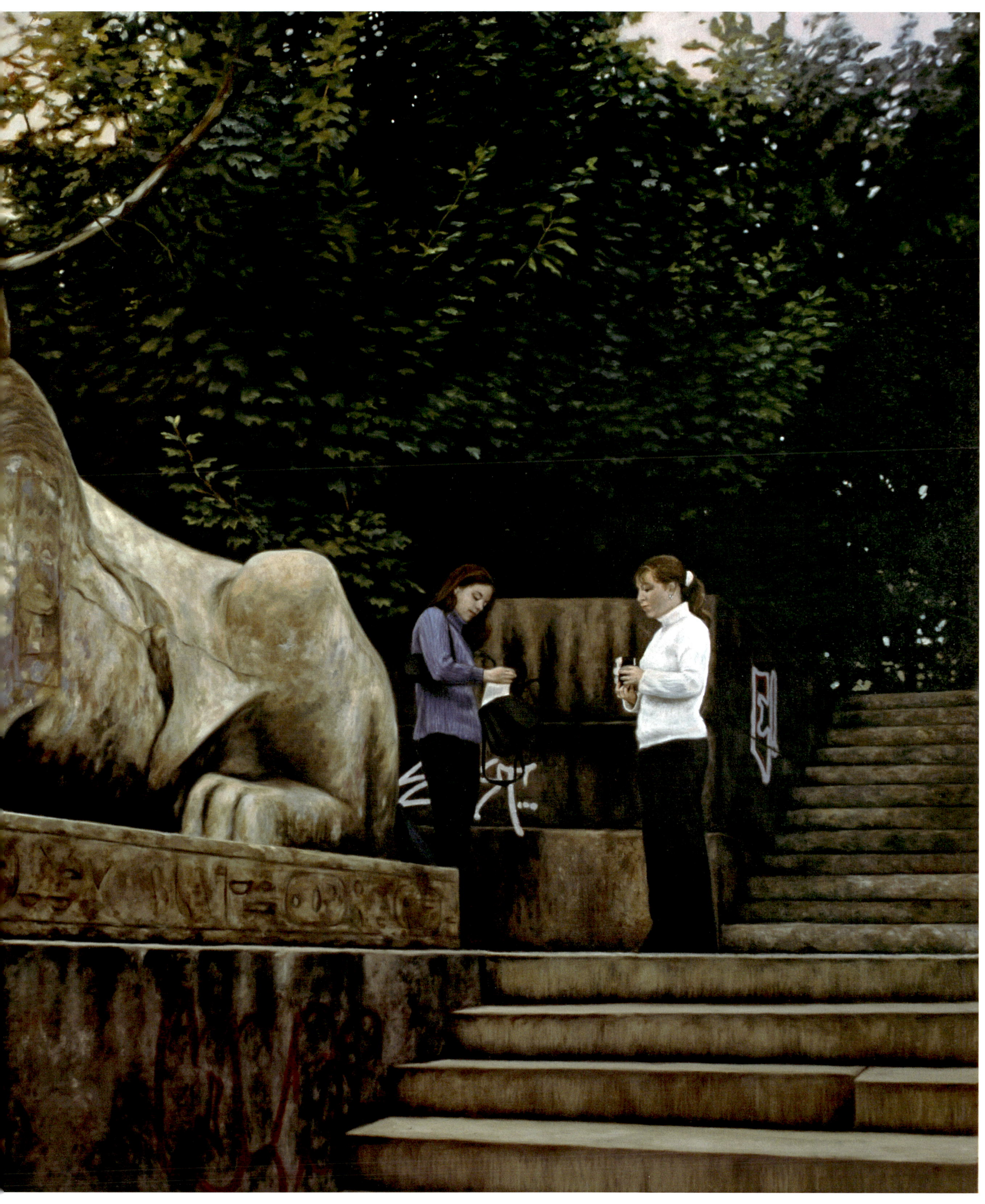

My Very Gestures
Installation view
Salzburger Kunstverein, 2008

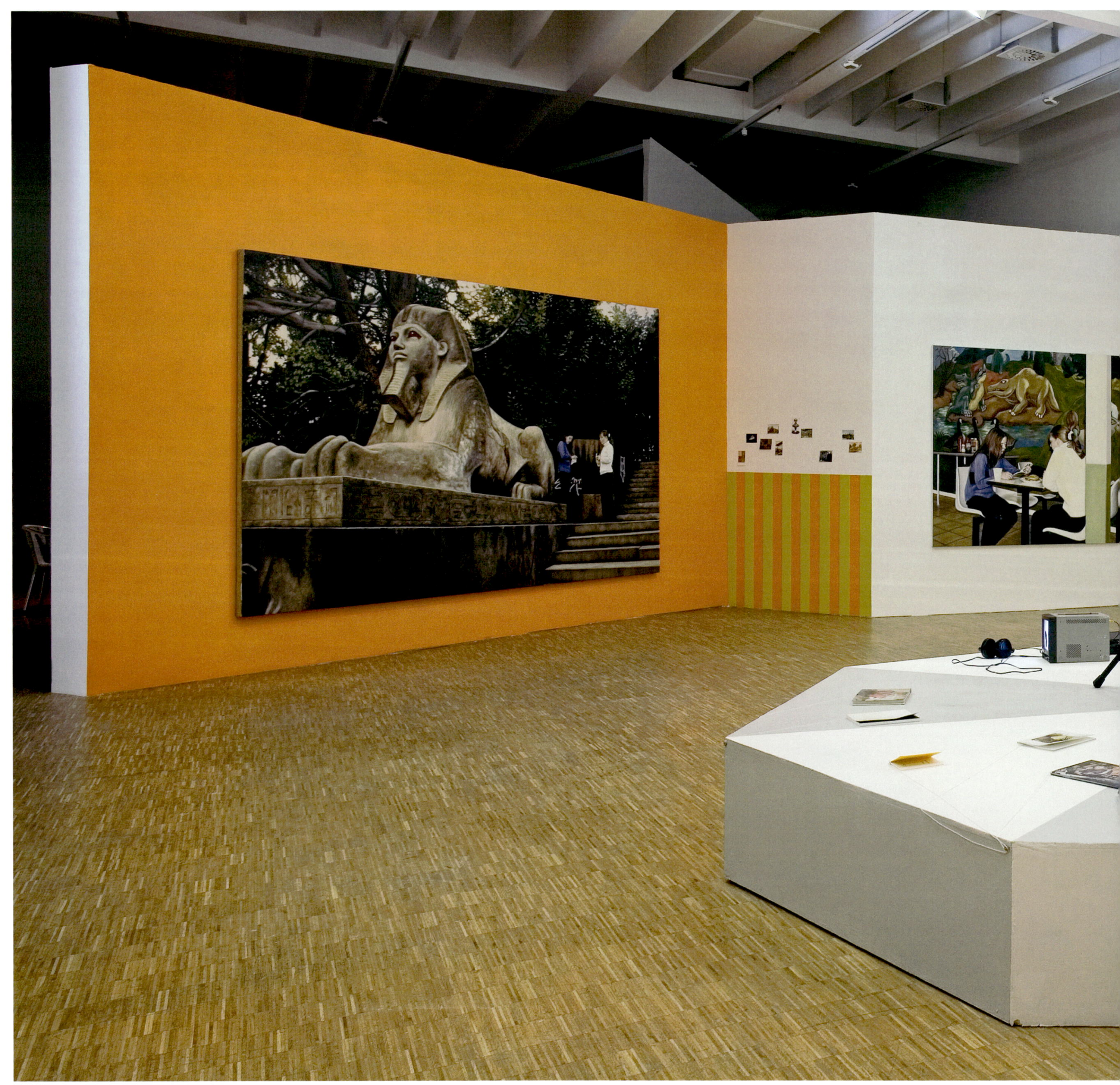

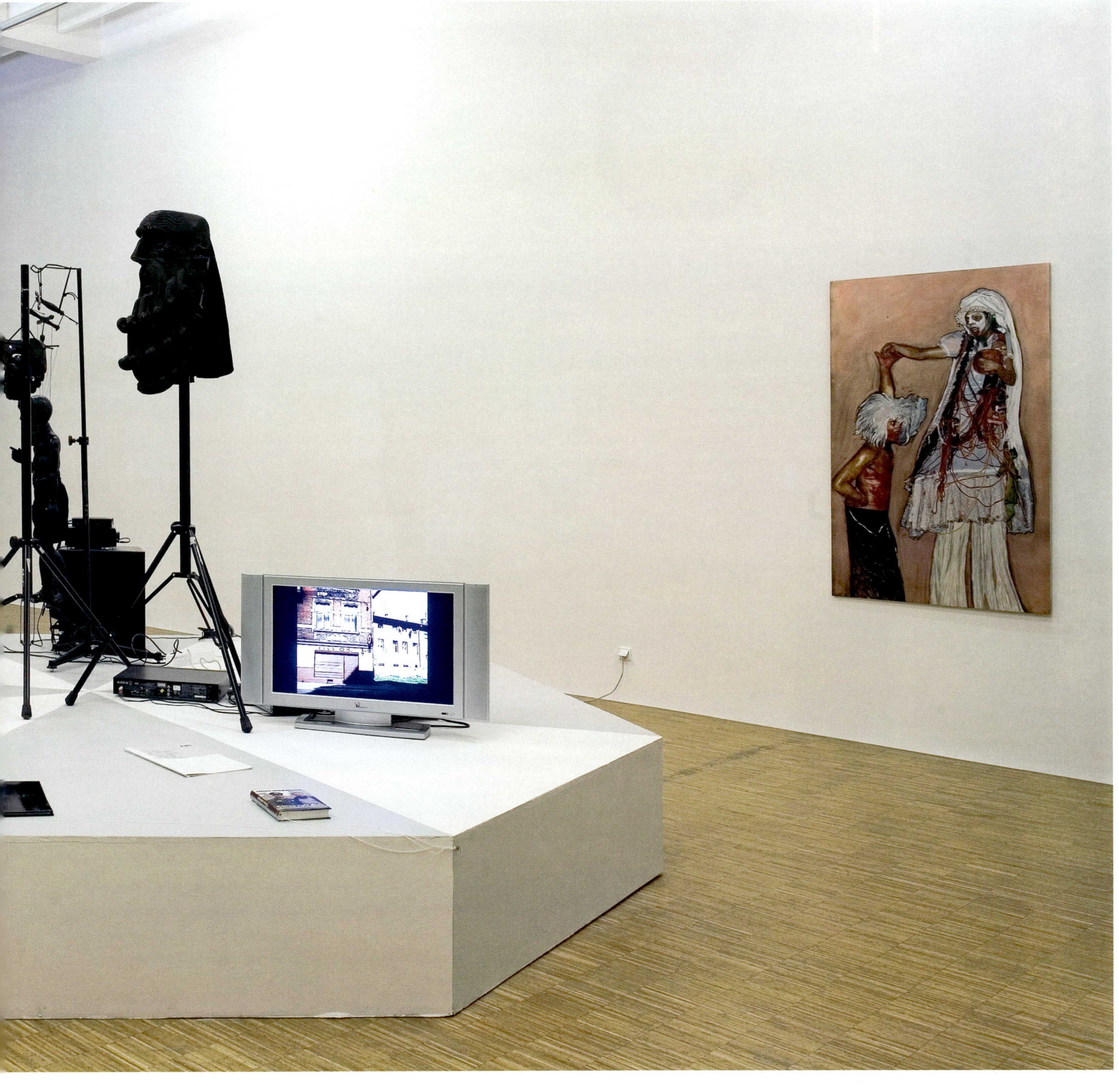

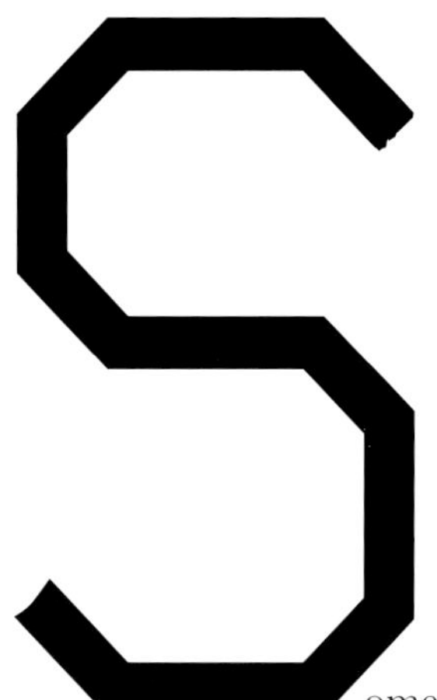

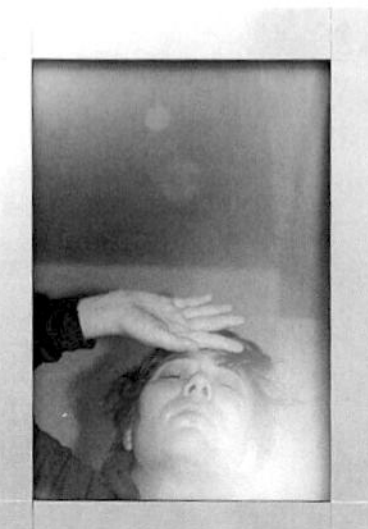

ometimes when we wake, regardless of what the day ahead might bring, the apparitions that have come to us in the night or early morning, cast a shadow in our heads. Looking at Antje Majewski's multifarious photographs, paintings, videos, and installations from the last fifteen years or so puts me exactly in that odd, in-between state of mind. A state, in which dream figures and their imaginative realm make their presence felt and color our perception of the objective world. Perhaps this is also what we are witnessing in the artist's self-portrait included amongst her series of black-and-white photographs mounted in mirror frames in *My Very Gestures… Enchanted* (2001). It shows Majewski holding one hand up to her forehead and with her eyes rolled partly back as if in, or performing that state when our sense of the real is inflected or haunted by visions. Apparently, and sometimes shockingly, the other-worldly, glowing protagonists or beings in these fading dreams or visions—whether statues or spirits and however strange, colorful or sexually-loaded they may be—are all aspects of ourselves. But they also exist outside of you, in your relationship to everything you have ever experienced, half-remembered, or projected onto the territory beyond what you think you know and have understood.

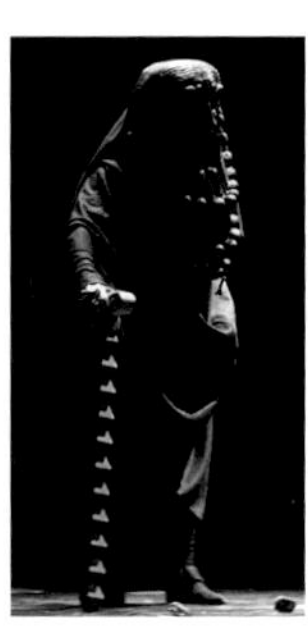

Take for example, the dark, changeable, and powerful Polish coal mine spirit called Skarbek in Majewski and author Ingo Niermann's 2005 collaborative dance theater piece of the same name, or the fake tribe of face-painted, robed, and hooded figures in the artist's series of paintings *L'invitation au voyage, Teil 4: Masken* (1999–2001). Works like these might be described as entailing the appearance of figures, whether their setting is a kind of heightened version of normality somewhere in the world, mythical, pure fantasy, or some kind of mixture of these. In the exhibition also titled *My Very Gestures* (2008), which, though by no means a complete retrospective, is nevertheless a kind of "looking back" or selected survey, these scenes and scenarios not only sit alongside each other, they coexist. Sometimes the artist achieves this through a fixing of their outline, contours, texture, and tone on the surface of a painted image. Elsewhere they come to life through sculptural props, costumes, and narratives of a video. There are other equally important thematic threads in her work, principal amongst them a kind of postmodern social realism in which the artist often uses television and travel images. But in the exhibition *My Very Gestures*, and this accompanying catalogue, it is the idea that art might offer a place where the real world mingles with the imagined one, that bring Majewski's varied works into conversation with each other. Pointing to the realism of other works, Majewski would say that these two aspects of her work are codependent, or won't exist without each other. Her imagination is not an escape from what can be experienced or observed, rather for the artist: "the imaginary or the visionary is kind of enfolded into the fabric of the real."[1] Perhaps the best example of how this works for the artist is Skarbek, a legendary spirit who has outlived his Socialist reformers and still haunts the mining towns that created him even as social and economic conditions deteriorate.

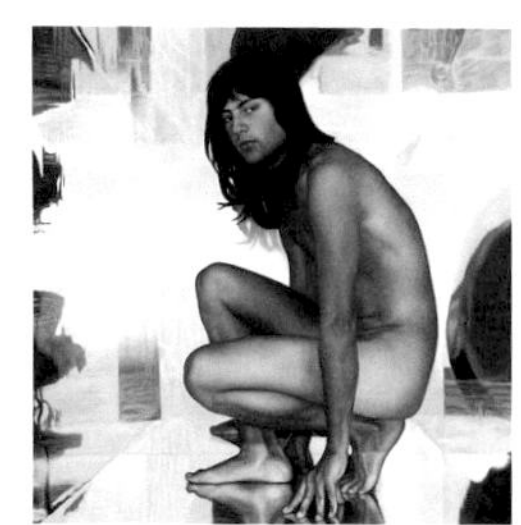

Bearing this in mind let's look more closely at one of the dream-like figures in the artist's work, for instance, the spirit depicted in the photorealistic figurative painting *Liebling* (1999), a work that hasn't aged in the way that oil paintings don't, if they're constructed well and treated right. (In conversation, the artist told me that one of her fascinations with oil painting was the way that they can defy time, or at least time measured by a human life.) The painting might be a present-day portrait of a young Dorian Gray—though without the addition of devilish, death-defying magic. Bound to the physical world the real model's misdemeanors won't ever sully its untainted surface. The work depicts a naked youth crouching in a mirror cube, whose front is open to the beholder. It is also through this virtual plane that the figure stares out of his two dimensional container or frame—where space is an illusion created by perspective—into our four-dimensional world. His body is reflected in multiple directions in the surfaces around him, a fact that doesn't seem to perturb this peaceful exhibitionist. (His gaze to the viewer doesn't suggest narcissist self-absorption.) A long mane and classically obscured genitals emphasize a certain androgyny and arguably make him available as a figure of pansexual fantasy, an alter-ego, or a flirtatious muse, existing as a tantalizing possibility beyond entrenched or proscriptive gender or sexual codes. He is painted, and it is the medium, which allows this apparition to remain in a constantly renewed present rather than to fade away in the imagination where he came from. Perhaps he came from a dream and perhaps he is meant to reappear in ours.

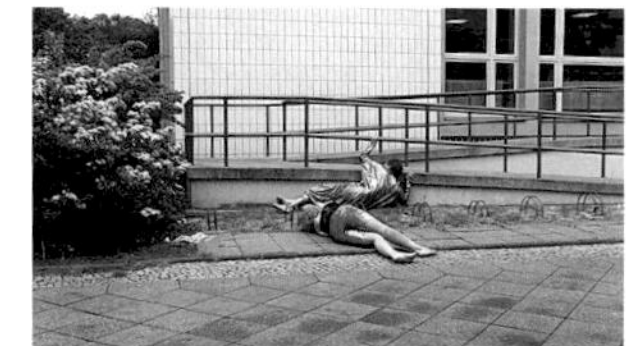

Turning to the outside world, in the video *Erde Asphalt Wedding* (2007), Majewski and collaborating artist Juliane Solmsdorf, crawl through the streets of the Berlin neighborhood Wedding, bare-kneed and absurdly costumed. Majewski is wearing a stretchy silver dress and Solmsdorf a black and gold sequin top and shorts—as if the two have emerged from a 1980s disco after a time lag. Partly, a disturbing endurance test that is sometimes painful to watch, it is not clear whether the artists have somehow regressed or are still evolving, or even whether their excruciating progress on all fours has any specific purpose other than their almost primordial movements. The tough and bleak streets of Wedding are completely transformed in the video through their performance, and appear like an alien environment or unfamiliar urban territory. The accompanying realistic painting *Säule Wedding* (2008) shows the two artists embracing while standing on top of what might be a water fountain, thus in a sense becoming momentary beacons for creative or unorthodox use of public space. The painting preserves and monumentalizes their fleeting performative gesture.

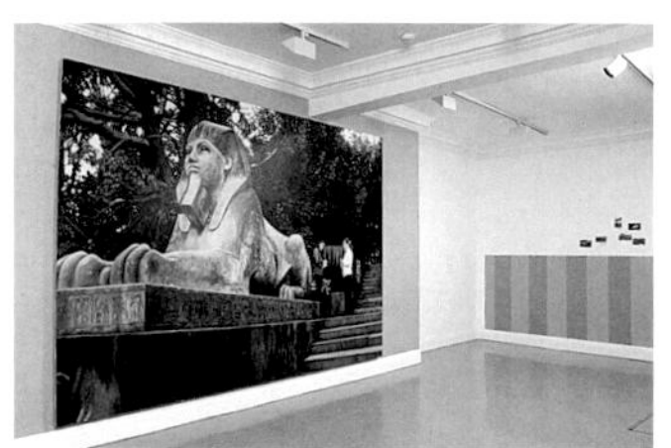

It is also the present condition and the cultural history of a particular public space, which inspired the artist's interest in the ruins of the 19th Century Crystal Palace grounds in London. The painting *Entrance to Crystal Palace* (2002), which has as a companion a wall painting with

[1] Antje Majewski in conversation with the author, August 2008.

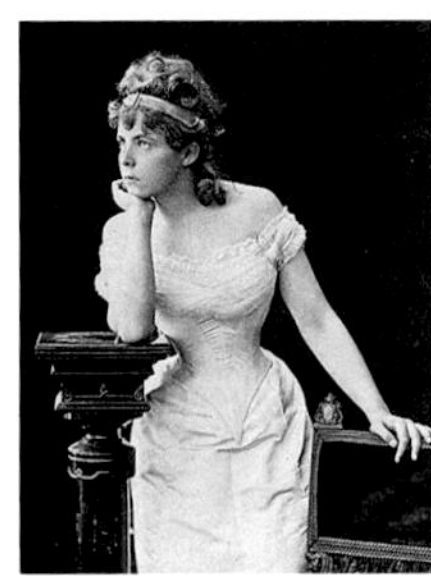

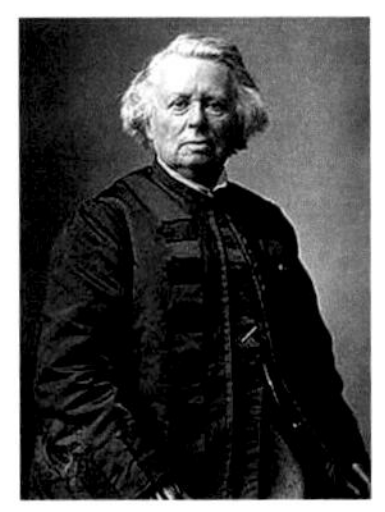

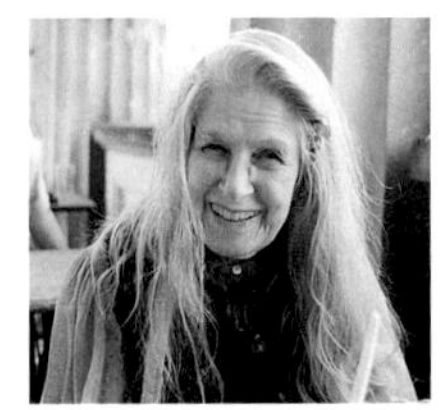

historical postcards illuminating the cultural and social history of the Crystal Palace, and the painting *Dinosaurs* (2002), direct the viewer's critical attention and imagination to both the past and present. In these works, the protagonists are some anonymous teenage girls who chat below a sphinx whose eyes have been defaced with red paint, and eat together in a cafeteria in front of a wall mural of dinosaur models—a depiction of one of the Crystal Palace's original and only surviving attractions. What we are offered are ordinary scenes with an extraordinary past. By painting them, the artist has achieved an instable convergence of the real and the fictional. In the exhibition *My Very Gestures*, the idea of the fairground or international exhibition is echoed in the display and exhibition architecture. The housing for the display of the video *Erde Asphalt Wedding*, for instance, recalls a freestanding fairground stand. The same goes for the striped octagonal platform elsewhere in the room, which provides visitors with an island to gather and rest and become part of the display and peruse the curiosities around them, such as the Skarbek puppet and masks.

It is perhaps useful to go back to the earlier days of her artistic production in order to locate and contextualize Majewski's artistic intention in relation to her divergent subject matter. In the mid-1990s, the artist published a text in one of the first issues of the still existing independent Berlin art, culture, and politics magazine *Starship*, which reads something like an untamed manifesto for a painter, specifically a woman painter. In fact, the text was constructed wholly from citations of texts from the women painters Rosa Bonheur, Marie Bashkirtseff, Louise-Catherine Breslau, and Tamara de Lempicka. The following excerpt gives an idea of its tone:

"As a young girl I squandered my time with excessive questions and eccentric inanities. There is a time when one feels naively capable of doing anything. [...] I smoke three packs of cigarettes a day and swallow tons of sleeping pills at night. The days are just too short. Sometimes I go to bed at night, come home at two in the morning and work until six under terrible light. [...] I have a goal, and I have a plan. After every second sold painting I will buy a bracelet, until the diamonds and jewels reach from wrist to elbow. You really have to have a lot of enthusiasm for your art to live in this ghastly milieu and among these clowns. I am only interested in the best.

I have a very black wig on and my eyebrows are also dyed black. I can spend entire nights sleepless, thinking about a picture or a statue; never has the thought of a beautiful man had the same effect.

[...] I am happy living here, far from the world, receive visits from a few intimate friends and work as best I can.

Had I been completely happy, I might not have worked." [2]

Two years earlier the artist had published the art historical text *Some Women Realists, Revisited* [3], considering the position of realistic painters of the 1970s including artists such as Joan Semmel and Sylvia Sleigh. I mention these early writings because to me they show how from

[2] Antje Majewski, "Pastiche," *Starship* 3 (Winter 2000): 124-125

[3] Antje Majewski, "Einige Realistinnen," *Starship* 1 (Autumn 1998): 24-35

the beginning Majewski made her allegiances, her inspiration, and critical perspective clear. Namely, that in terms of thinking about the fantasy figures, performance, roles, and costumes in Majewski's work, the theoretical backdrop is informed by a progressive form of feminism. In particular, Judith Butler's thesis about the importance of performance and performativity in the construction of gender should be taken into account. Again, the vibrant and mysterious images *Masks* are perhaps a good example of how this thought is taken on board in an un-dogmatic exploratory way in some of Majewski's work. The series depicts a group of friends and other artists with wildly painted faces in geometric abstract patterns and clothed in jar-ringly patterned, non-gender specific clothes, sewn from inexpensive fabrics by the artist. The painting on untreated copper *Masquerade* (2006), which suggests that the painted image involves some modicum of magic and alchemy, is also a celebration of a potentially liberating form of performance.

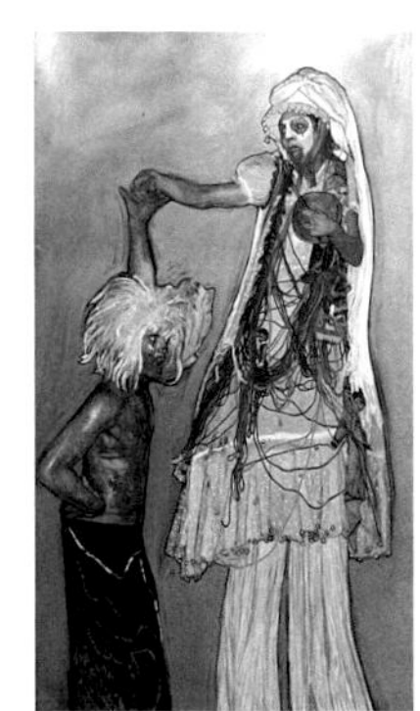

But to return to the recent past, it is also important to remember that back in the mid-1990s, painting (for which Majewski became principally known in the late 1990s) and, even worse, realistic or figurative painting wasn't featuring large amongst emerging artists' practice. Al-though, this unofficial moratorium on interest, on the part of curators and, to a lesser extent, galleries, was about to be done away with in a major way—in Germany, for example—as a result of the commercially driven rise of what's known as the Leipzig school. In sharp distinc-tion, much closer to home for Majewski were the protagonists of the nascent Berlin scene—still relatively small and self-referential, by comparison to today. Artists more specifically important to the context for Majewski included Lukas Duwenhögger, Ull Hohn, Michel Majerus, and Katharina Wulff, —all of whom in their own admittedly highly divergent ways, approached painting with a discursive vigor and a new affection for the problems of paint-ing and addressing the troubled status of figuration. That is not to suggest that there was any sense of a Berlin school or movement, just that at that time, there was a lively discussion about what was seen as defensible rather than kitsch or conservative or otherwise retrograde in con-temporary painting. It's important to appreciate Majewski's work in terms of that context and intellectual climate of those years.

The exhibition title *My Very Gestures* is taken from the Frankie Goes to Hollywood album *Wel-come to the Pleasuredome*. In particular, some lines which paraphrase a passage from Friedrich Nietzsche's *The Birth of the Tragedy* (*Die Geburt der Tragödie, 1872*): "In song and in dance I ex-press myself as a member of a higher community. I have forgotten how to walk and speak. I am on the way toward flying into the air... dancing. My very gestures express enchantment. I feel myself a god. Supernatural sounds emanate from me. I walk about enchanted, in ecstasy, like the gods I saw walking in my dreams. I am no longer an artist, I have become a work of art." The artist wrote to me that this perhaps "summarizes more than anything else what I would like to get at." To me this suggests that at the core of Majewski's practice is the idea of a celebration, the performance and living out of joy. The figures and characters in her art spring forth from the ordinary in order to show us a different imaginative trajectory.

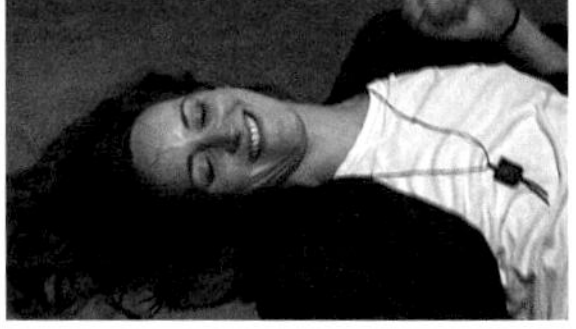

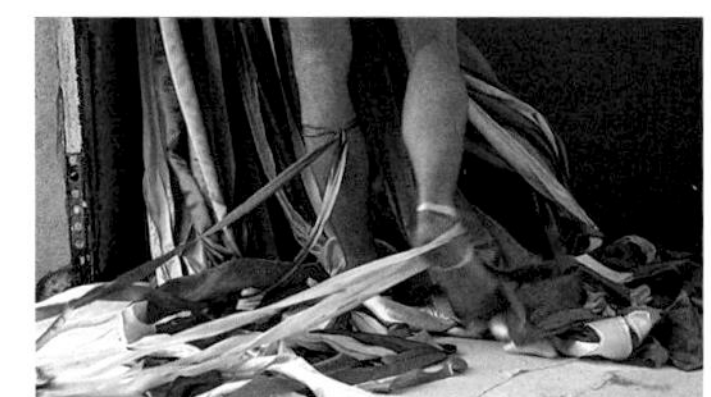

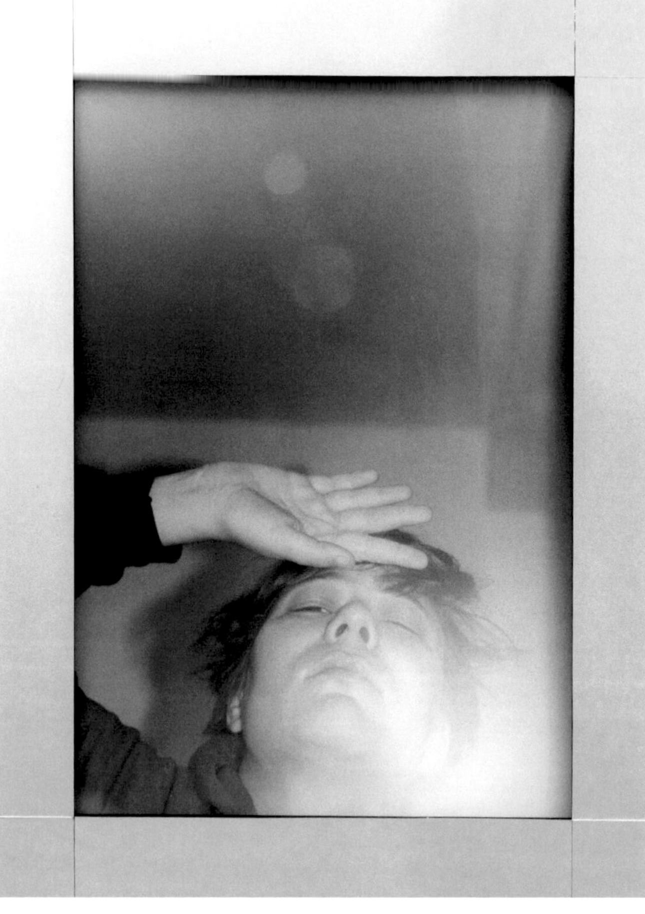
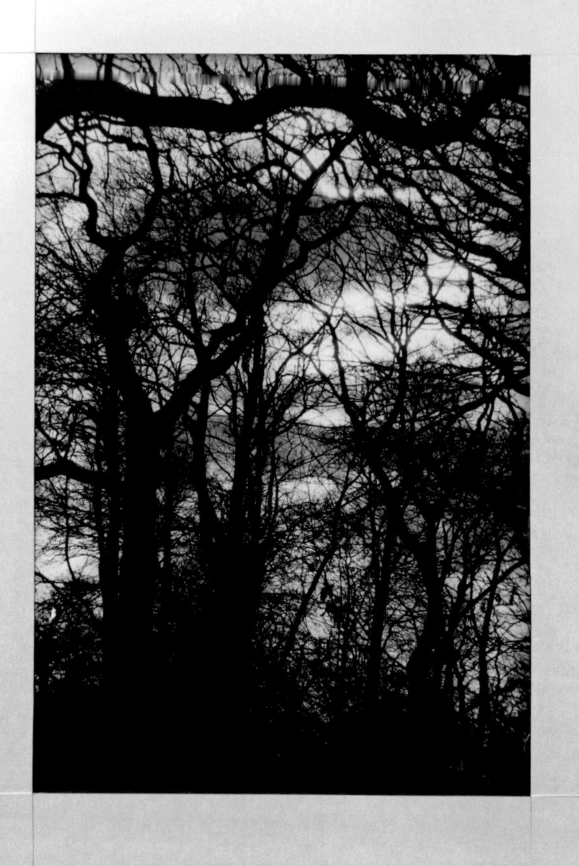
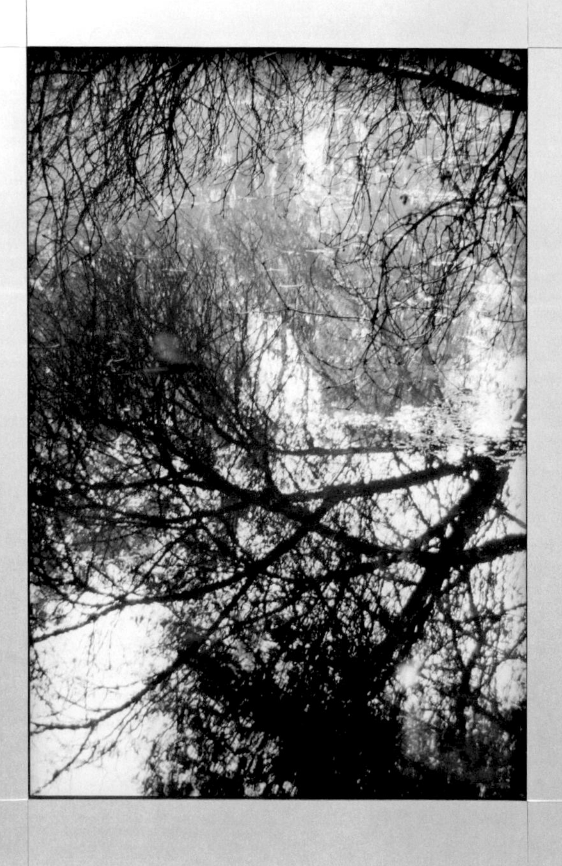
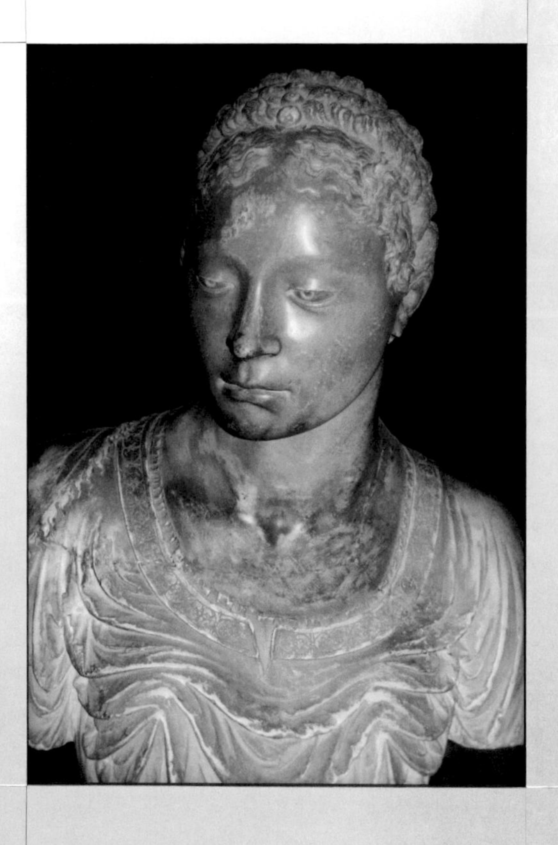

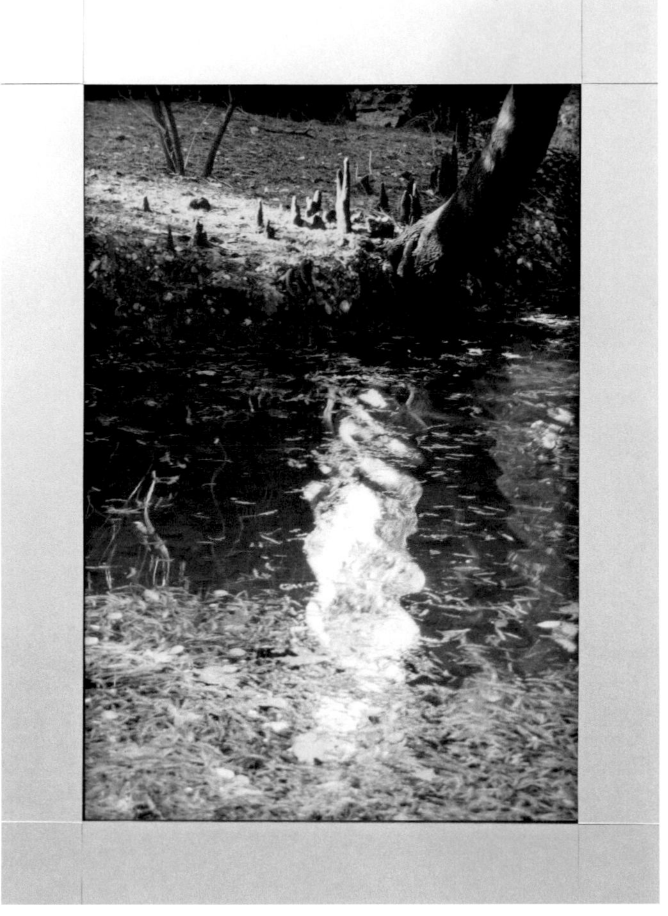

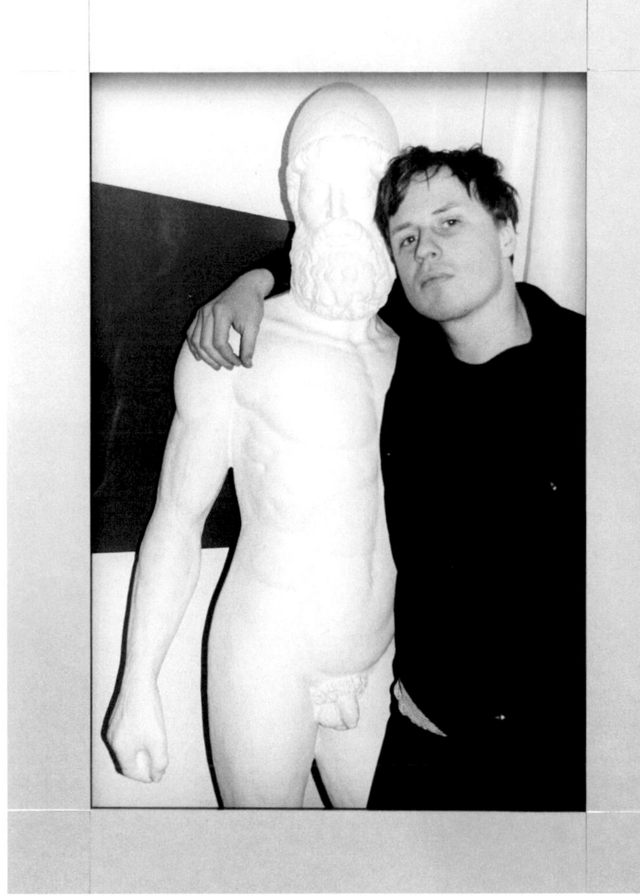

*My Very
Gestures…
Enchanted*
8 b/w prints,
mirror frames
41 x 30.5 cm
2001

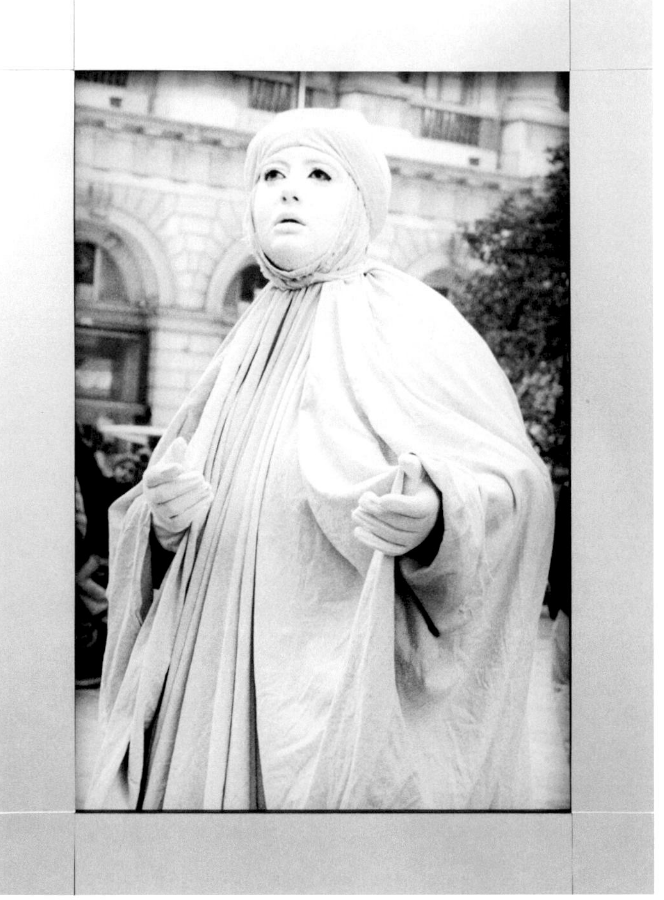

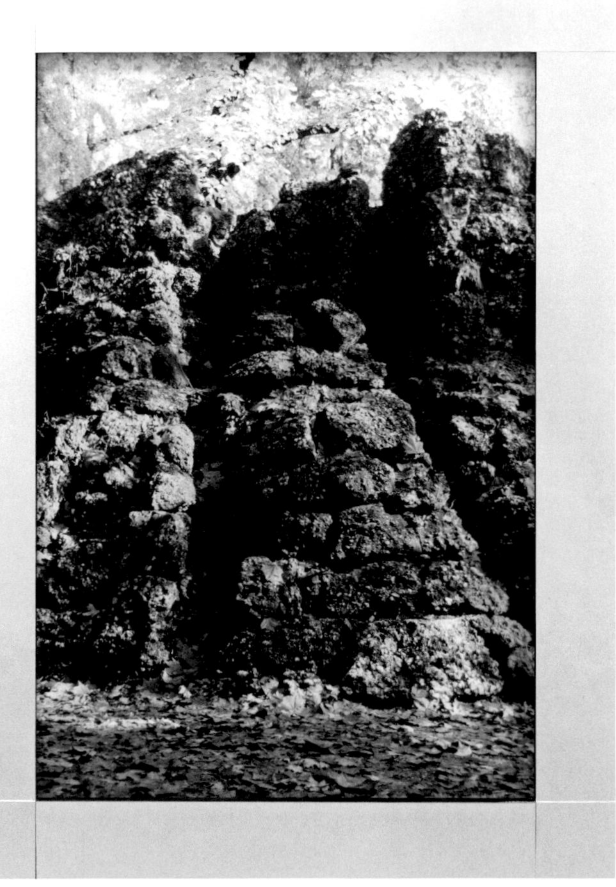

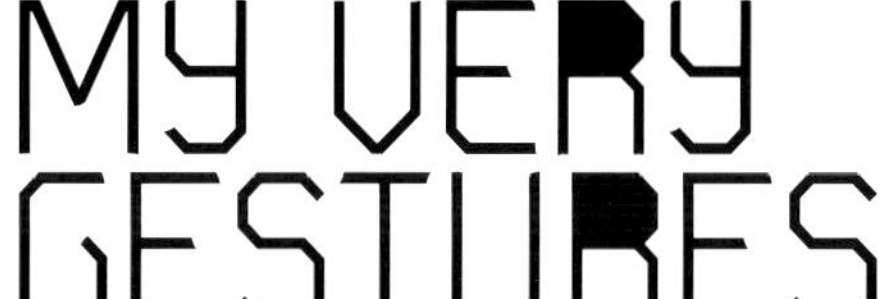

THE ROYAL MUMMIES

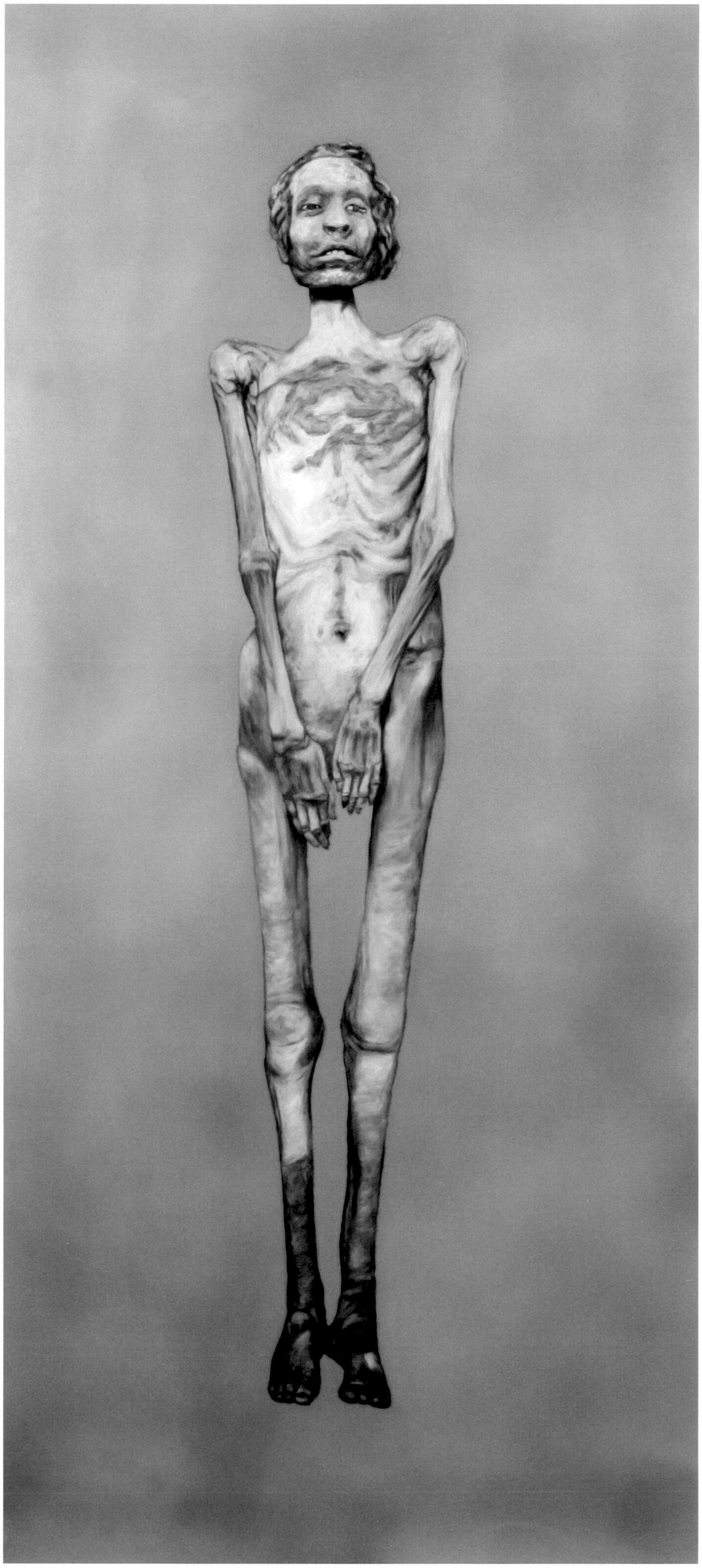

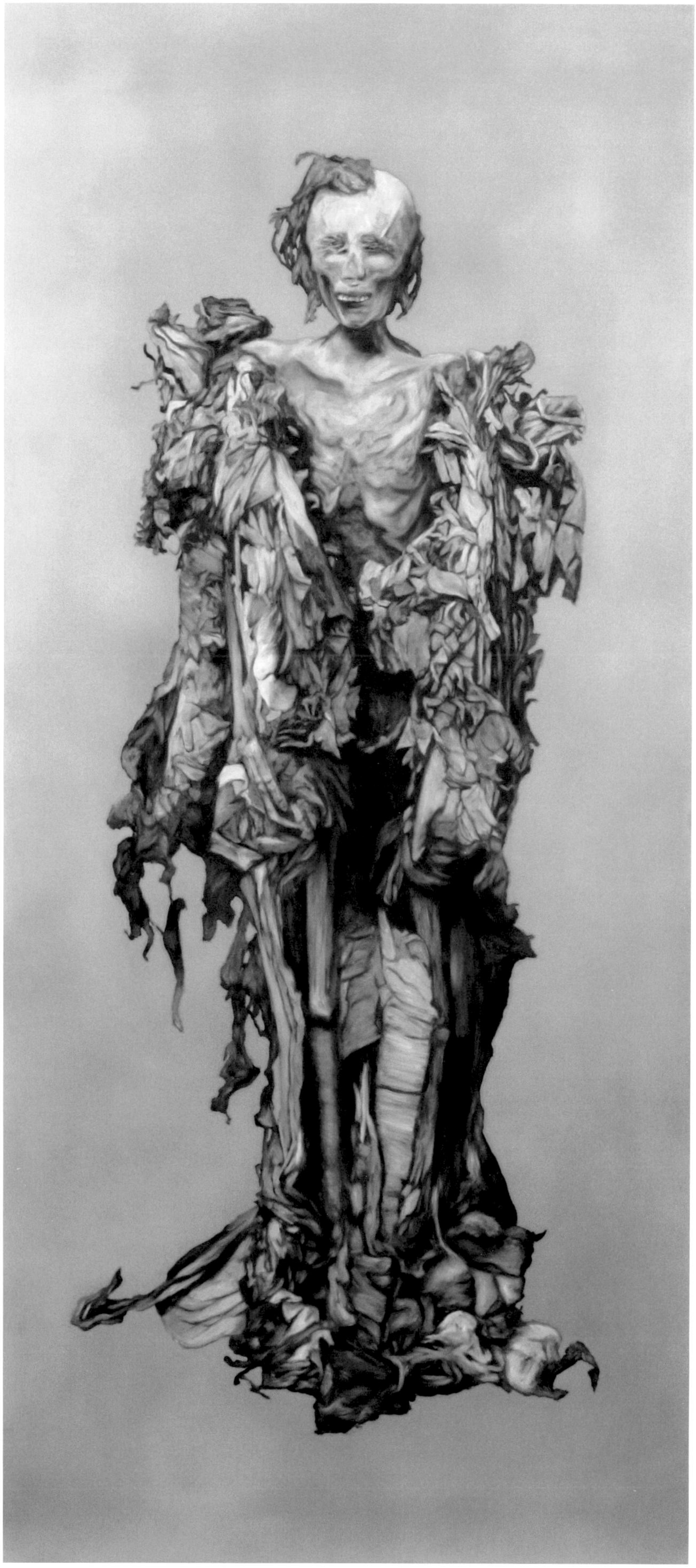

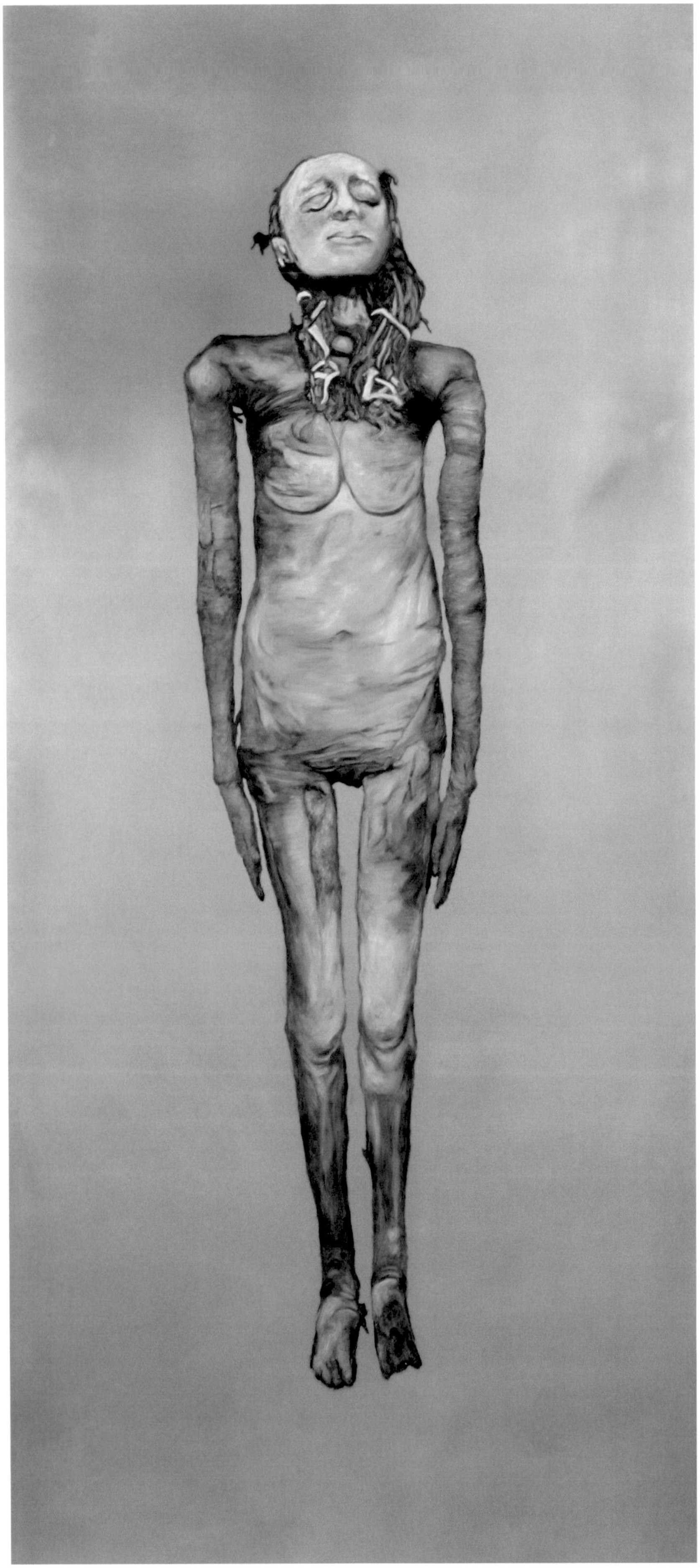

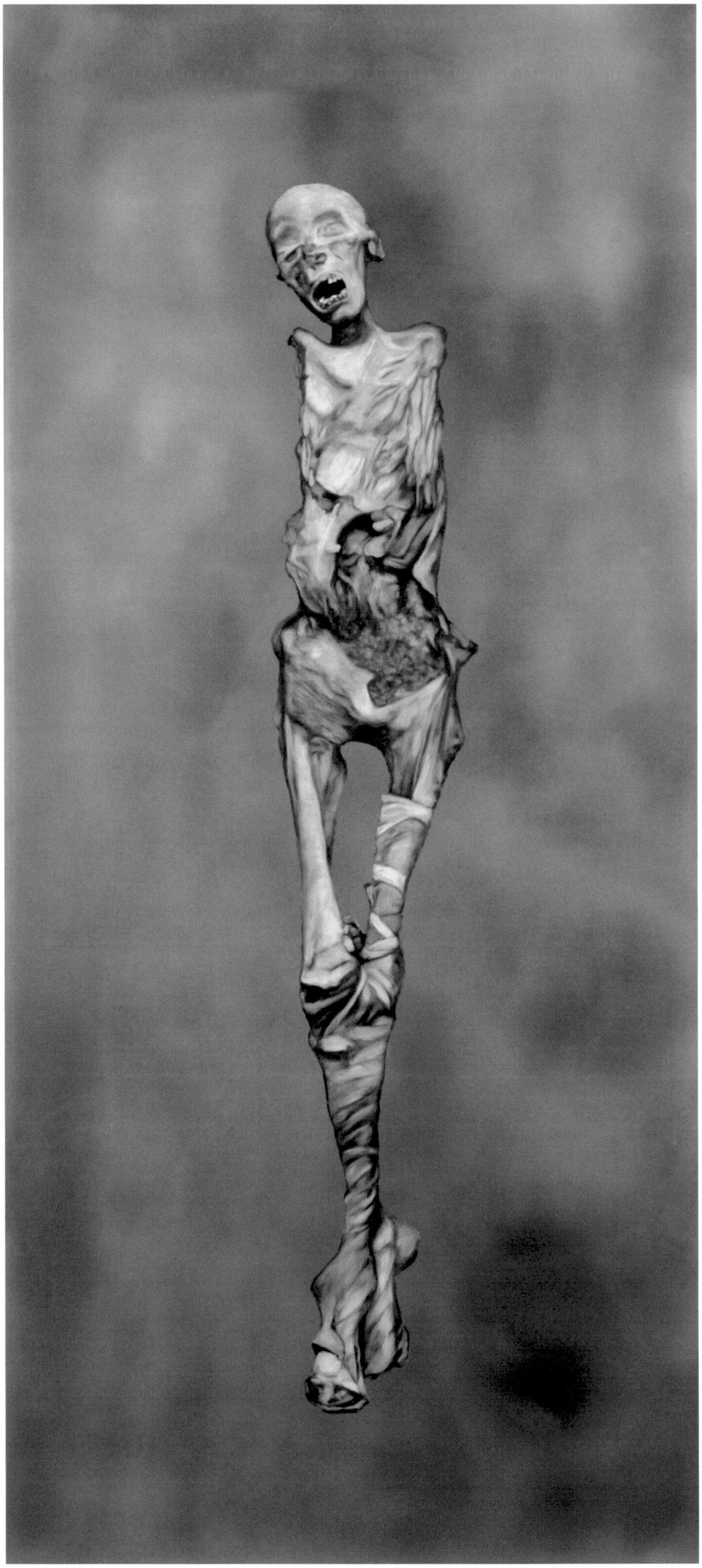

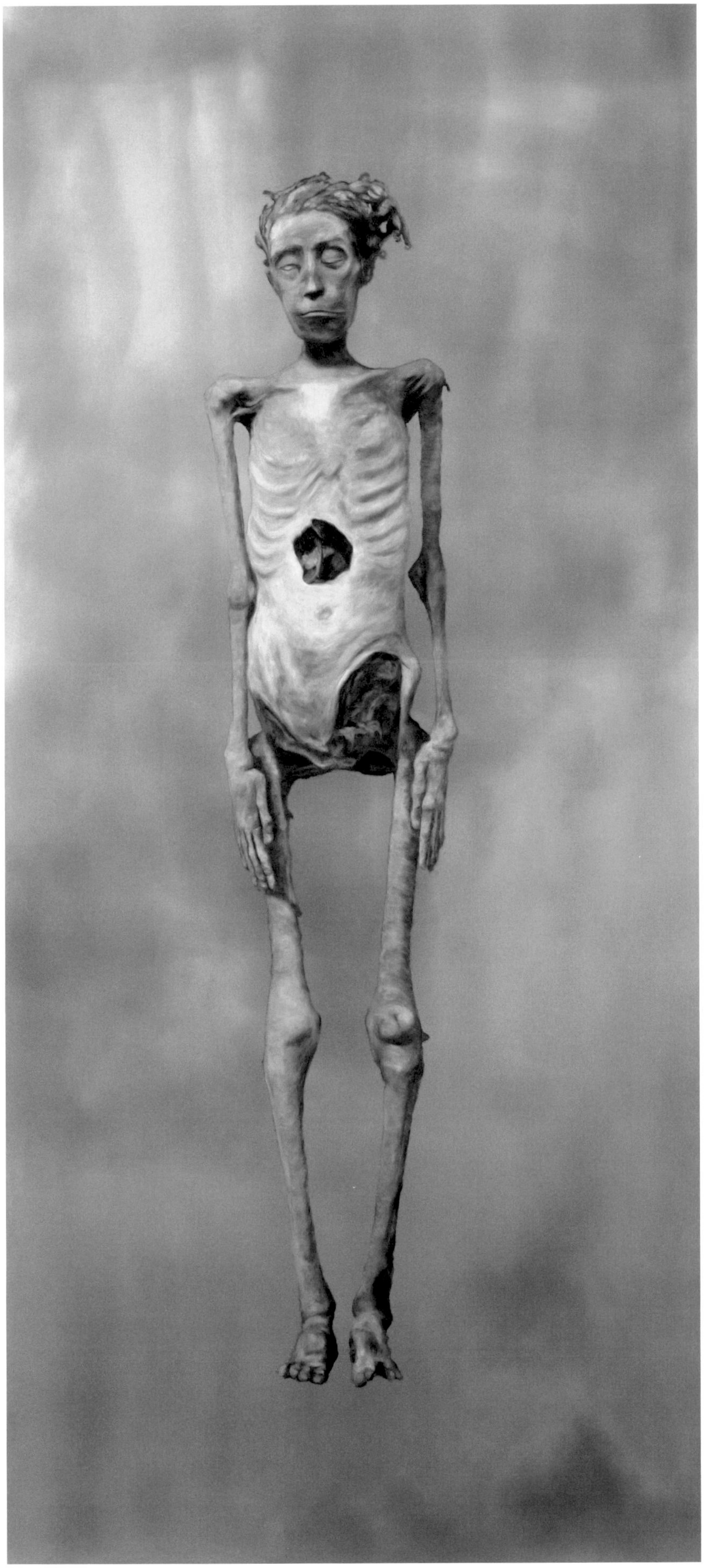

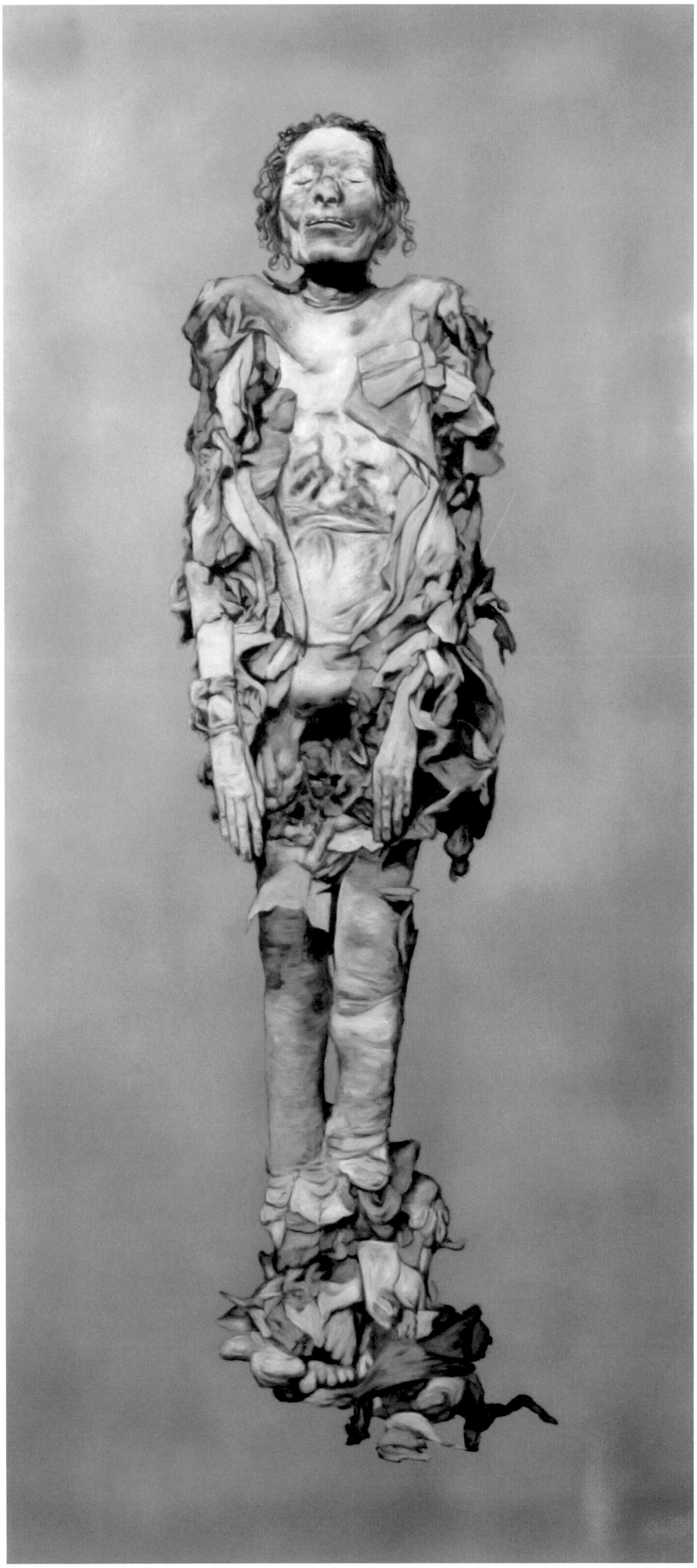

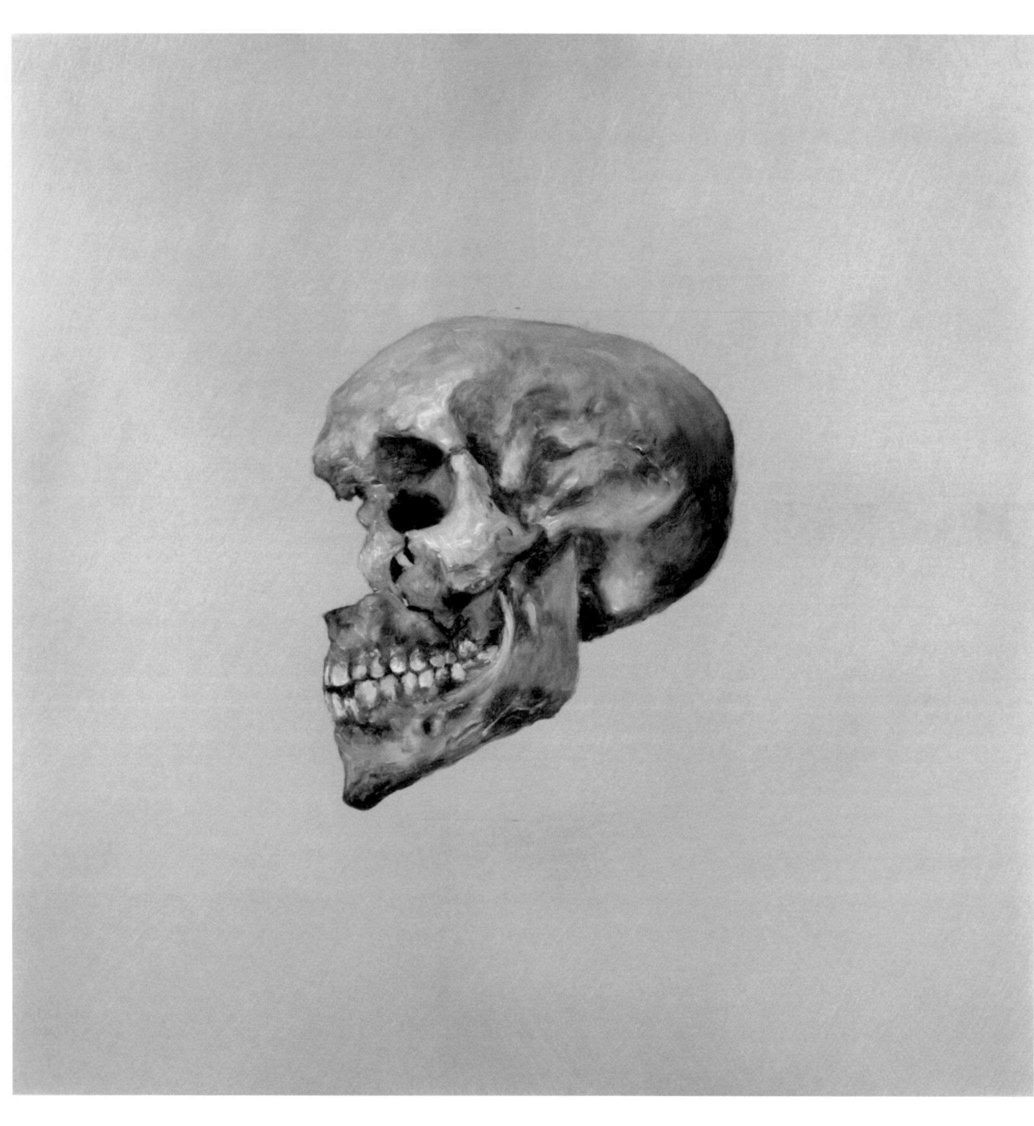

This page:
Unknown Man (Akhenaton?)
Oil on aluminium
40 x 40 cm, 2006

Right page:
The Lady Rai
Oil on aluminium
100 x 60 cm, 2006

This group of paintings attempts to "remummify" the stunning black-and-white photographs, mostly taken by the Egyptologist Emile Brugsch, in Grafton Elliot Smith's *Catalogue Général des Antiquités Égyptiennes du Musée du Caire* (1912). The Egyptians had wanted to conserve themselves for eternity; by bringing them to the light of day again, the Egyptologists of the late nineteenth century set the same wheel of destruction in motion again that the embalmers had tried to halt. They unwrapped the mummies, sometimes in a very crude manner—extremities like fingers, ears, or the penis frequently broke off and were lost—and the humidity in the museum made the skin turn dark.

The photos of Emile Brugsch conserve the state the mummies were in when they were first made visible after millennia. The time span of the photos is very short in comparison. The original negatives, prints, and catalogues will wither soon.

The aluminum "canvases" were chosen in the hope that they would survive better than canvas. The colors that were used for the paintings are lead white, carbon black, and a fake "mummy brown." "Mumia egyptica vera" was a pigment made of ground mummy limbs that remained very popular with painters until the nineteenth century, partly because it contained natural asphalt (bitumen), which made this brown very fluid and paintable. Other ingredients, such as linen oil or dammar, were already in use by the Egyptians for both the conservation of bodies as well as paintings, and we still paint with them today. Grafton Elliot Smith, who was the founder of "Hyperdiffusionism," might have been delighted by the idea that not only did painters' recipes diffuse from ancient Egypt into modern Germany, but also the Realism first invented by Akhenaton (or his wife Nefertiti), whose (probable) skull can be seen on this page. *A.M.*

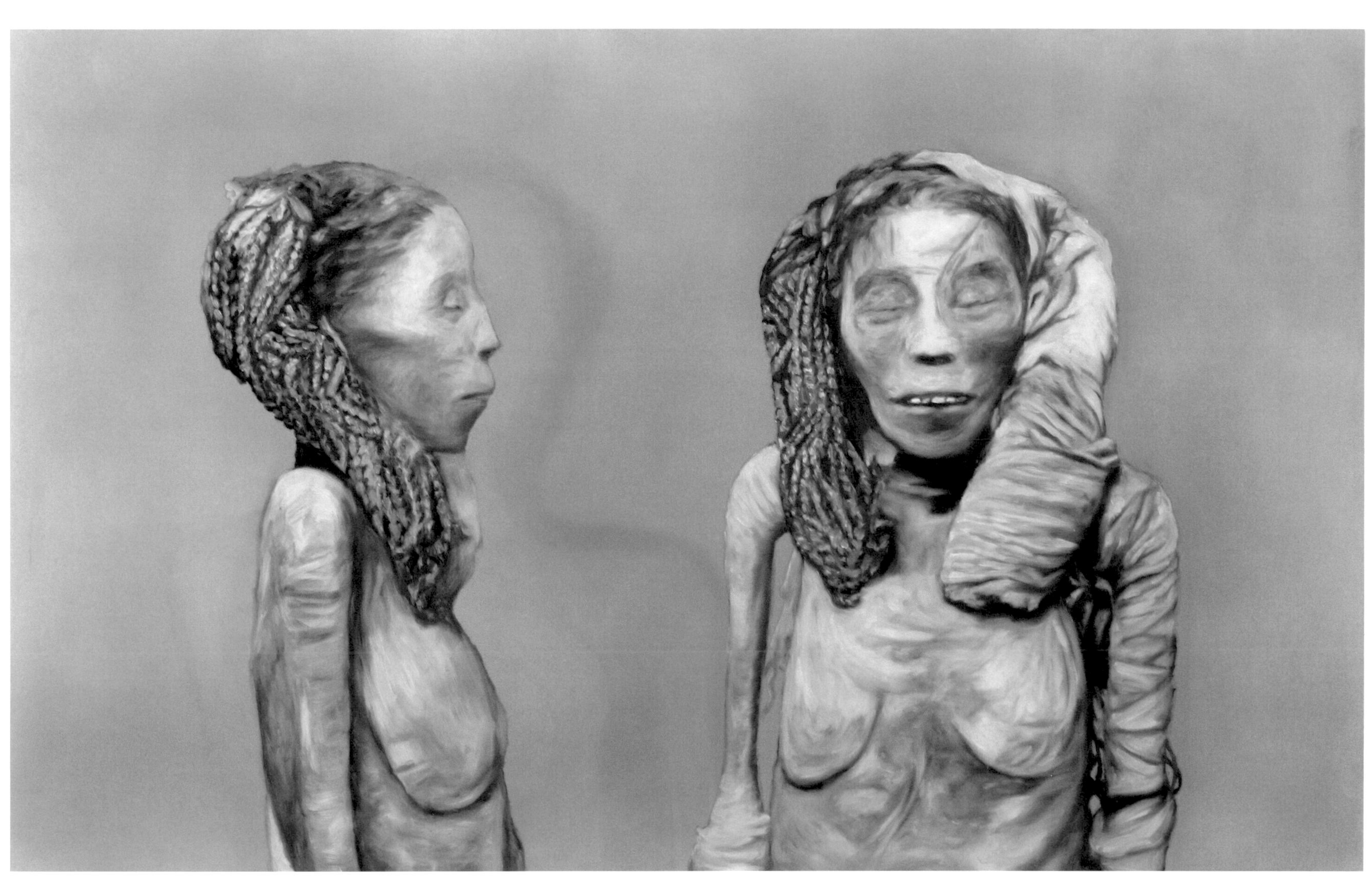

SKARBEK

Bytom is a Polish city in which, for centuries, the mining of ores and later coal was the main source of income. Many houses are standing oblique, have cracks or have collapsed, because the coal was even excavated underneath the city. Today, nearly all of the mines have closed. Progress has left the inhabitants of this formerly prospering mining city behind. The people in *Skarbek* don't want to wait any longer. They hastily go down into an abandoned mine and try to wring another treasure or adventure out of the earth. The lack of air and stimuli makes them dizzy, their sense of proportions of space and time is disturbed. They move on the border to death, and it seems as if by their intrusion the abandoned mine starts to move as well. Skarbek and the treasures of the earth—gold, silver and crystal—make their appearance. Skarbek is a figure of the fairy-tale world of Upper Silesia, a gnome who lives in mines and keeps watch of the underground treasures. Being an earth spirit, he relates to death and the dead. He guards over the miner's ethos and punishes those who don't respect the mountain. Skarbek makes his presence known with noises and can take on various shapes. In the play he materializes as a mouse, a dead miner, and three figures with masks: a very large one, one of human size, and another very small one, which was used for the head of the marionette. All three masks were bought in Mexico. With their dramatic Gothic carvings, they stylistically reflect the time in which the Spanish conquered Mexico and its rich gold and silver mines. In Real de Catorce, the miners had to expect to meet El Jergas. Stories about earth spirits are plentiful wherever men dared to confront their natural fear of dying, deep down in the earth. Sometimes Skarbek plays harmless, amusing tricks on people, but he can also become vengeful and very dangerous. He is unpredictable for the human beings in our play. Belonging to the realm of the inorganic, he follows its laws, which are alien to human beings.

A.M.

Skarbek, 2005
Play by Antje Majewski and Ingo Niermann

Directors	Antje Majewski and Ingo Niermann
Libretto	Ingo Niermann
Choreography	Tomasz Wygoda
Dancers	Witold Jurewicz, Anna Maria Krysiak, Iwona Olszowska, Beata Owczarek, Jacek Owczarek, Janusz Skubaczkowski, Anita Wach, Tomasz Wygoda
Marionette Player	Włodzimierz Pohl
Stage design and costumes	Antje Majewski
Music	Katrin Vellrath
Light design	Piotr Pawlik
Assistant director	Dorota Sajewska
Dramaturgical collaboration	Götz Leineweber
Set construction	Jerzy Cieŝlicki
Costume tailor	Krystyna Szczepan
Music production	Christoph de Babalon
Marionette	Rafał Budnik
Mouse	Martine Maffetti
Production	Galeria Kronika, Bytomskie Centrum Kultury, and Büro Kopernikus

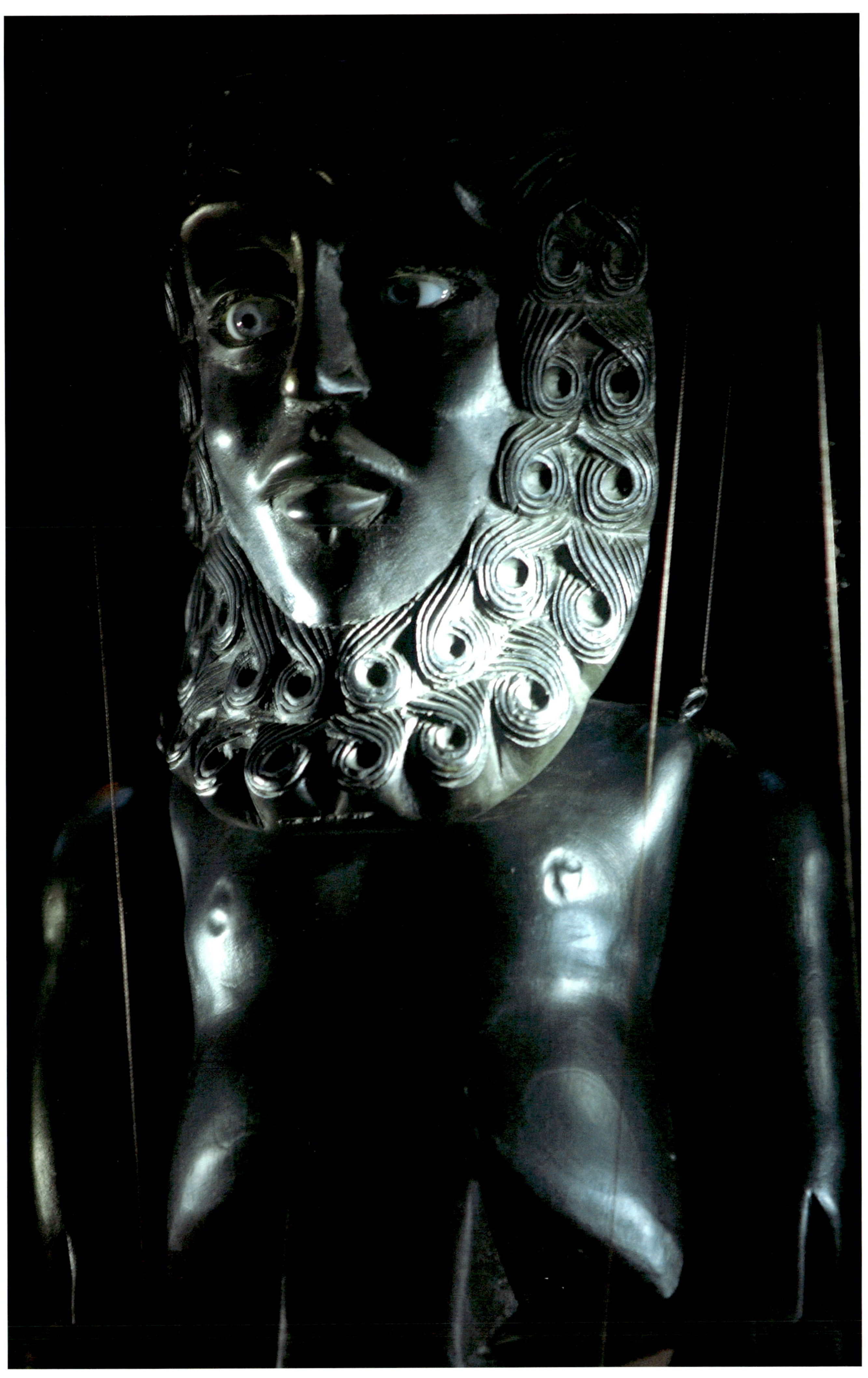

Skarbek
A play by Antje
Majewski and
Ingo Niermann
Photos of the
performance at the
Volksbühne am
Rosa-Luxemburg-
Platz, Berlin, 2005

53

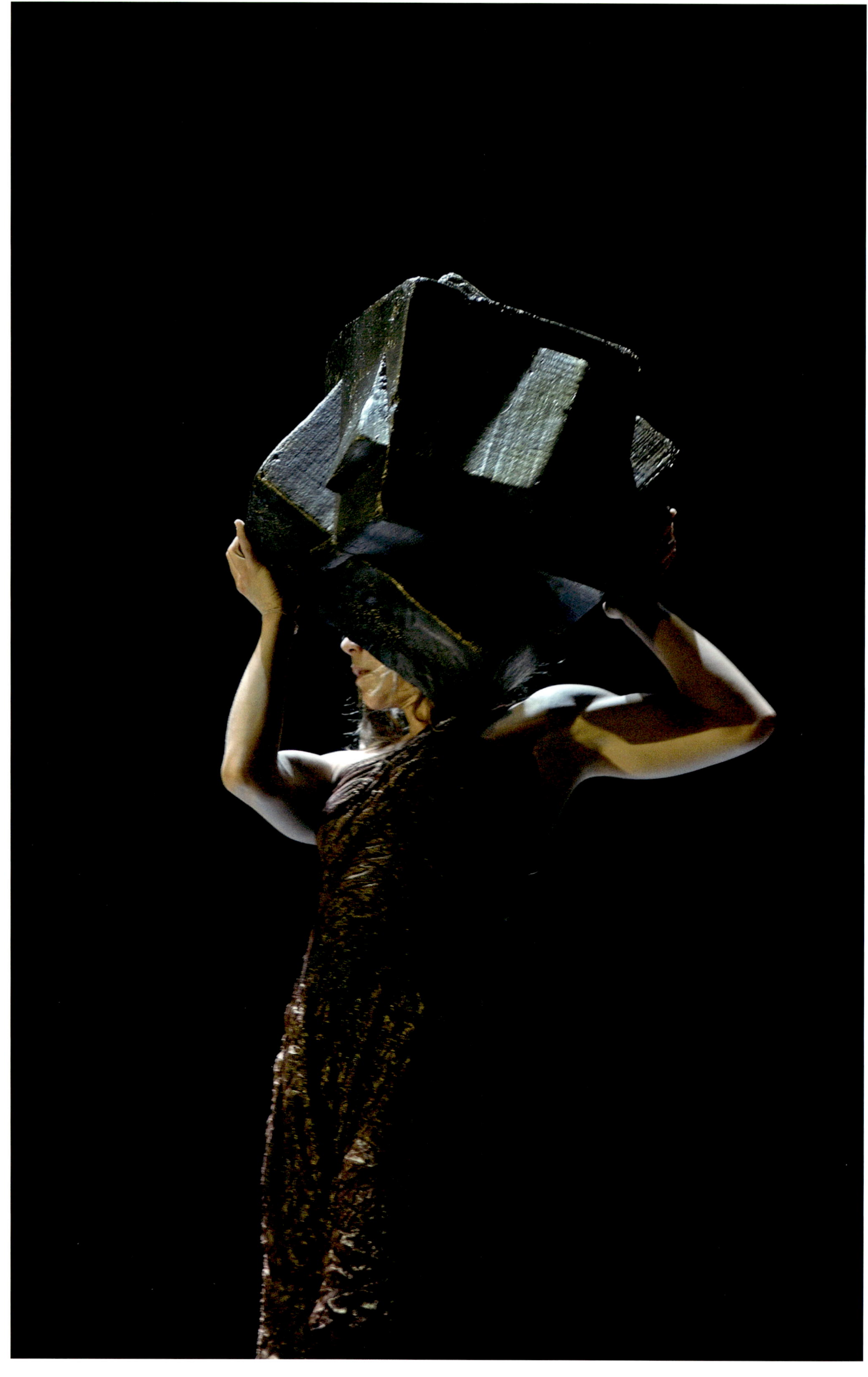

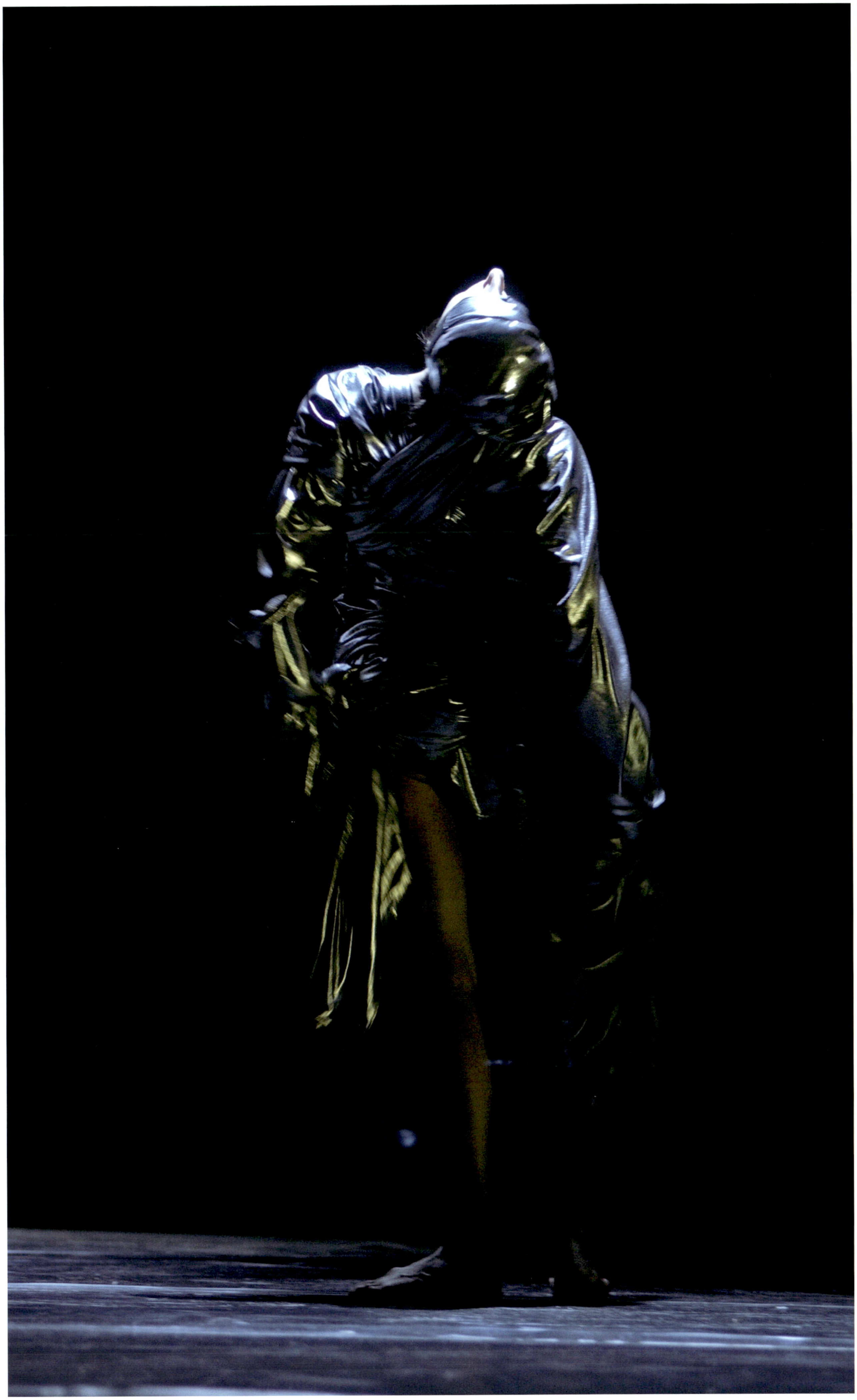

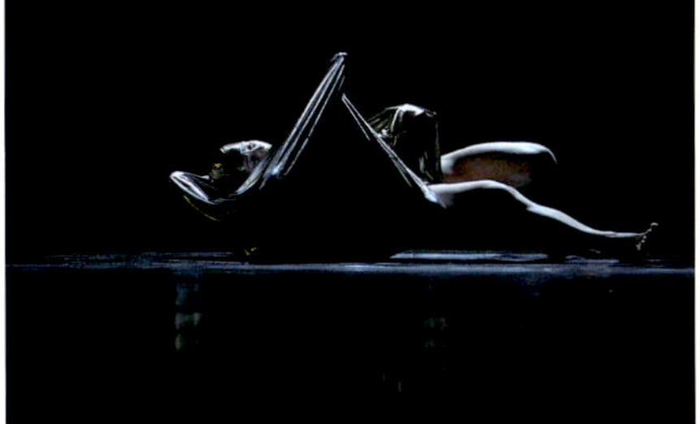

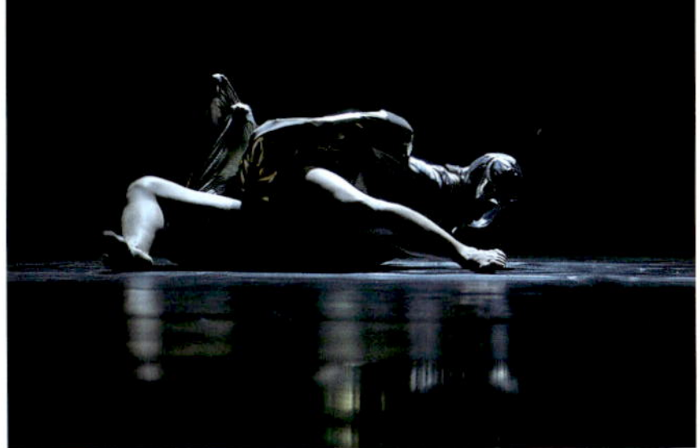

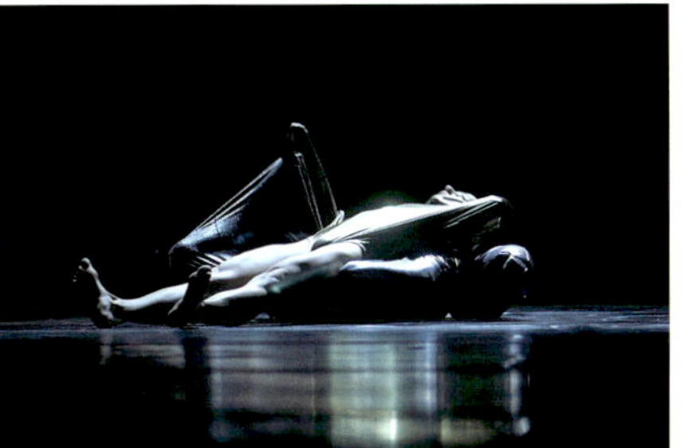

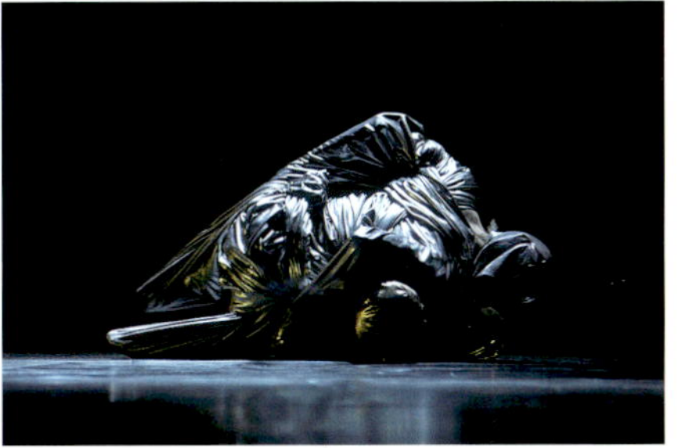

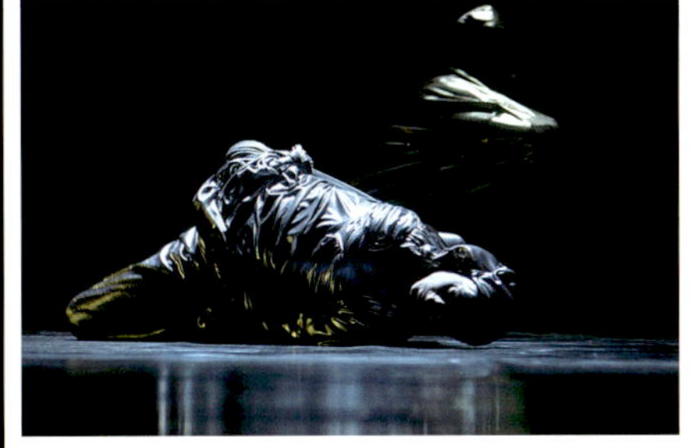

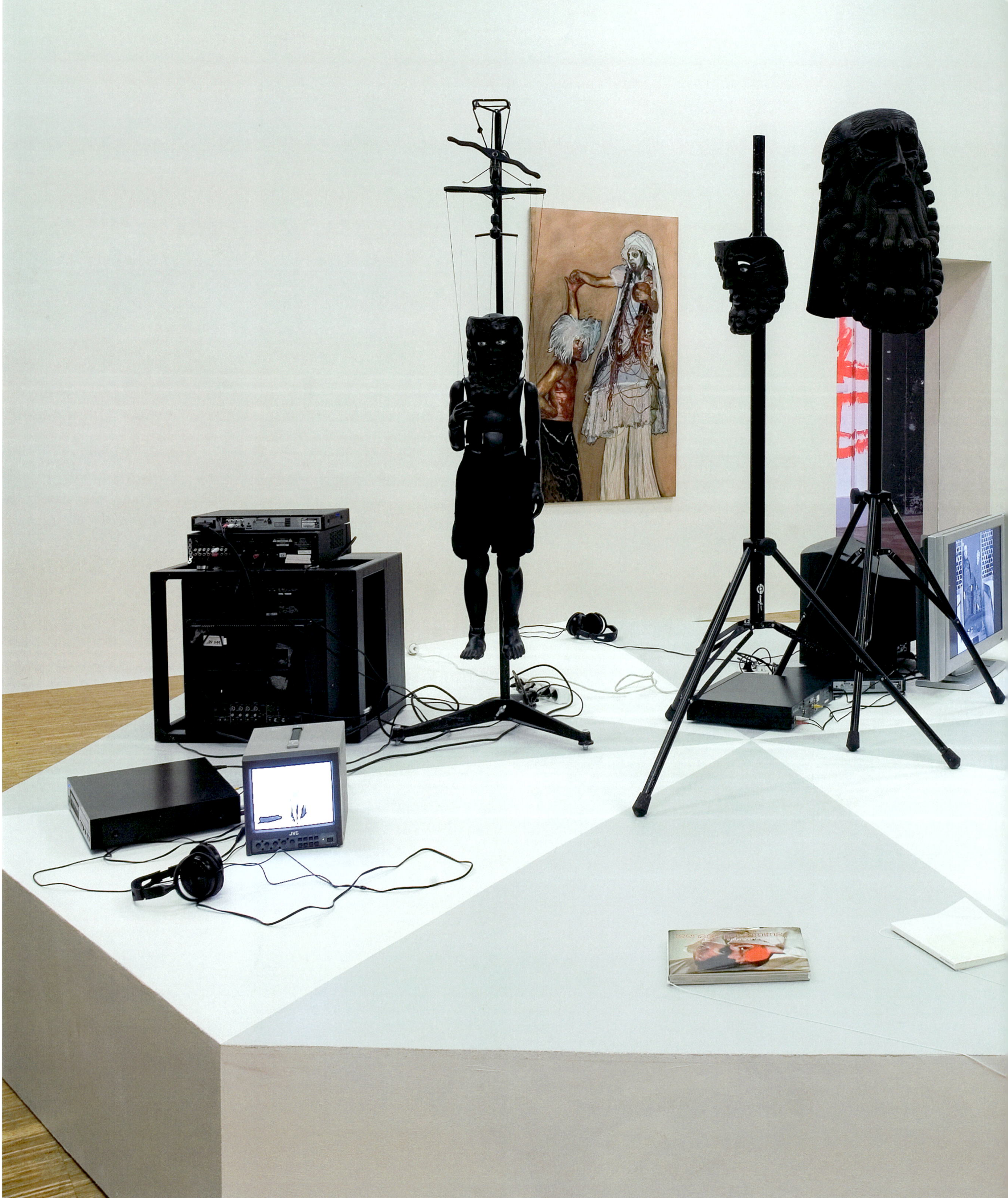

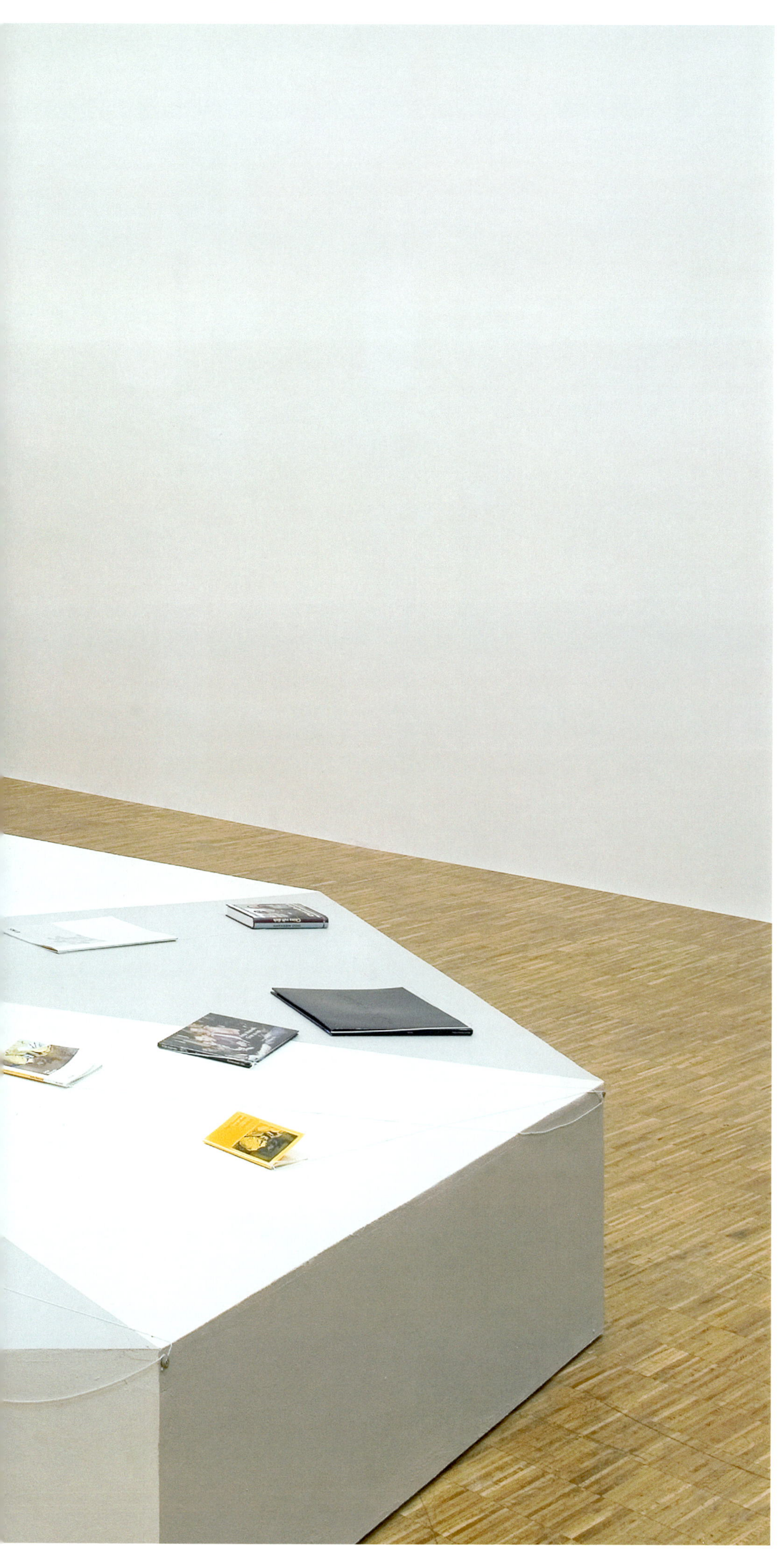

My Very Gestures
Installation view
Salzburger Kunstverein, 2008

Masquerade
Oil on copper sheet on wood
168 x 100 cm, 2006

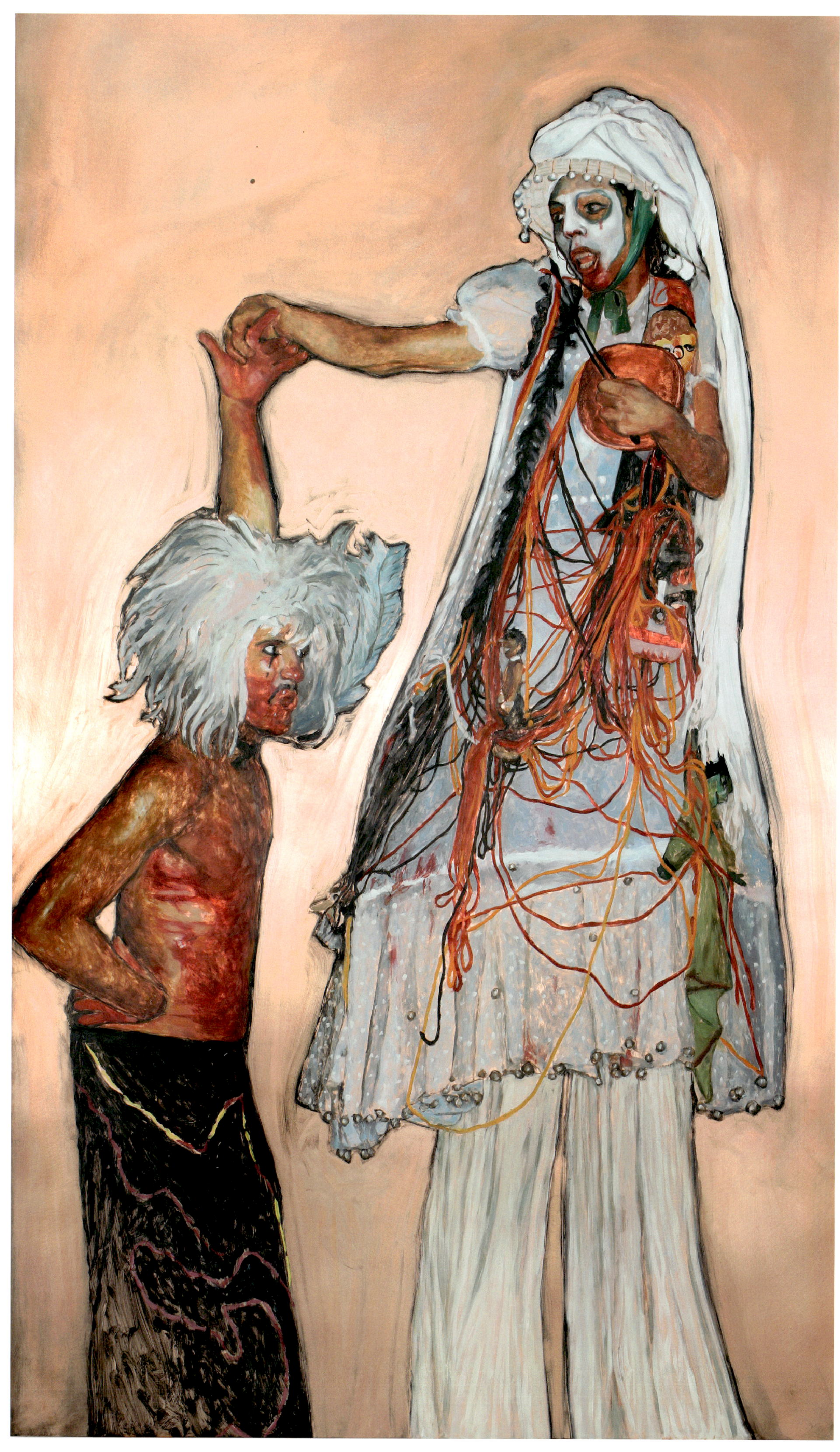

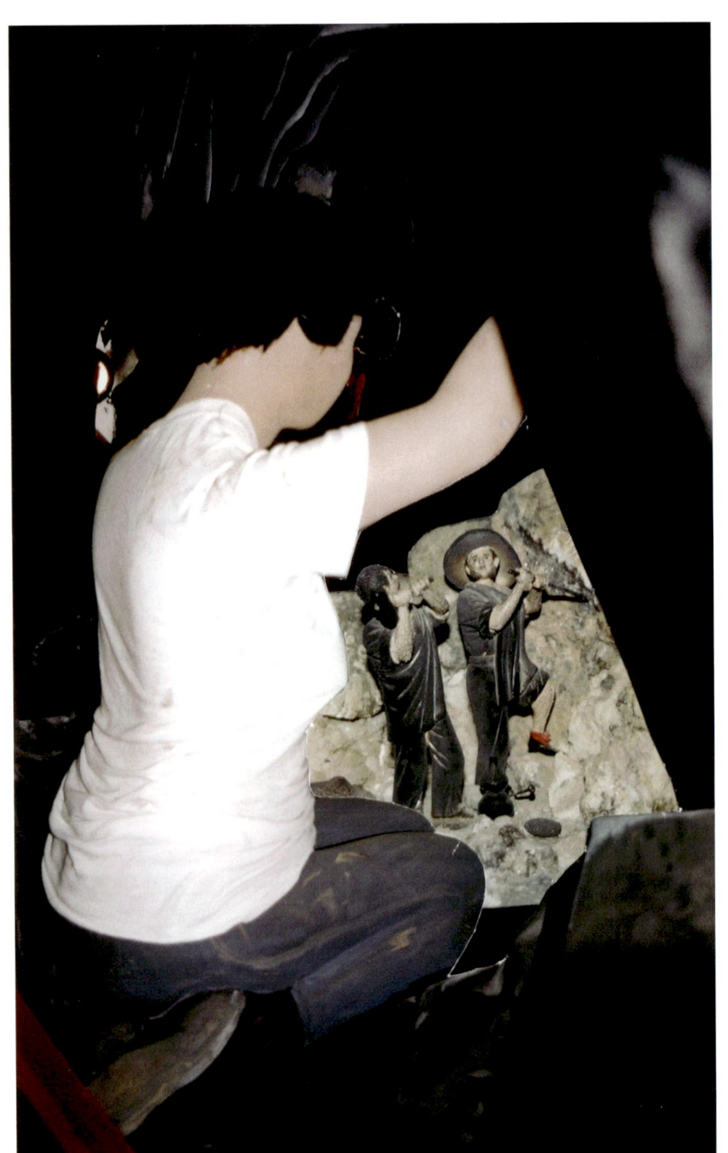

MAL
DE
OJO

Die Bergleute
C-prints, collage
29 x 18.5 cm, 2005

60

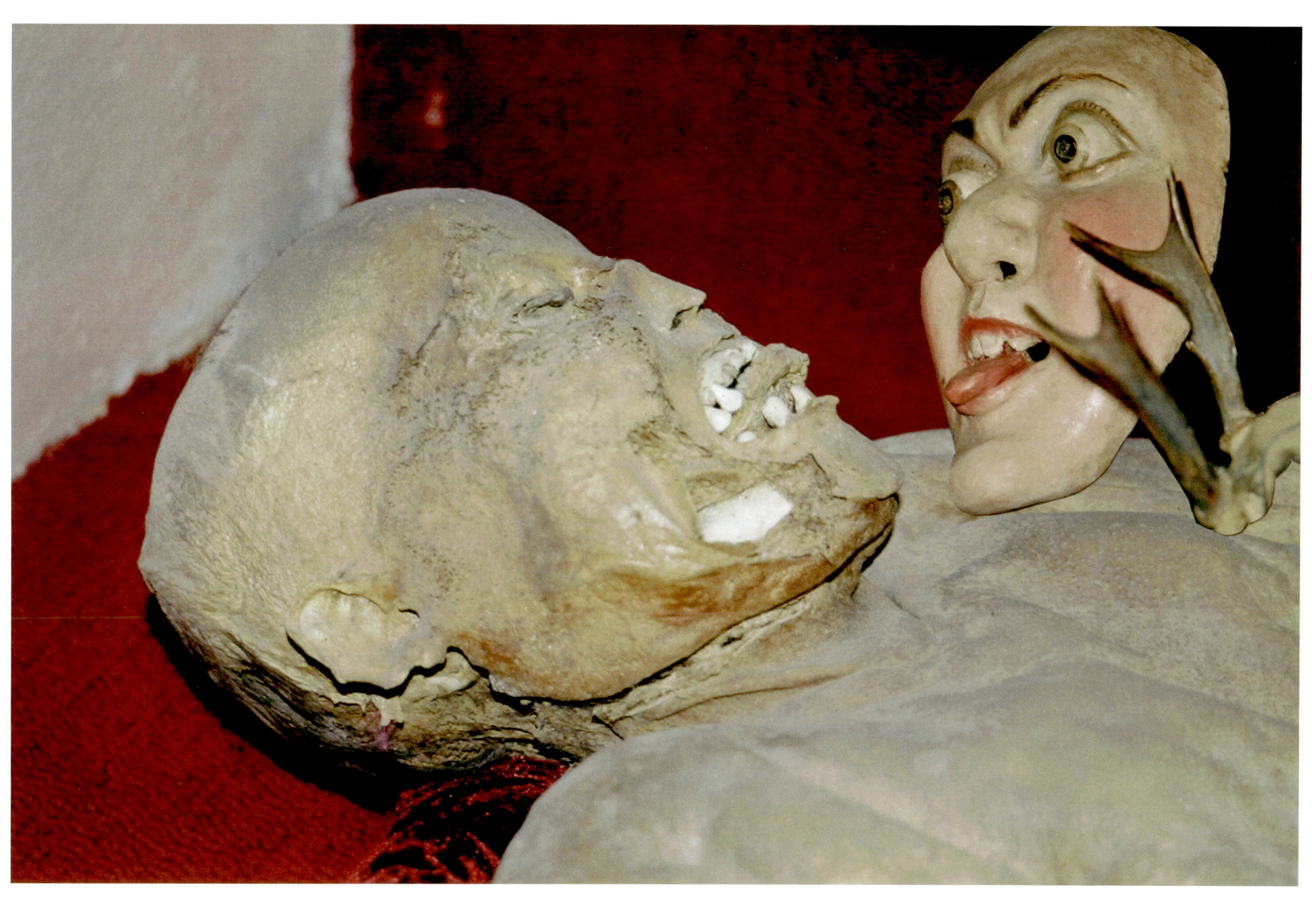

"??"
C-prints, collage
18.5 x 29 cm, 2005

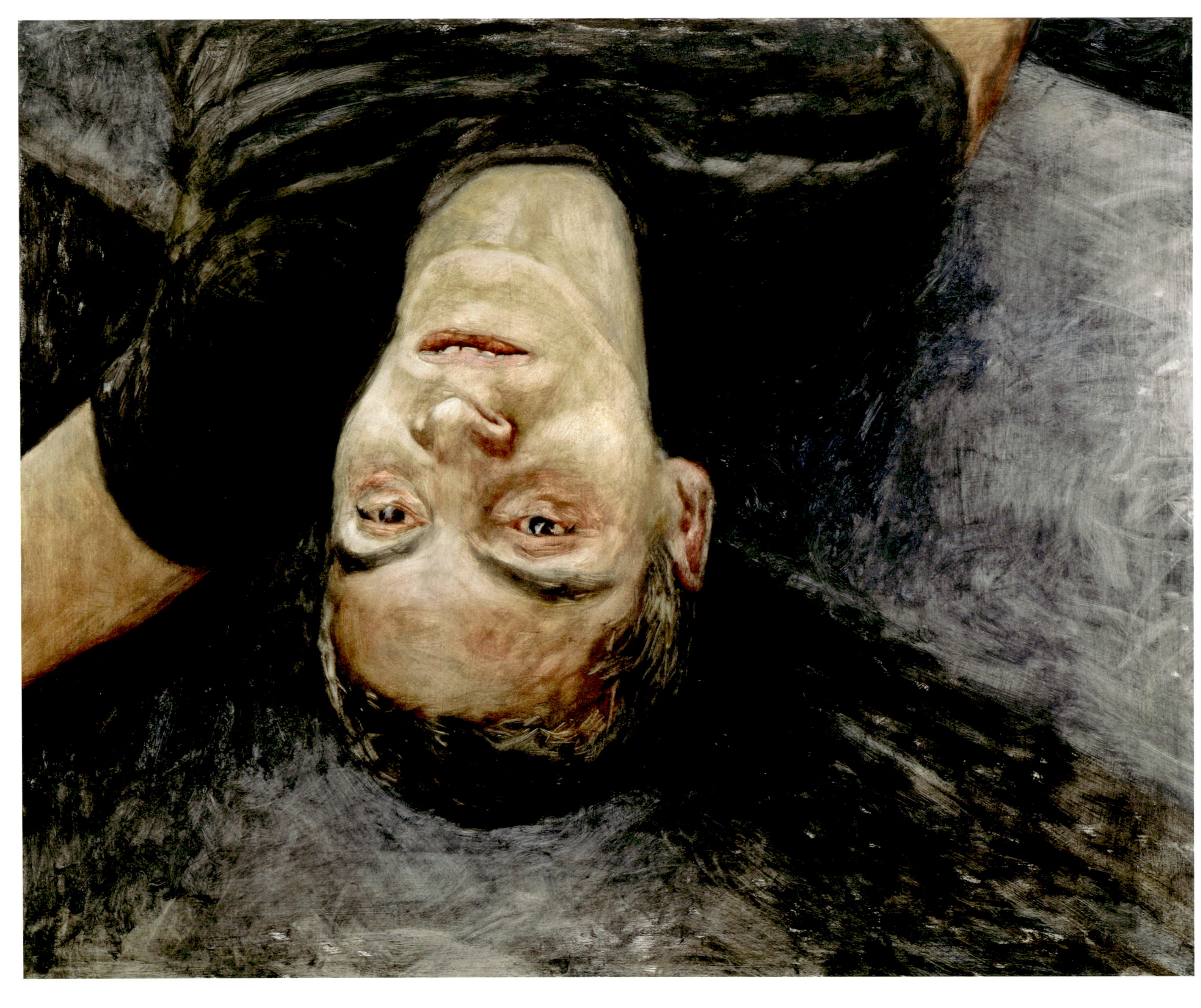

Der Schauspieler Kaveh Parmas stellt einen Toten dar
Oil on macrosel
50 x 63 cm, 2005

62

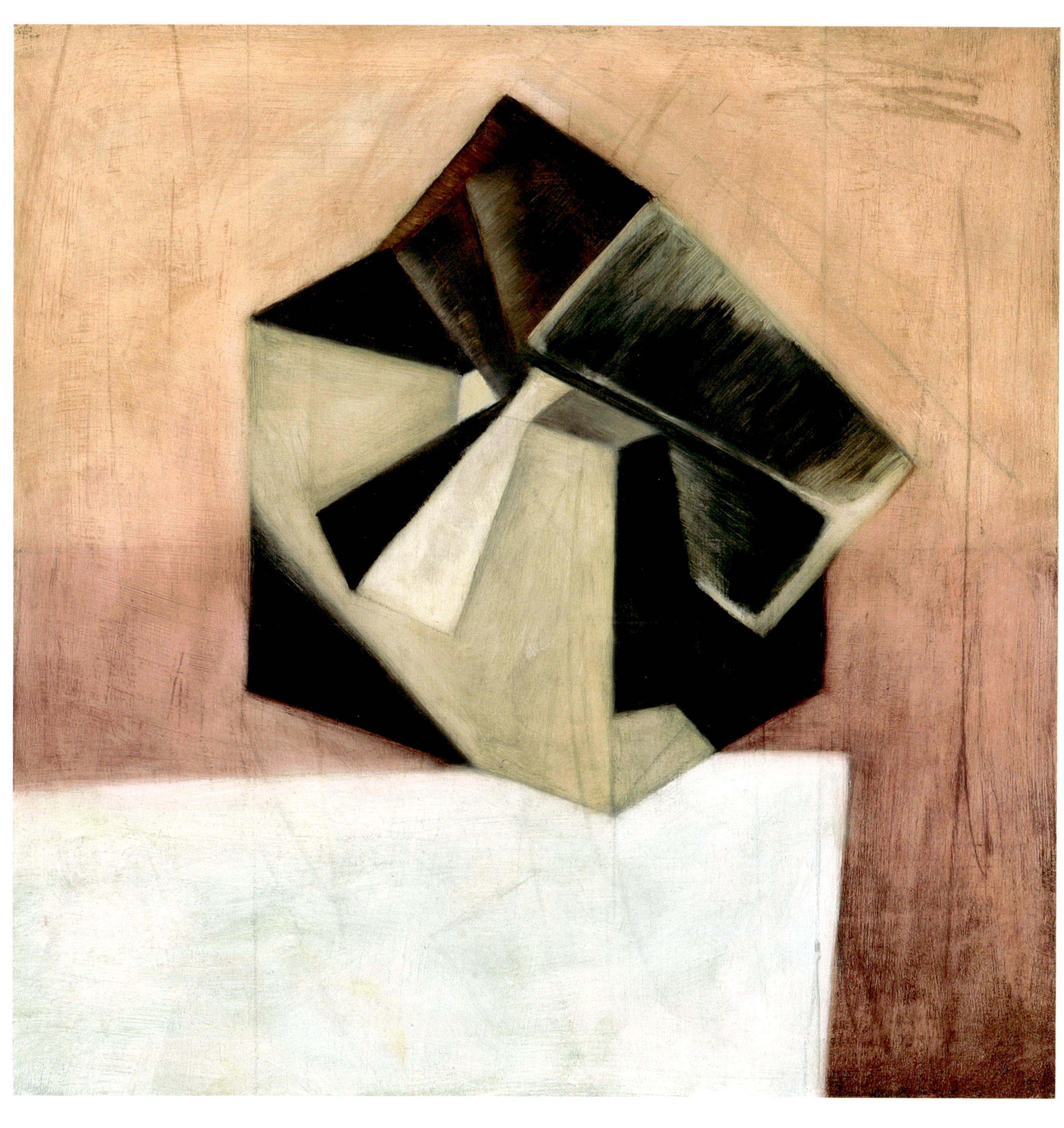

Pyrit
Oil on macrosel
43 x 43 cm, 2005

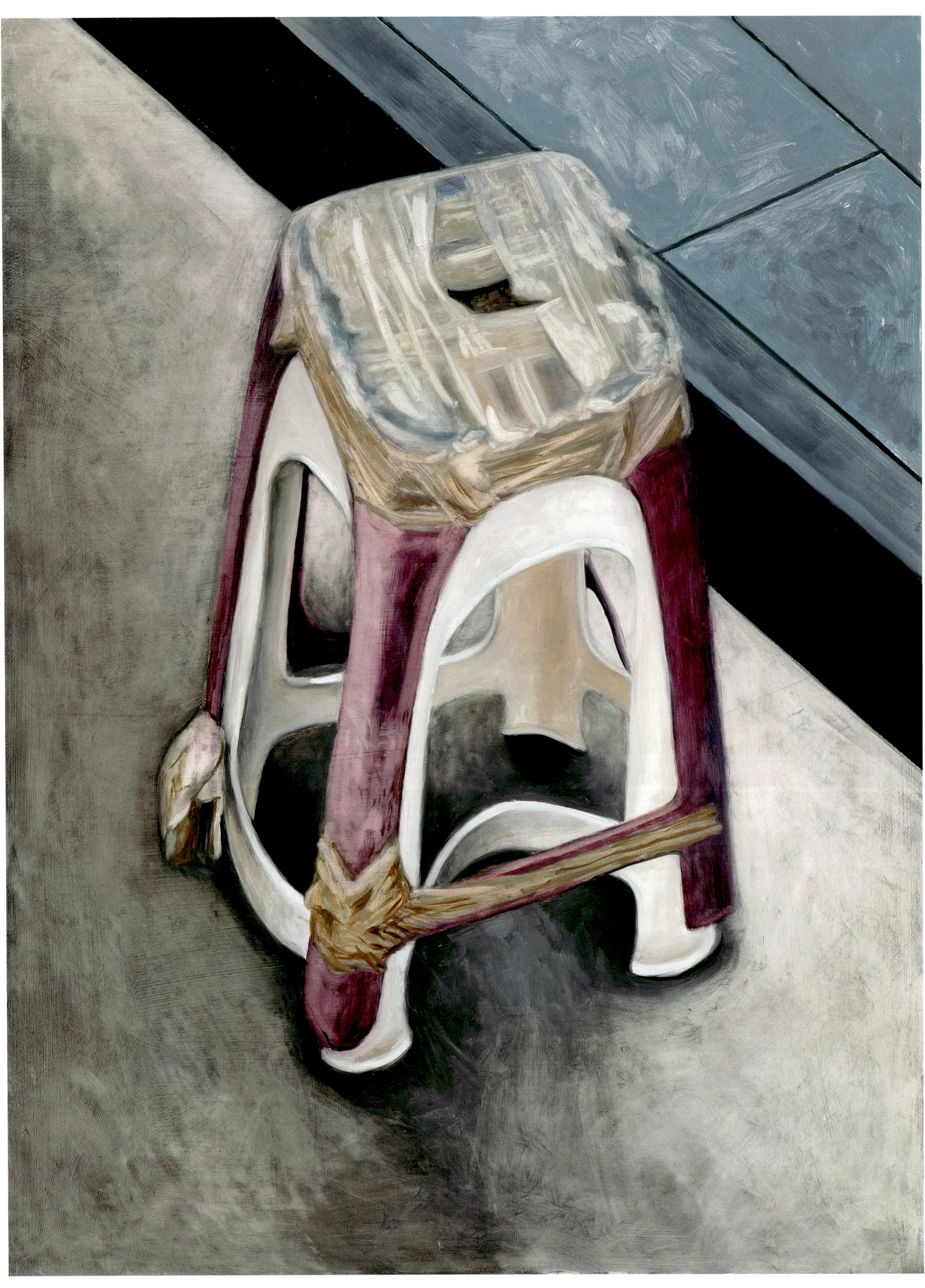

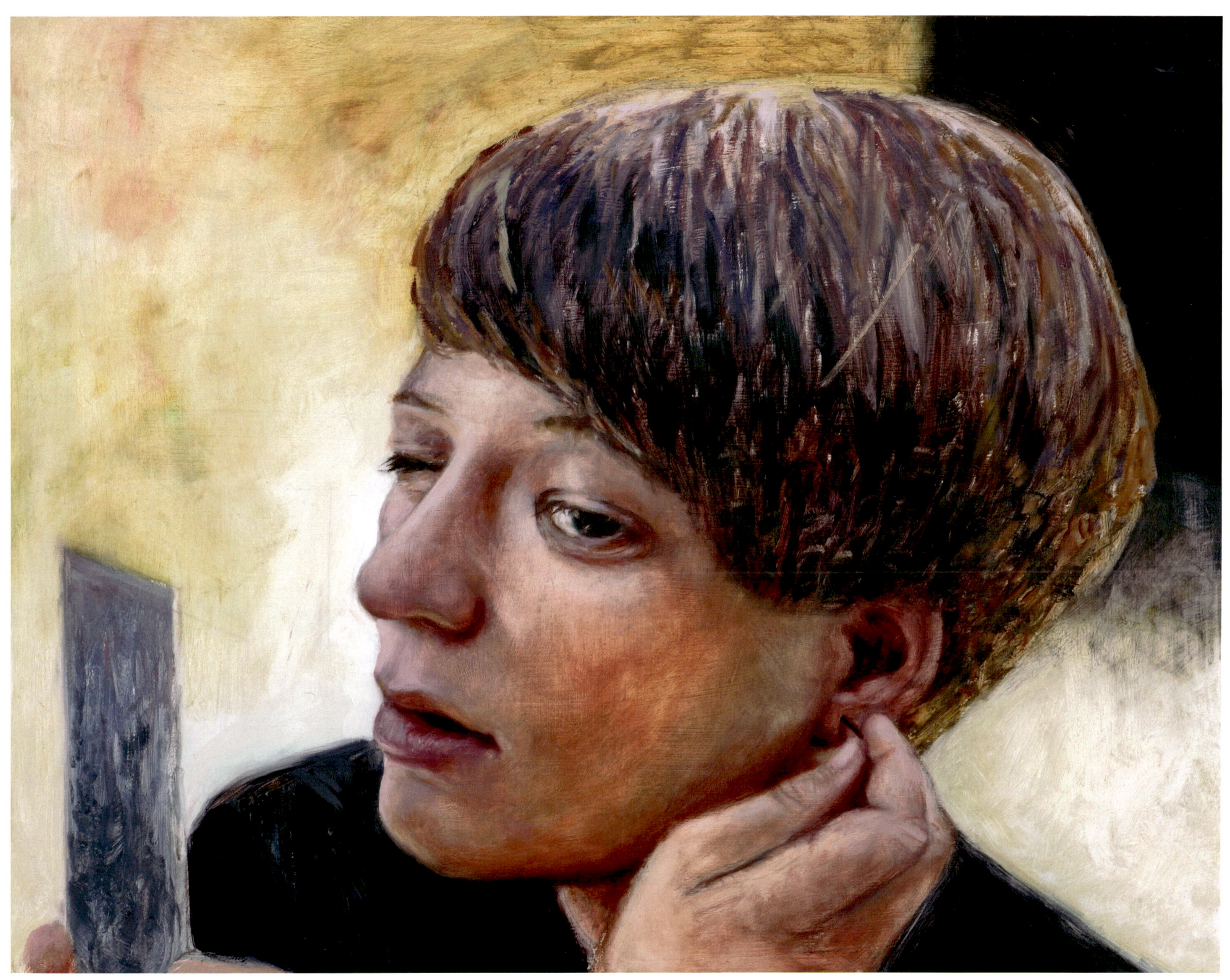

Ich steche mir ein Ohrloch
Oil on macrosel
43 x 56 cm, 2005

Zwei Plastikhocker
Oil on macrosel
86 x 64.5 cm, 2005

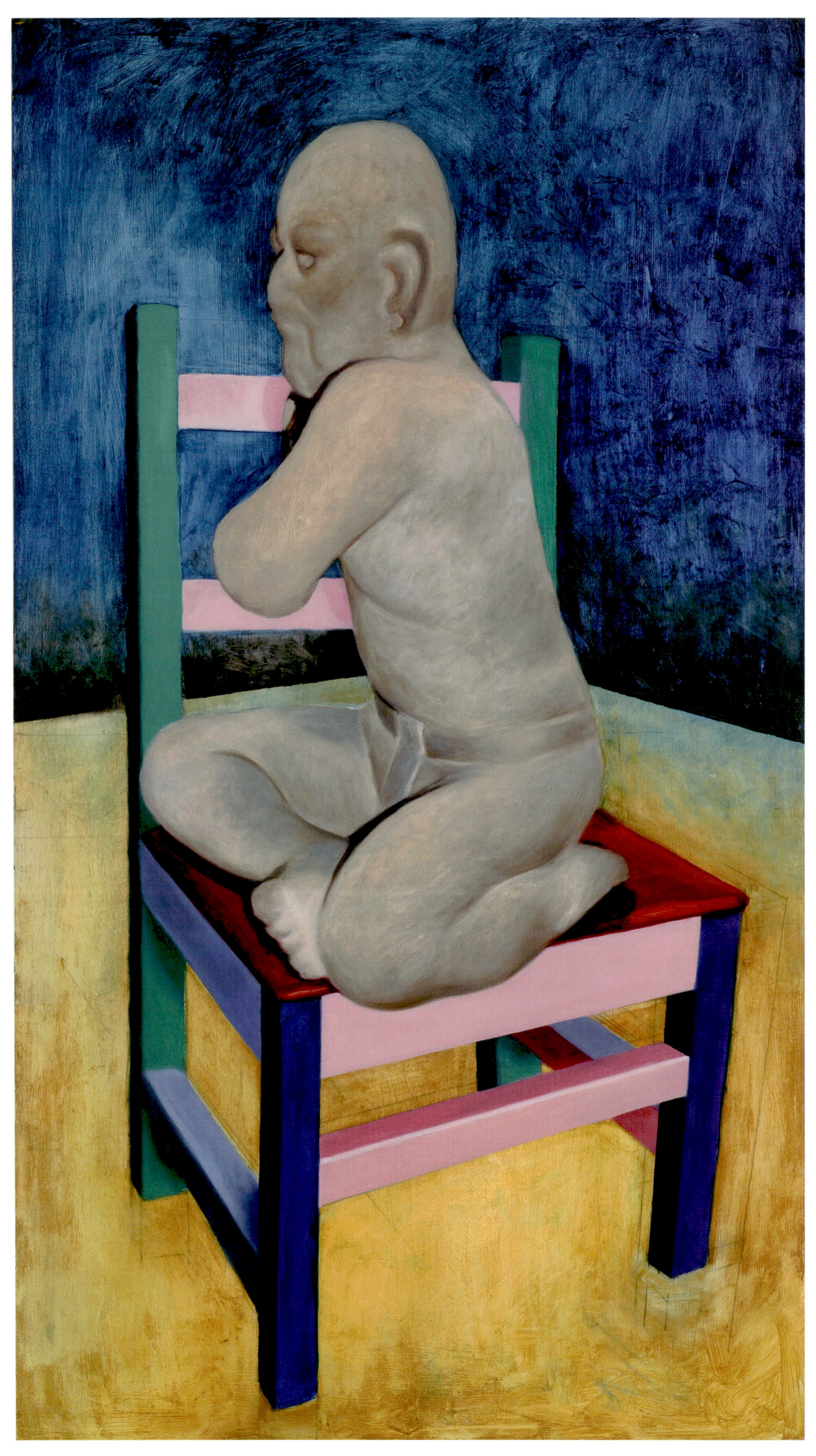

Der Steinmann
Oil on macrosel
112 x 64.5 cm, 2005

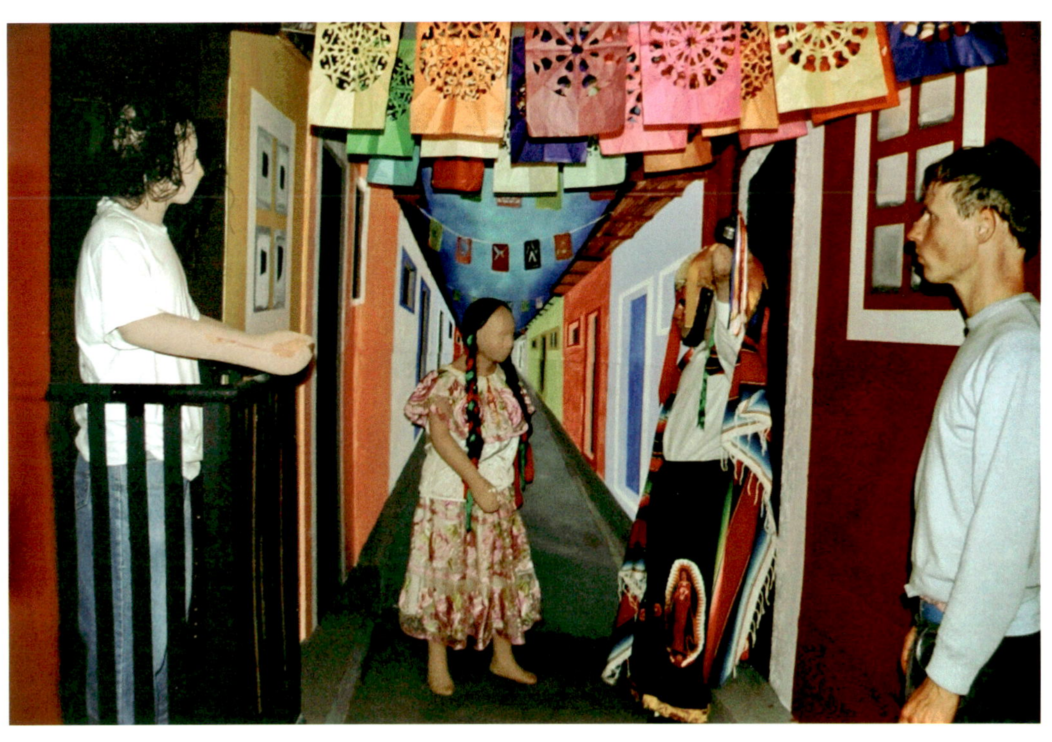

Karnevalsszene mit zwei Beobachtern
C-print
18.5 x 29 cm, 2005

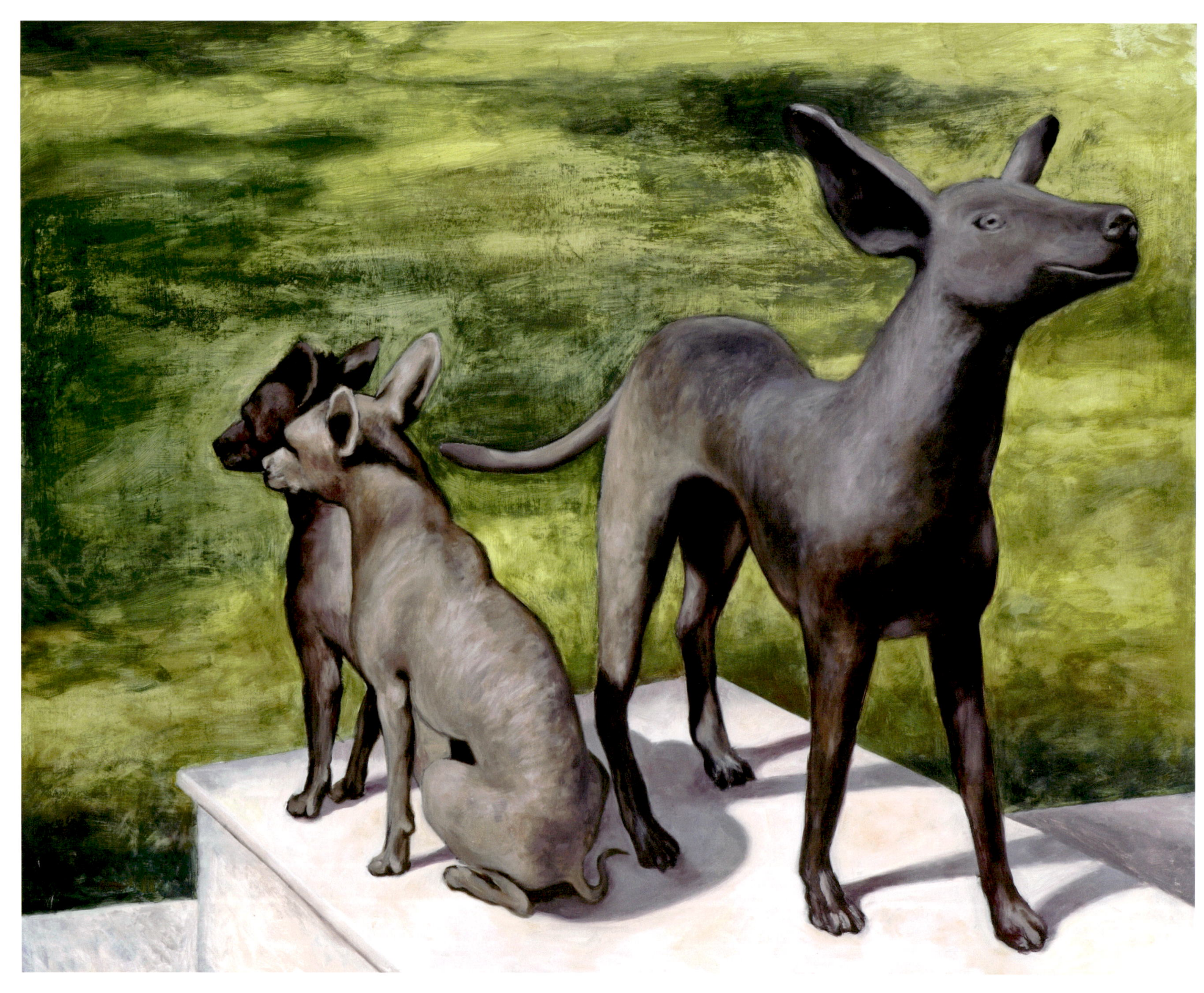

Xoloitzcuintles
Oil on macrosel
84 x 107 cm, 2005

68

What Is with the People?

Ingo Niermann

Not only man builds himself a shelter. Utters to make himself understood. Uses devices. Recognizes himself in the mirror. Lies. And yet only a human being has the will to be someone other than he is. He paints himself, dresses himself, works out, commits suicide. Even artifacts decoupled from the body serve a magical and thus not only gratifying, but manipulating function for them and other beings.

The more people accomplish in the world, the more they understand themselves as devices whose exteriors are to be designed for the greatest possible functionality—versatile and clean. Even for festivities, they paint their faces only decently. The art that they buy or look at in exhibitions and theaters is indulged more extravagance because they don't need to look at it constantly and consider it largely irrelevant.

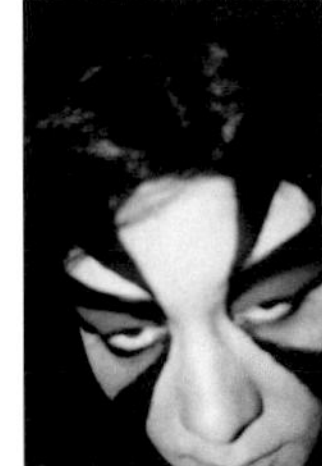

It is only when machines operate increasingly in secret and require hardly any human assistance, but by contrast are capable not only of repairing human beings, but also reconfiguring them, that man's appearance breaks free of man as machine. Until then, actors can become

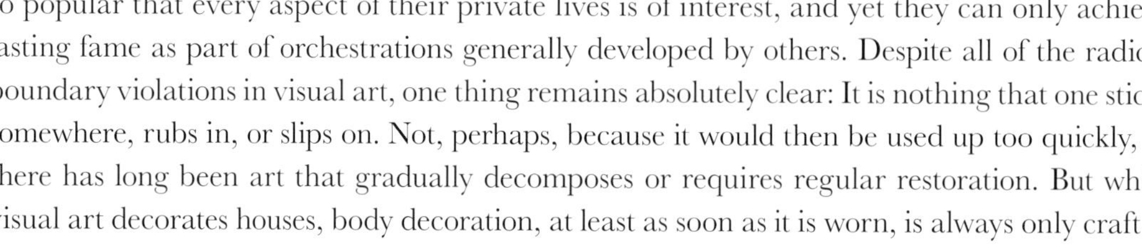

so popular that every aspect of their private lives is of interest, and yet they can only achieve lasting fame as part of orchestrations generally developed by others. Despite all of the radical boundary violations in visual art, one thing remains absolutely clear: It is nothing that one sticks somewhere, rubs in, or slips on. Not, perhaps, because it would then be used up too quickly, as there has long been art that gradually decomposes or requires regular restoration. But while visual art decorates houses, body decoration, at least as soon as it is worn, is always only craft.

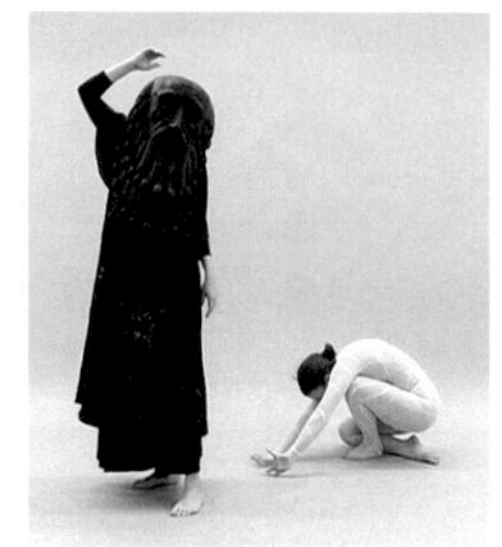

Antje Majewski doesn't allow these boundaries to apply. As a collector, she stores opulent clothing and fabric just as carefully as photos and paintings, but they are also worn by herself and friends. As an artist, she not only paints and films, but also designs the makeup and many of the clothing items related to her underlying orchestrations. When she later sells the paintings, but not the clothes that appear in her videos, then it is not because she sees the latter as a lesser artwork, but because they will continue to be worn as part of her personal collection. For the typical collector, this can be enforced only conceptually at best.

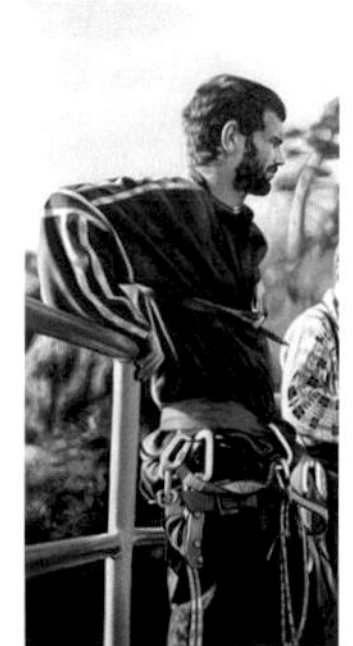

Whether Antje Majewski paints people in their everyday appearance or a staged one, she subordinates herself. Whatever can be seen stays with the people. They are the actual images whose real presentation is only a fleeting one. Even on the photos used for the paintings, they are only snapshots. Painted by Majewski, the visible seems plastic and contrived. The weekend mountain climbers, the museum visitor in a fur coat, the carnival, the temporarily settled vagrant—the human pursuit of self-design is everywhere. Contemporary art, on the other hand, is an epiphenomenon claiming eternity.

In the exhibition *Mal de ojo* (2005) and the dance theater piece *Skarbek* (2005), objects appear prominently for the first time. Treasures of the earth come alive and plastic stools, curtain, and lamp—painted on a smooth, slick piece of fiberboard, smeared and scratched—become the relentlessly waiting undead. Elsewhere, the Xoloitzcuintles, Mexican hairless dogs, already resemble weathered sculptures, and the actor Kaveh Parmas plays a dead man. Like in animism, there is no essential difference between that which is living and the things. This lunacy can also befall animals (cats become enamored of catnip), and yet its systematization into the "evil eye" made art possible, and is conveyed to non-believers as only art. Majewski retraces a possible beginning on herself and re-pierces an earhole from her teenage days.

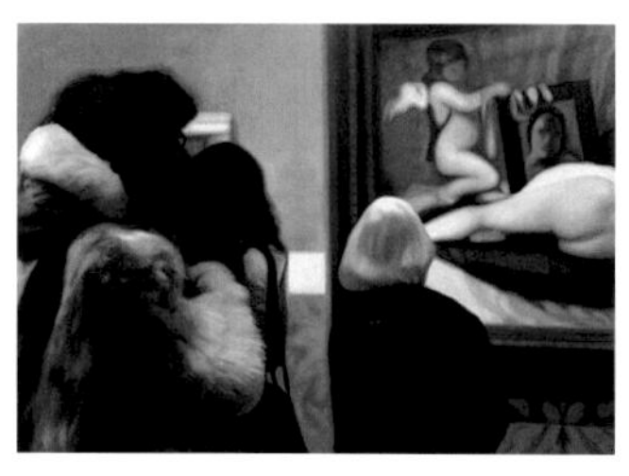

The painting *Entrance to Crystal Palace* (2002) shows a sphinx that once adorned the entrance to the Crystal Palace in London, the eyes of which had been painted red by a stranger. Velázquez's *The Rokeby Venus* seen in *Venus* (1997) was slashed by a suffragette in 1914. The Egyptian mummies in Majewski's *The Royal Mummies* (2006) were supposed to stay concealed forever, but their wrappings were sliced open by researchers. People not only mask and uncover themselves, but also artifacts, and develop new relationships with them. What once evoked reverence is now referred to only casually and vice versa.

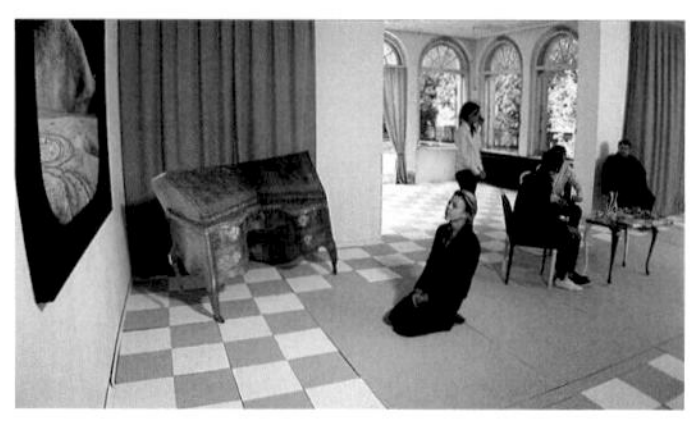

In the video *No School Today* (2005), a child lets an adult move through his high-rise apartment according to new rules. In *Dekonditionierung* (2008), five actors and lay people distill essential human behavioral patterns, such as power and closeness. Majewski's pictures, painted as part of the film's set design, are like everyday décor that the actors can either engage with or ignore. Then in the exhibition, film and paintings stand together as equals. The paintings step forward or the plot steps back as likewise art.

In *Säule Wedding* (2008), Antje Majewski and Juliane Solmsdorf stand together on a defective drinking water fountain in front of the entrance to the Berlin subway station Pankstraße. The artists erect a memorial to themselves in their own lifetimes. But holding onto the column quickly becomes a struggle, and every other passerby can climb onto it for a few minutes, or, like the two artists in the film *Erde Asphalt Wedding* (2007), only crawl forward.

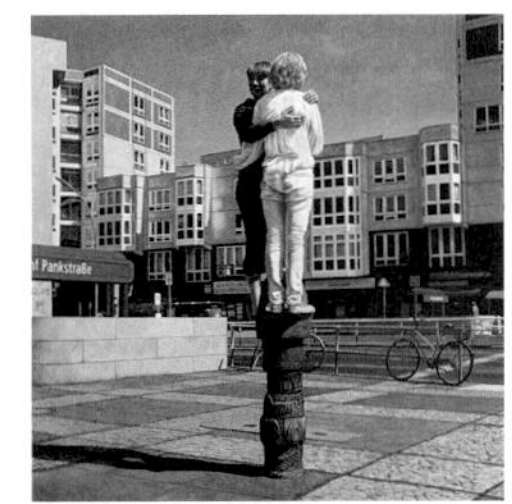

Time and again, the task of art was supposed to be to find the absolute correct forms, and, in doing so, echo man's own mortal and finite measure. This belief has waned. What remains are official norms for how wide an airplane seat should be and how high an apartment should be or how brightly a billboard may shine. But these ordinances are arbitrary, because every single person can decide again for himself at any time what is for him too small, too big, too bright, or too dark. Majewski wants to explore the mutability of this measure in a series— a single image that she will paint over and over again while under the influence of various drugs.

Drugs are the only things, in the course of a human history piled with an inconceivable number of things, that have lost hardly any of their transcending effect on the everyday. They do not surround man, but penetrate him.

The same could also be said of Majewski's ideal of an art that, like in the short story *The Winter Market* by William Gibson, is transmitted directly from one brain to another. As a mask turned inward, it is no longer perceptible to the senses and could, in the most extreme case, completely obscure the other stimuli—man would lose himself in his own mutability.

But what interests Majewski about a directly transmittable art is less the totality than the precision. At the beginning of her career, she toyed with the idea of locking the exhibition visitors in by surprise to defy the meaninglessness of contemporary art. It wasn't long before she realized that she wanted more. She should succeed in no less than a splendor, the measure of which can be seen in a Velázquez, Vermeer, or likewise the spectacles of a forest stroll.

ATOMKRIEG

Silber auf Kupfer (Denkmal für Paul Rosbaud), which translates as *Silver on Copper (Memorial for Paul Rosbaud)* was part of the group show *Atomkrieg (Nuclear War)*, curated by Ingo Niermann and myself at Kunsthaus Dresden in 2004. The painting is done on untreated copper, and shows a piece of jewelry made by Frank Frink (born Fink), a character from Philip K. Dick's novel *The Man in the High Castle* (1962), and is my Medal of Honor for the German spy Paul Rosbaud.
In my text for the exhibition catalogue, I combine my own historical research on the story of Paul Rosbaud who, towards the end of WW II, tried in vain to betray the secrets concerning German nuclear bomb research to the Americans (which, had he succeeded, would have made the American deployment of the nuclear bomb inexcusable) with the Philip K. Dick novel, a world scenario in which Germany and Japan have won the war. Frink, a secretly Jewish, American artisan, suddenly manages to create a piece of jewelry that the Japanese see as containing *Mu* (or, in Chinese, *Wú*)—the emptiness of the spirit, or the Nothing sought by both Chinese and Japanese philosophy, which is supposedly incomprehensible to the base American race. This piece of jewelry also allows Frink a glimpse into the real world in which the Japanese have actually lost the war.
Since Frank Frink doesn't exist and I didn't dare claim to have invented something with inherent *Wú* myself, the piece of jewelry is, in fact, a piece of natural silver from a mineralogical museum.   *A.M.*

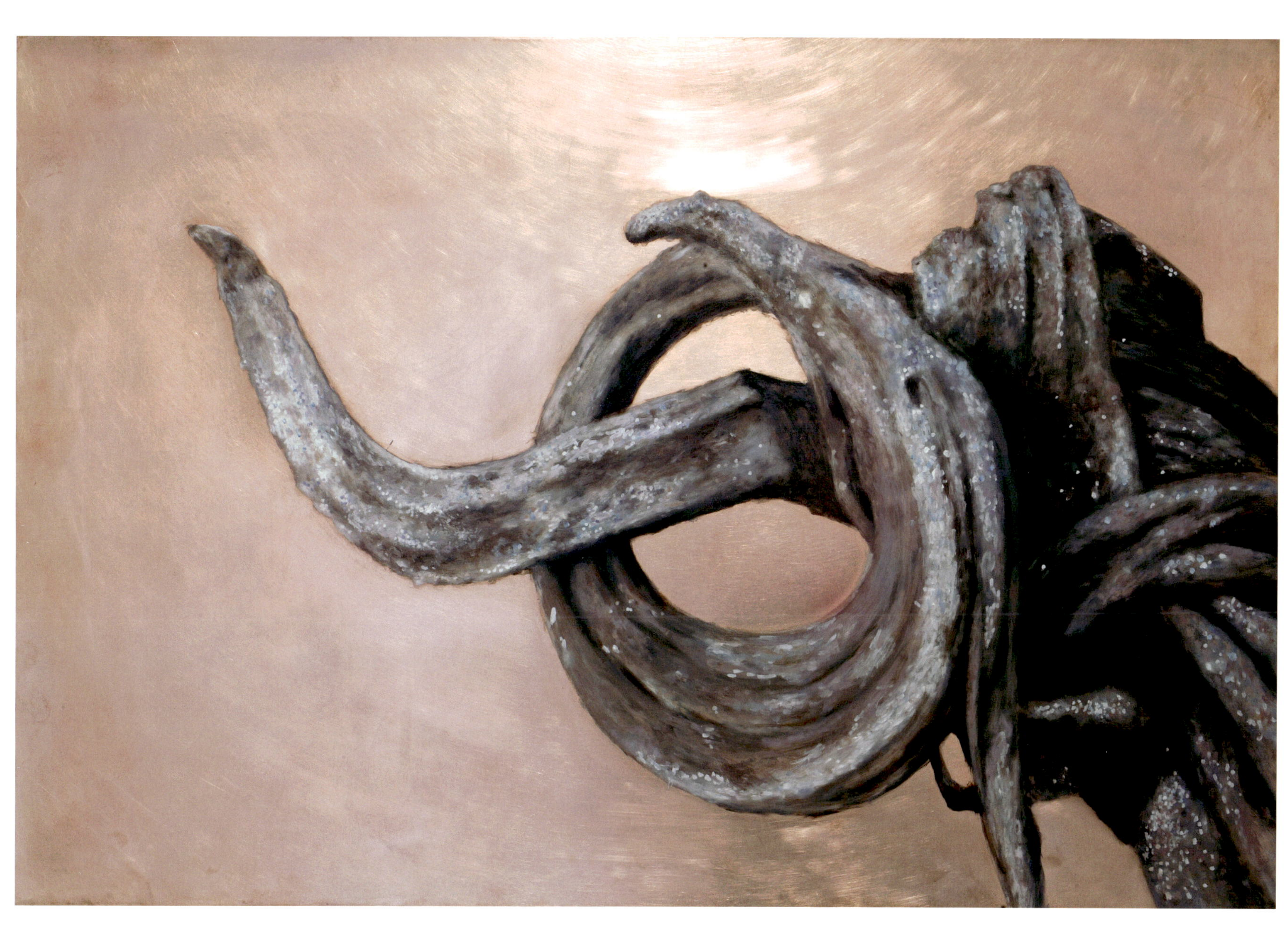

Silber auf Kupfer (Denkmal für Paul Rosbaud)
Oil on copper, wooden board, 80 x 120 cm, 2004

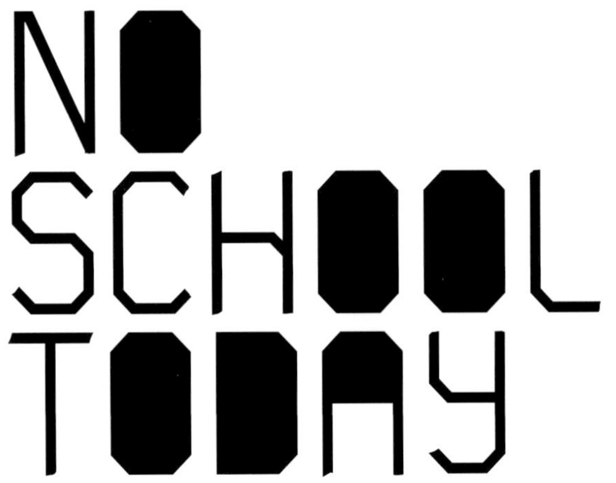

No School Today
Video, color, sound, 12 min, 2005

Director	Antje Majewski
Adult	Cui Tao
Child	Zheng Chenggong
Production Manager	Jan Kern
Director's assistant	Amy Wan Meng
Camera	Di Shen
Camera assistant	Zhang Liang
Sound	Huang Dong
Editing	Antje Majewski
	Barbara Gies
Music	Katrin Vellrath
Painting	Antje Majewski

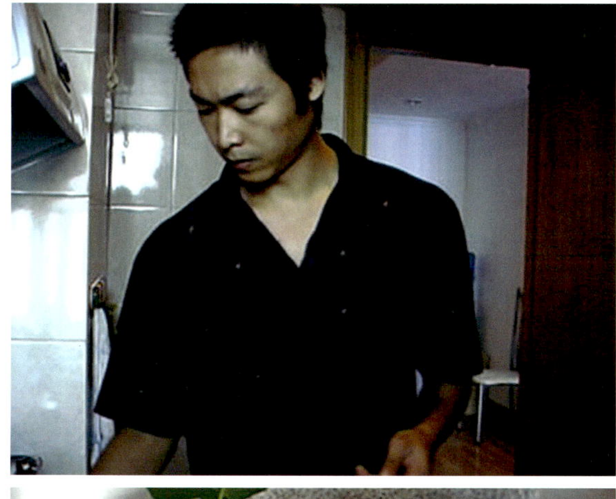
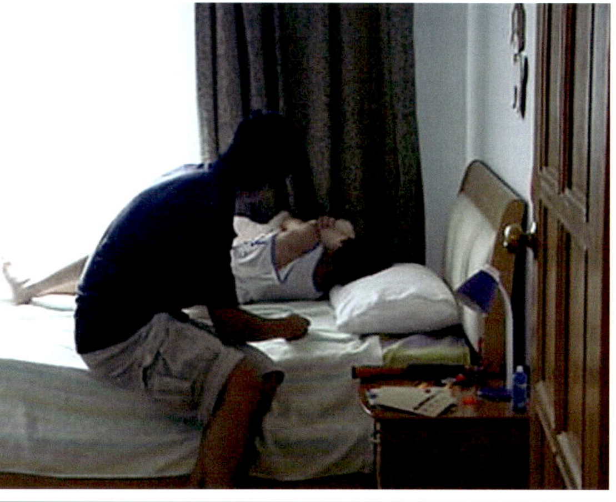
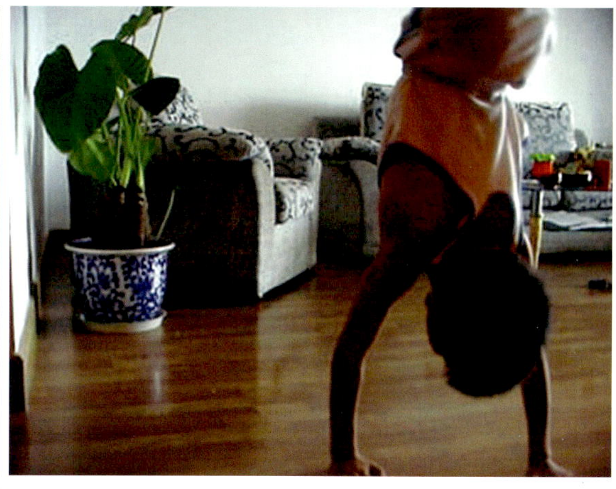
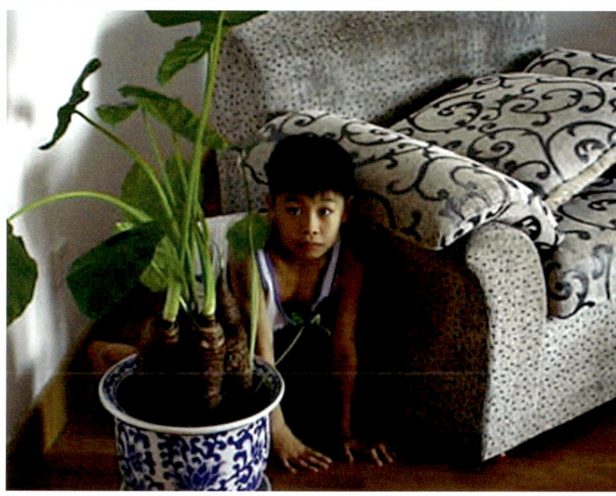
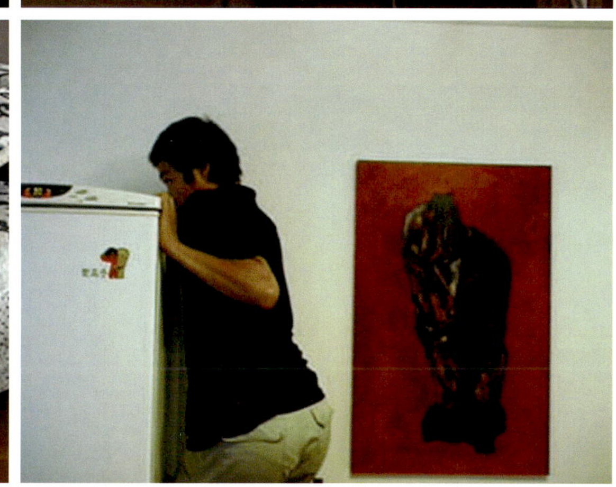
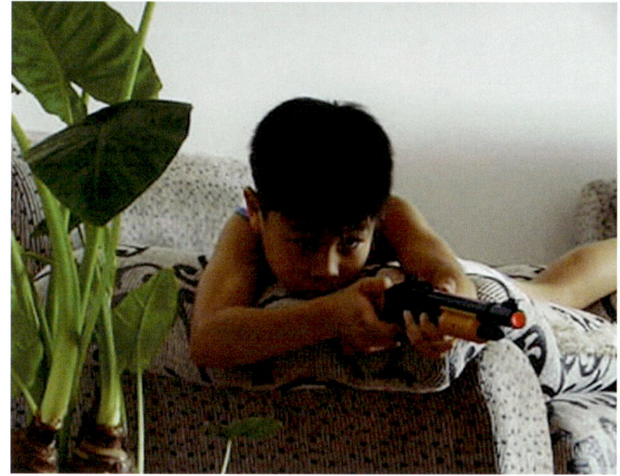
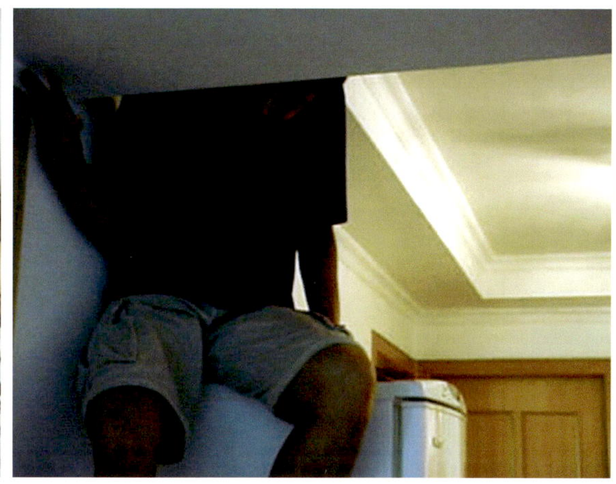
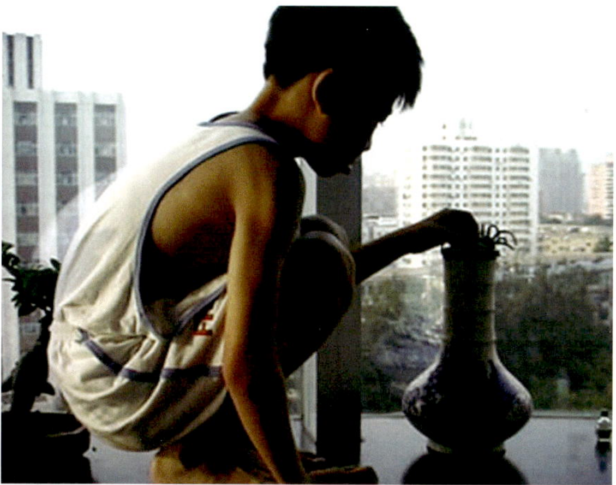
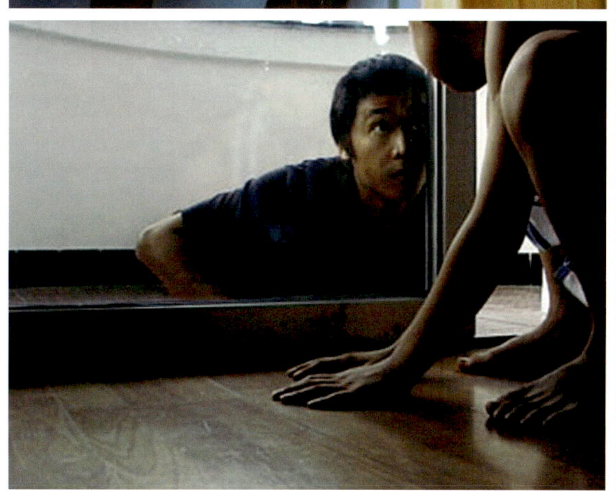
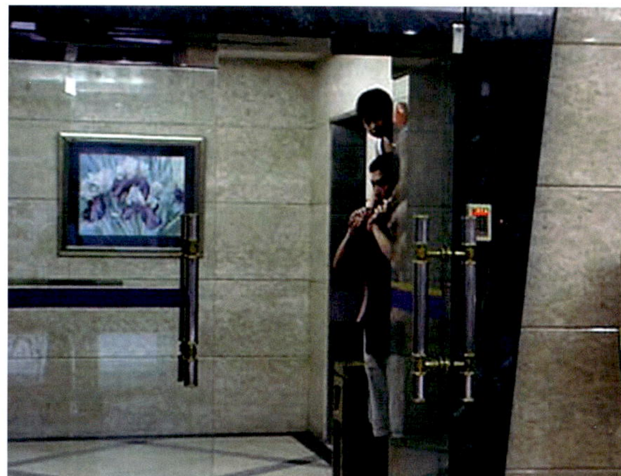

Growing up is about learning the rules of the current civilization. Part of that consists of reducing possible movements. A small child can still climb walls, jump, and fall flat on the floor in public. If an adult did the same thing, people would stare at him. The process of civilization ensures that an adult would not even think of trying to move strangely in private, hidden from view, with the exception of exercise or sports, which also follows its own set of rules.

Daily life routines are changing rapidly in Beijing, transformed not only by new working conditions but also new floor plans for private apartments. In *No School Today*, I wanted to try out what happens if the rules of movement are changed within the confined space of one of Beijing's new, anonymous flats, so that it gets used in an unintended way.

A man and a child are living in one of the new apartment blocks. The flat is furnished "international style" with no specific taste, with the exception of an oil painting showing a *gongshi*, and hanging on the wall next to the fridge.[1] They start a chasing game in which the man has to catch the child. He can only move with his whole body close to the floor and furniture, while the child is allowed to do acrobatic jumps.

No School Today was an experiment based on improvisation. I was working with Cui Tao from the Beijing Modern Dance Company and ten-year-old Zheng Chenggong from Dongcheng Sports School, where he is a martial arts student.   *A.M.*

[1] *Gongshi* (rare stone) or *guaishi* (strange or fantastic stone) are small stones collected for their shape and placed in a shallow tray filled with sand, fine gravel, or water. From the time of the Song Dynasty (960–1279) on, they were put on beautifully carved wooden stands resembling roots. The fashion has spread throughout Asia. In Japan, they are called *suiseki*; in Korea, *suseok*; in English, they have been called "scholar's rocks" or "viewing stones."

As in many countries around the world, mountains were considered sacred in China. Rocks were seen as the bones of the earth, maybe the bones of prehistoric dragons. When garden design developed into an art form, no garden was complete without a uniquely shaped garden stone. The stones were considered the backbones of the garden, while the soil was thought to be the skin. Stones with holes in them were highly valued, since they allow the cosmic energy to circulate. Scholars then used even smaller stones for meditating on the cosmos, placing them next to landscape paintings of mountains or calligraphy. These abstractions allowed the imagination to focus and be purified. In 1131 A.D., the scholar Tu Wan wrote the *Stone Catalogue of Cloudy Forest*, which lists 116 different kinds of rock formations that could be distinguished by connoisseurs.

To me, the stone that I painted represents a Western adaptation of a Chinese tradition based on a deep connection to nature. Beijing at first sight is the absolute opposite of the Chinese love of nature; never have I seen a city that is as gray, polluted, concrete jungle-like as Beijing. But a closer look shows that each of the new apartment blocks is laid out around an extremely manicured garden. Even the young people love huge aquariums with rock landscapes.

The man and boy in my film use movements reminiscent of animals, and they do it with ease, because we are after all animals. The Chinese scholar's stone is an extremely cultivated way to look at nature—a nature seen not as an opponent but as something human beings are only a tiny part of. Even though the stones seem very small and tame on their nice pedestals, they are not small to the thought of the scholar. Human beings are small, like in the landscape paintings. Today, the relative size of men and nature will have to be re-thought in China, as all the latest developments make use of nature in an extreme way.

Rare Desert Stone (No School Today)
Oil on panel, 80 x 50 cm, 2005

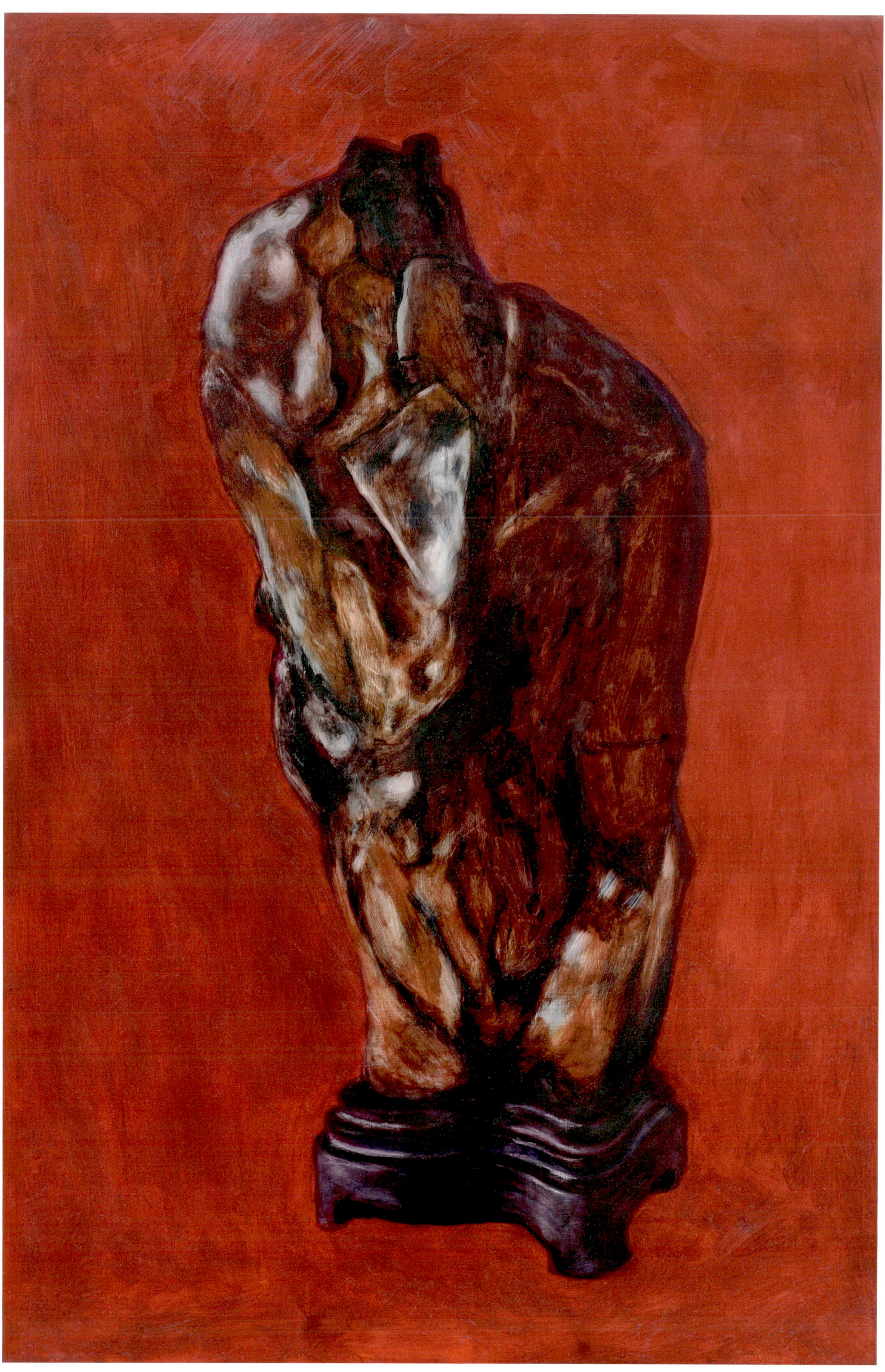

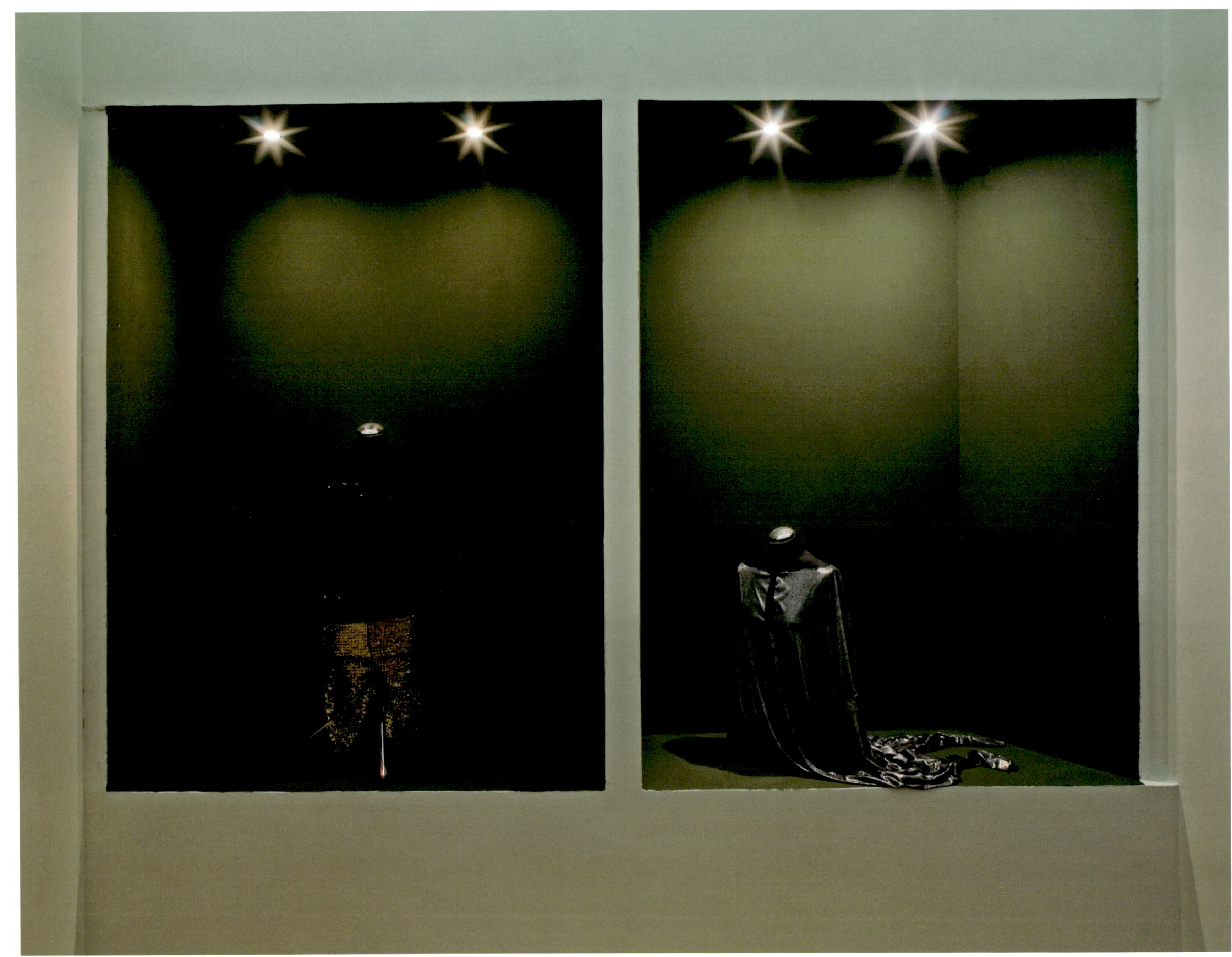

ERDE ASPHALT WEDDING

My Very Gestures
Installation view
Salzburger Kunstverein, 2008

Antje Majewski & Juliane Solmsdorf
Kostüme (Erde Asphalt Wedding)
Cloth, sequins, mannequins, 2007

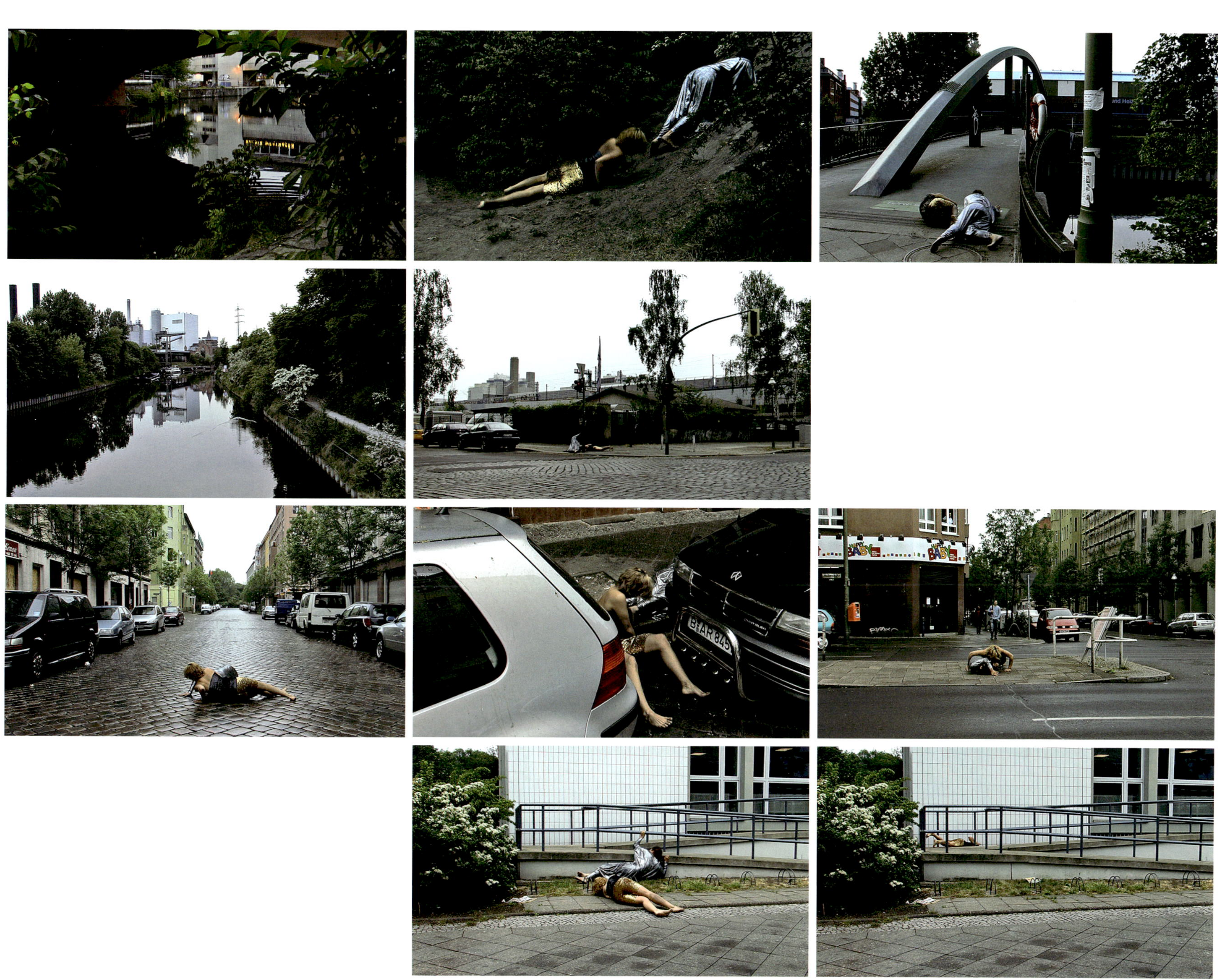

Antje Majewski & Juliane Solmsdorf
Erde Asphalt Wedding
HD video, color, sound, 8 min, 2007
Single channel projection in wooden construction

Creatures	Antje Majewski, Juliane Solmsdorf
Idea	Antje Majewski
Cameras	Patricia Lewandowska, Nana Rebhan
Costume design	Antje Majewski, Juliane Solmsdorf
Assistance to Antje's costume	Martine Maffetti
Editing and sound mixing	Antje Majewski, Juliane Solmsdorf
Editing and sound mixing assistance	Marian Otto, Elmar Vestner

Antje Majewski & Juliane Solmsdorf
Erde Asphalt Wedding / Säule Wedding / Nichtstun

Two strange creatures come out of the canal at Westhafen in Wedding, one of Berlin's seediest
districts. Their shiny costumes twinkle in the early morning light and the noise of the streets
becomes louder as they continue to crawl on the ground, and then up to the street, over a bridge,
across crossroads, and past cars, until finally vanishing again behind a concrete ramp.

The bar stools stand out on the sidewalk, ready to be picked up and taken to a place where you'll
have to pay money to sit on them. But in this very moment, they serve no purpose, have a nice
shape. Beautiful white foam strips from the packaging are blowing in the wind. May I use them,
as long as they are still standing in public space?

We install ourselves into this space, becoming a sculptured column. We measure the height of
the buildings behind us with our bodies, the width of the road.

A 1976 photo series by Valie Export shows her performing curves, lines, and corners in the city.
They are ambiguous photos: she could also have been the model after which the city was built,
in which case the houses and streets would huddle against her, not the other way round.   *A.M.*

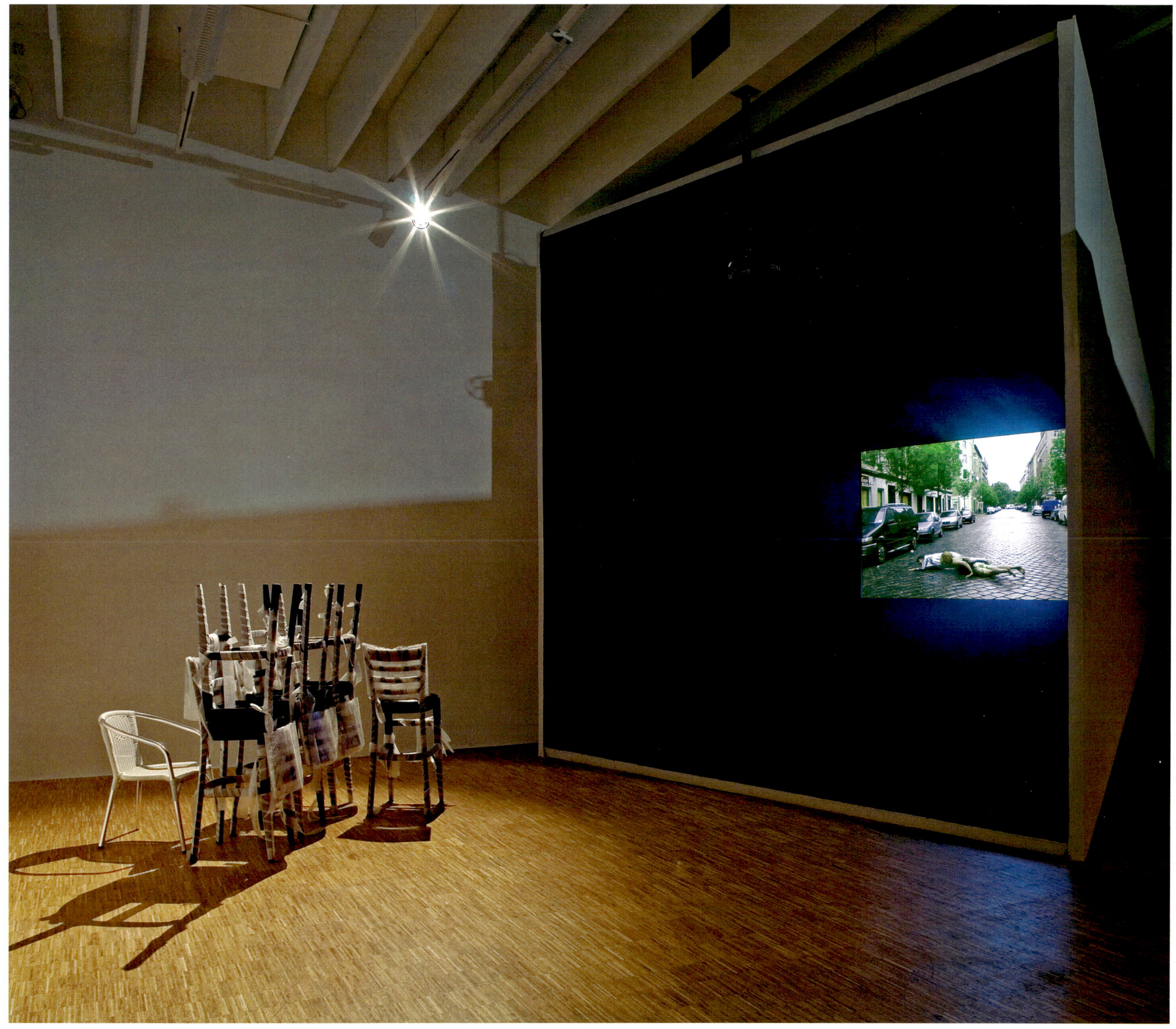

My Very Gestures
Installation view, Salzburger Kunstverein, 2008

Juliane Solmsdorf
Nichtstun
Aluminum, plastic, wood, varnish, synthetic leather, foam foil, bubble wrap, 2007–08

Antje Majewski & Juliane Solmsdorf
Erde Asphalt Wedding
HD video, color, sound, 8 min, 2007, single channel projection in wooden construction

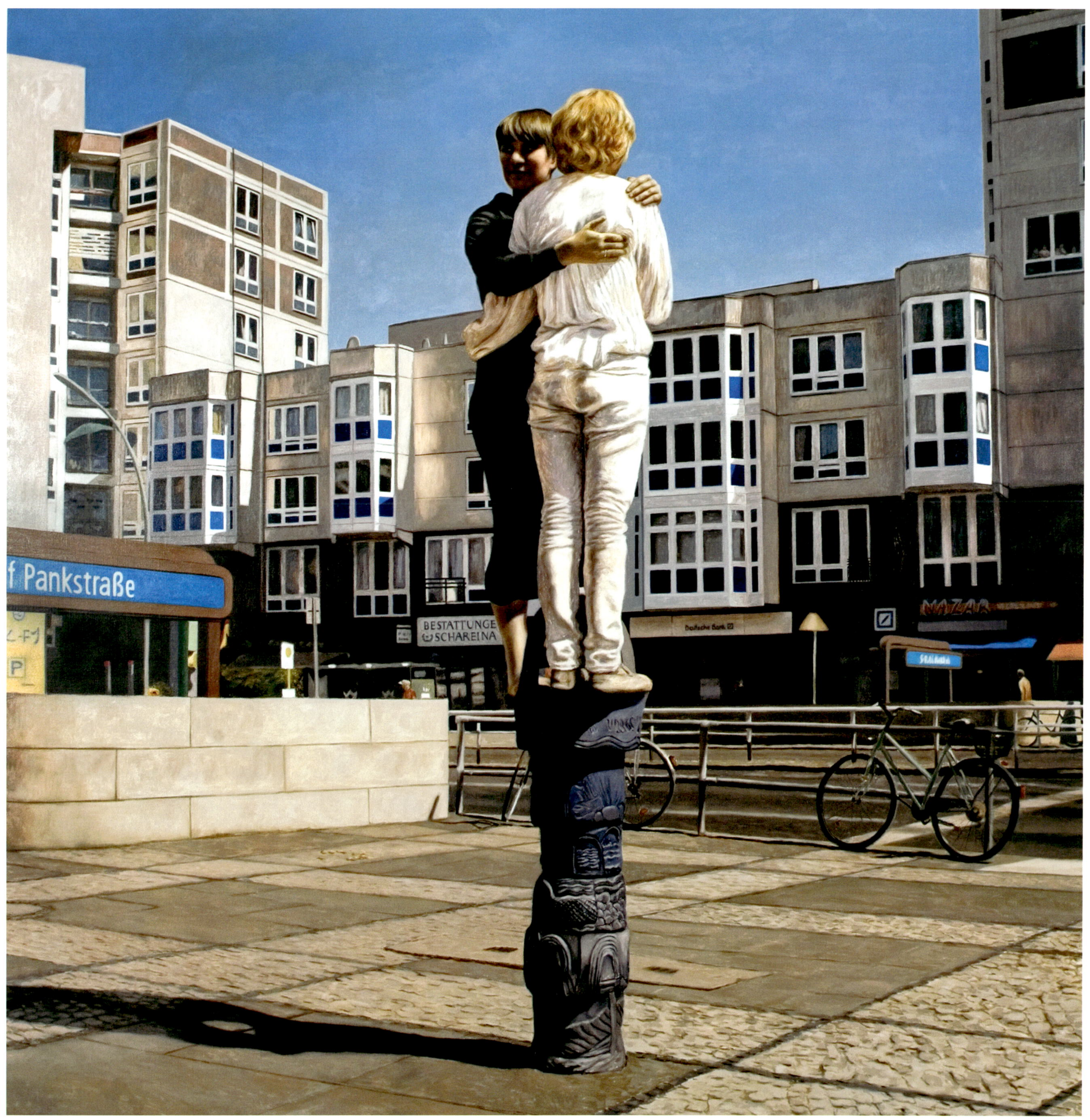

Säule Wedding
Oil on canvas
280 x 280 cm, 2008

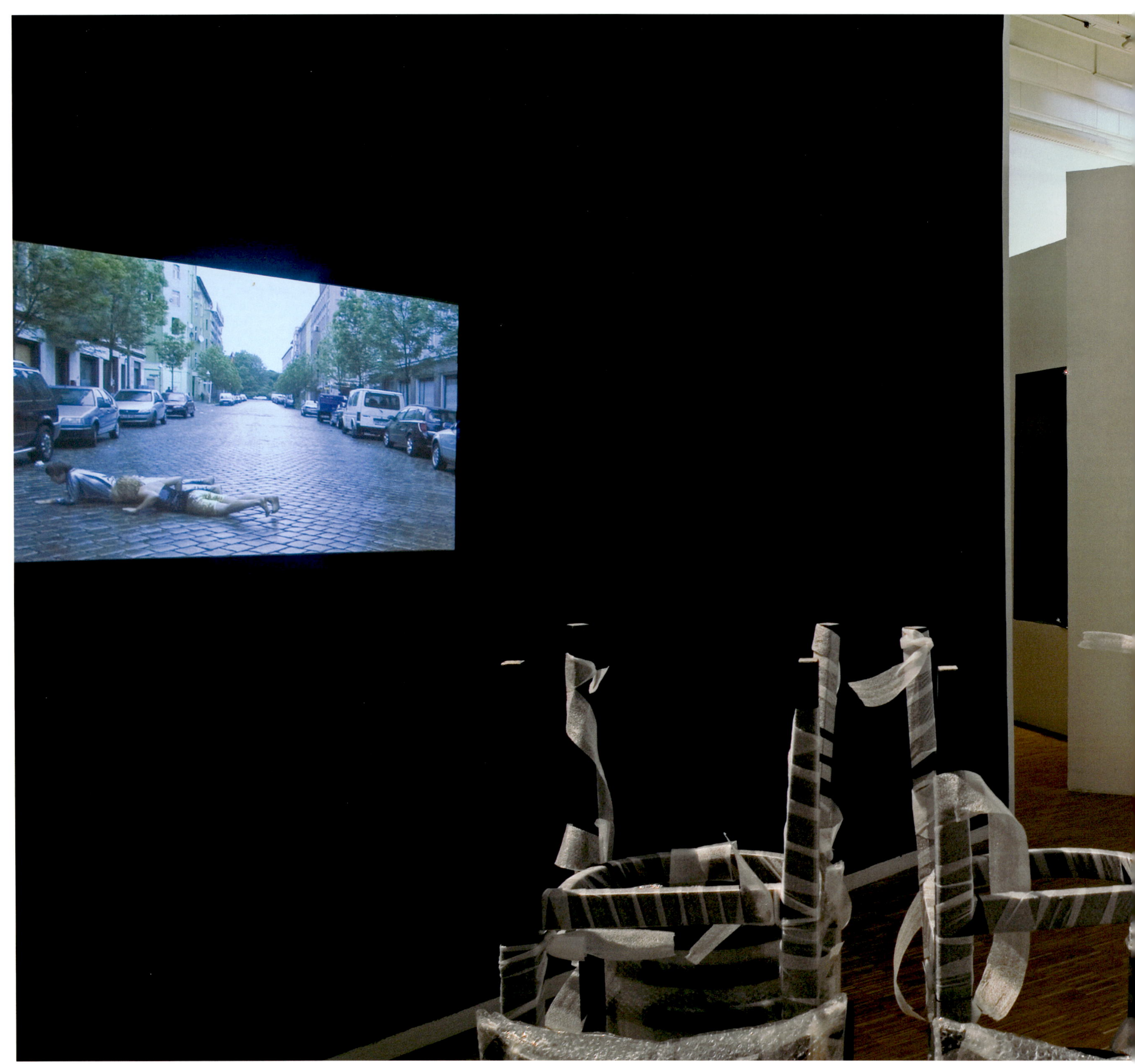

My Very Gestures
Installation view, Salzburger Kunstverein, 2008

Antje Majewski & Juliane Solmsdorf
Erde Asphalt Wedding
HD video, color, sound, 8 min, 2007
Single channel projection in wooden construction

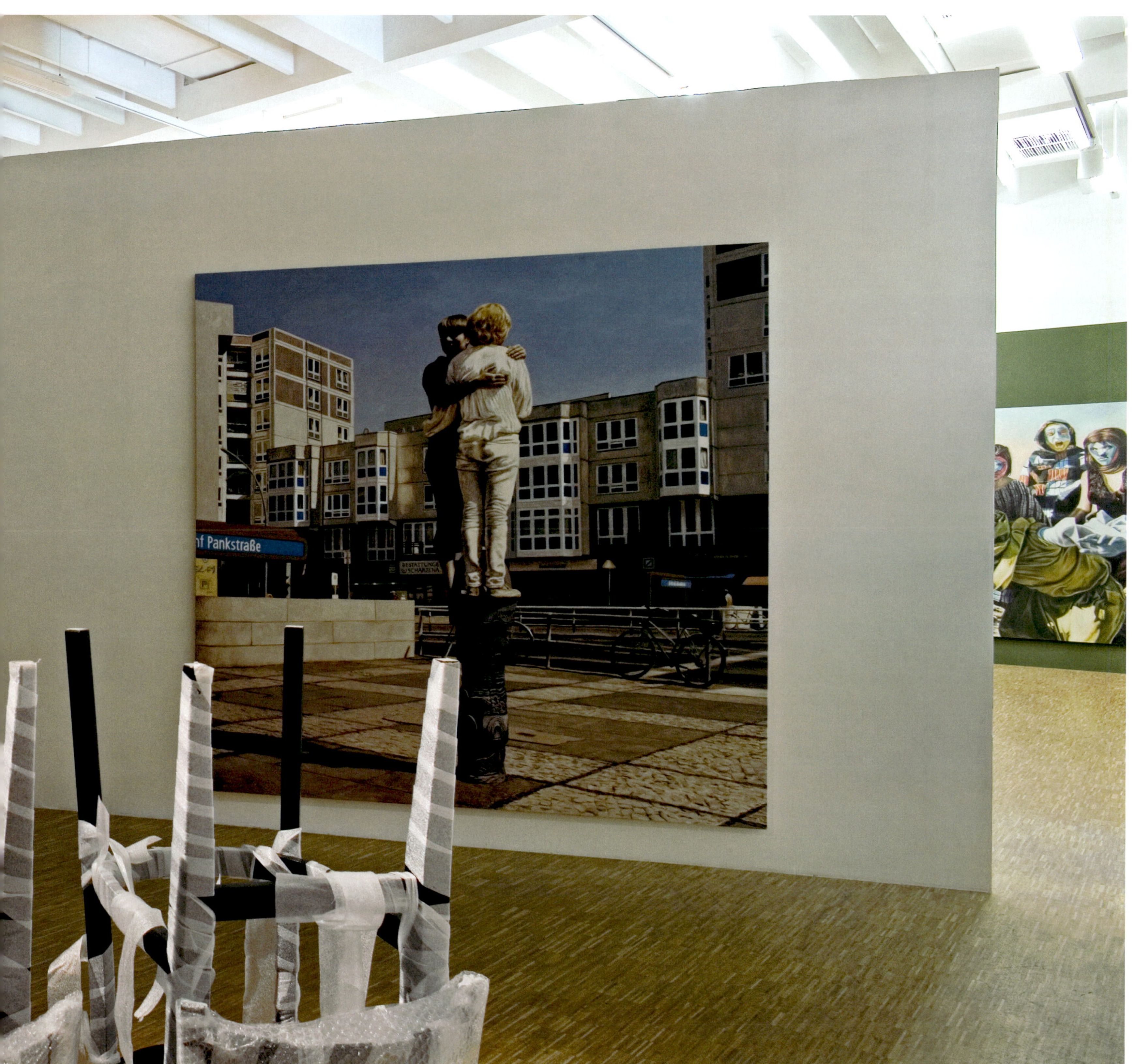

Juliane Solmsdorf
Nichtstun
Aluminum, plastic, wood, varnish, synthetic leather, foam foil, bubble wrap, 2007–08

Antje Majewski
Säule Wedding
Oil on canvas, 280 x 280 cm, 2007–08

TW:

I'd like to start this conversation by thinking about the painting *Masken* (2001), which was more or less responsible for our meeting in the first place. I'd like to take it again as a point of departure for this talk. Let's see how far we can get, keeping our focus and our conversation centered around it, and to what degree this allows some of your other works to be drawn in, too. Several points of reference come up for me when I look at this picture again. On one hand, it reminds me of Watteau. The staginess recalls a theatrical setting, but it's not so much that the figures presented here would actually inhabit or activate a stage. This staged quality begins at the moment of disguise and encompasses the figures' gestures and masks as well. The signifiers have been freed from content here, like with Watteau. If the costumes, gestures, and masks were bound together in a theater piece, in one single narrative, they would be loaded with specific meaning. But here they remain signs, which are powerfully set down, which evoke meaning, but remain suspended. As illegible, quasi-hollowed out signs, they grab our attention; as a viewer, I can only reach the conclusion that what they indicate is absent.

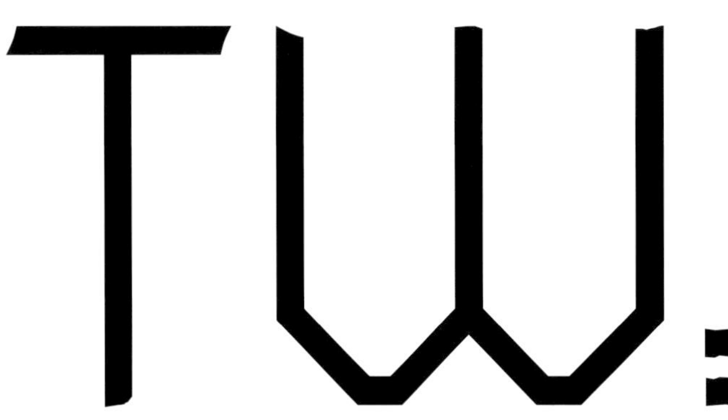

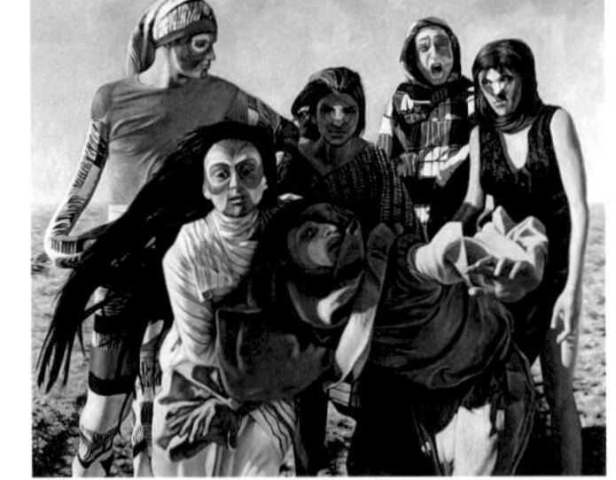

The group that appears before me carries with it a promise of unrealized utopia, and evokes the free experimental theater groups and socially critical formations of the 1960s and the 1970s. At the same time, the faces of the figures, some of the materials, and the painting style really feel contemporary. As the viewer, I feel that the image appeals to and addresses me personally, but just the same multiple boundaries are drawn. It's exactly the theatricality, the group dynamic, and the location of the scene in the painting that render the exhibition space

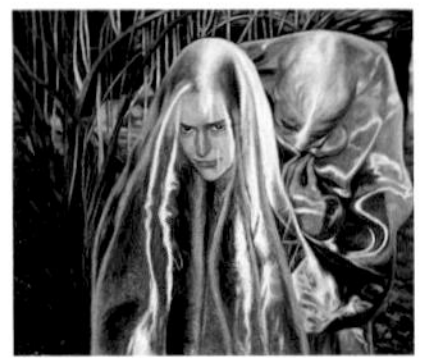

fully un-dramatic, quotidian, and sober. In a similar way, the collectivism of the group also feels foreign and distant. In this ambivalence between appeal and distancing, between the mundane and the extraordinary, a maelstrom opens that cannot be closed, a recurring phenomenon in some of your other work as well. What constellations of groups and relationships are you invoking?

AM: I think your description is really interesting. In fact, it wasn't until these last few years that I noticed that my childhood in the early 1970s was really influential for me. I was born in 1968 and went to an anti-authoritarian kindergarten. We played with mud, painted the walls, and were allowed to run around naked in the woods. My parents devoted serious thought and discussion to our upbringing, and a goal was definitely to make us into free individuals who were in a position to deal with each other in a nonviolent way. The quest for an ideal society was even embedded in our children's books, by Friedrich Karl Waechter or Alexander Sutherland Neill, for example. Besides that, we would play dress-up a lot, my mom would shoot Super 8 movies, and we would put on little plays and photo-narratives. When I was looking at Masken, *it brought up memories about those photos, and that's how the book* Teenage Pantomime *(2002) came about.*

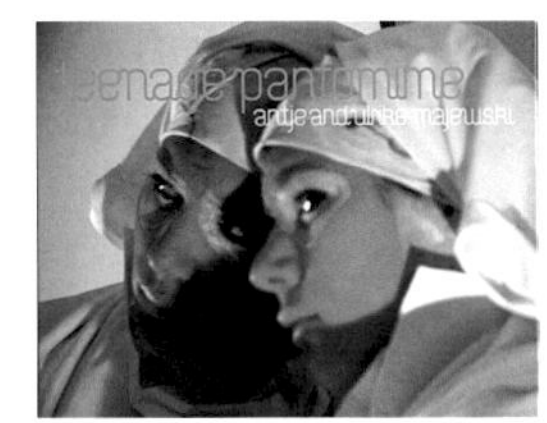

Later, we moved from the country to the suburbs, and I suddenly became a brooding loner. It was the social life and relationships of my early twenties that first brought back those feelings of community that I'd had in childhood. But love and friendship in young adulthood are very complicated affairs. On top of that I was reading Nietzsche, Barthes, Elias, and Wittgenstein. And I got really involved in studying the theory of social and mentalité history, which is based on the assumption that there can't be an objective description, but which is nonetheless made up of the tedious collection of evidence for one particular version.[1] What came out of this for me was not the desire to make art about the impossibility of truth (in the representation of reality or the inherent rules of the medium), but rather to create my own realities. I started by making photo-collages that had a very convincing effect, but were spatially or temporally confusing. Then I staged images with actors, and took photos. These served as the basis for my paintings.

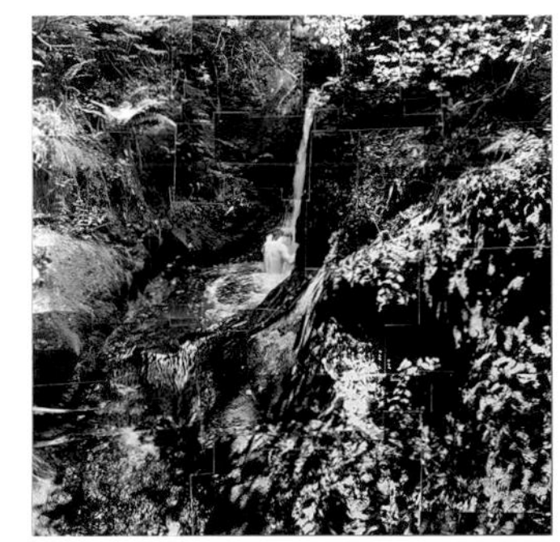

The series titled L'invitation au voyage *(1999–2001) attempts to evoke rather than symbolically represent interior conditions. I noticed after I finished the first part,* Freunde und Liebende *(1999), that it wasn't enough for me to portray the individuals from the outside. Feelings weren't so much embodied in the later paintings as they were "enacted" or "performed" because it wasn't supposed to be about my feelings in relation to the world or about how I could convey these by means of a painterly hand. It was about the representation of something that was in the world and in other people—and more than anything that took place between them.*

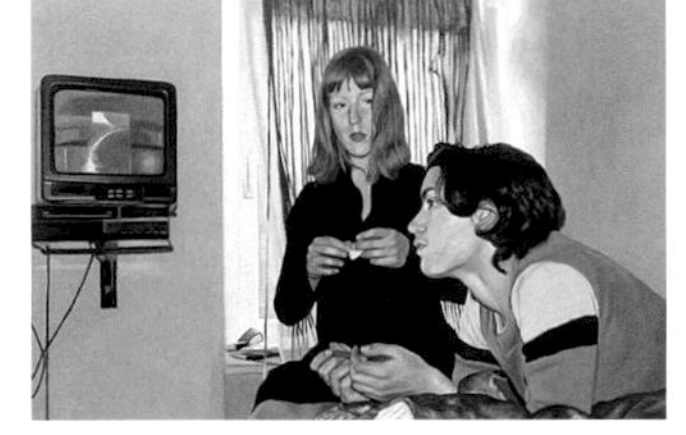

TW: Let's look at this question of performance. Could you elaborate your definition of it? What does it mean for you that whatever is translated into the images, whether it's feelings or specific constellations, evokes a desire for specific historical ideas of the ideal society and shifts it to the now, while at the same time not being embodied by the represented figures? Neither embodiment, in the sense of a complete and uplifting identification, nor (self)-realization seems to me to be called up in your work. For me, the thing that maintains the suspense in the experience of your work is exactly this strange simultaneous layering of distance, evacuation, and hollowing-out on top of a recharging.

---

[1] *In the beginning I was fascinated by the history of long stretches of time (the longe durées of Fernand Braudel and the mentalité history of Philippe Ariès). I wrote my M.A. with a very respected German professor of social history, Jürgen Kocka.*

Performing, in my opinion, also always implies a takeover, a transference: whatever creates the possibility for dislocation. This non-identifying gesture also ties in with a challenge to the sometimes even too idealistic sense of self-realization as it sometimes appears in 1960s' concepts. What I'm more interested in is a position like the one Judith Butler proposed. In this questioning of the possibility of a "practice of freedom," what her position doesn't lose sight of is the constitution of a self through codes, rules, norms, etc., which precede and affect us. Clearly though, the formation of the self isn't really entirely determined by this field of norms; they can still be reflected and challenged. In this regard (and in relation to Foucault), Butler speaks of a similarity to something "like an originary freedom ... Something similar, indeed, but apparently not quite the same." [2] I think this dislocation is really important for me in your work, in the framework of a fiction, the staginess we were discussing before, etc.

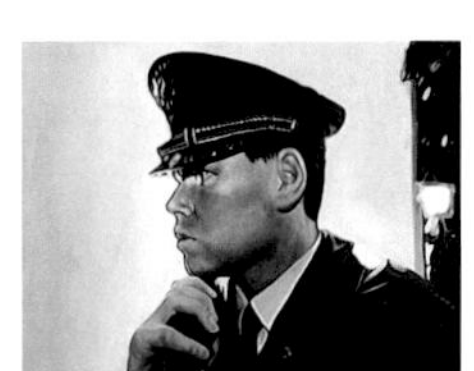

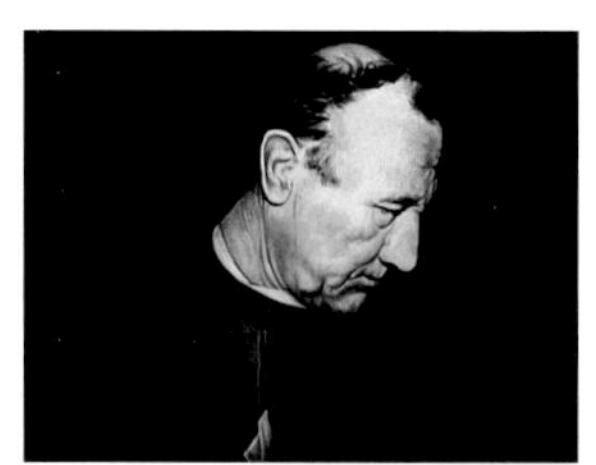

AM: An answer is hard for me to formulate here, because you're asking for something which has to defy any description and/or fixed meaning, which takes place in another realm. But I'll try it like this anyway: for me, really important terms like freedom and happiness can't be brought into representation. Because of this, the pictures with their actors can only enact something. The idea that something unrepresentable becomes perceptible can only be reached through the "as if." The unrepresentable has to do with being outside of yourself: a condition I'm really interested in. I find it really dreadful being trapped in your own body, in your own head, in mortality. But also in cultural conventions, in an adherence to the rules that always forgets it's historically changeable, in ascriptions of identity. Where I paint people or work with them in film, I get a little "outside of myself" and into the artwork, into which the viewer, in turn, can remove himself as well. That works best with a protagonist who's already inclined to position himself "outside." This could be a drag performer, but also the bum that positioned himself on the fringes of society. So my sympathy goes out to anyone who wants to create a new persona for himself, especially in fields that will never belong to high culture. Like the street mime in Video *(2001) and* My Very Gestures… Enchanted *(2001). She perfected her art to the degree that she could hold her eyes open for minutes at a time. At the beginning, she cries with open eyes, because they stay moist that way. This is melodramatic, but the pathos seems fitting to me.*

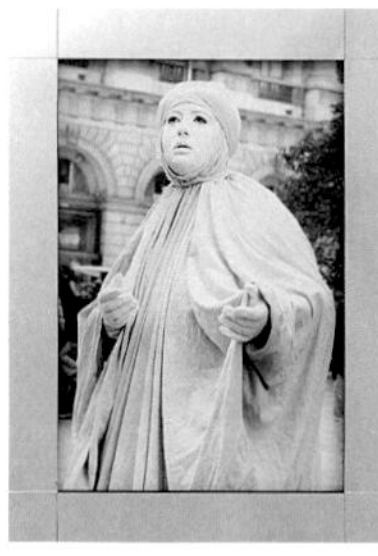

TW: I think this performance is interesting because the demonstration of a capacity to hold your eyes open is a performance of nothing, but a nothing that still stirs the body, calls up affects, which still appears as a pathos formula. This leads me directly to Warhol's early work in film and the screen tests. Here as well nothing was represented, it was potentiality that was presented: a kind of a visage, a surface, a machine. Complexity emerged, though, in the relationship between elements and power, and at the same time a maximal reduction, through the meeting of pure surfaces and affects queering time. Group constellations become a central factor in his productions, which allowed for the reflection of both the working order of Hollywood and contemporary artistic settings. The specific use of the camera gave Warhol the option of having the group, the individuals always in view, to record as well as to promote the circulation of desire, and the formation of the self in the capitalist machine.

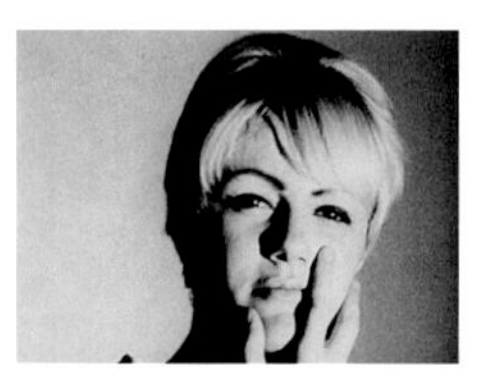

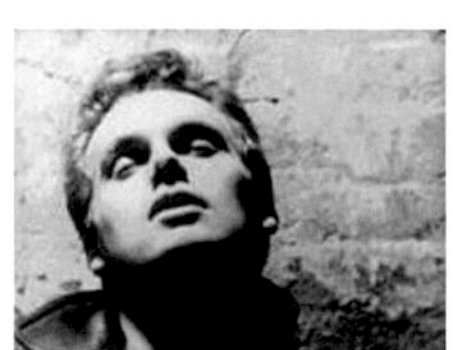

*AM: I just reread Warhol's books. I find the films really funny; they're almost like slapstick ideas. Like when someone's face is filmed while he is been given a blow job (*Blow Job, *1964). It's an experimental scenario but one that has no other goal than to give you the chance to see what you really want to see. Or*

[2] Judith Butler: "What is Critique? An Essay on Foucault's Virtue," available online at: http://eipcp.net/transversal/0806/butler/en.

Sleep *(1963): he explained that no one slept anymore, so he wanted to hold on to the experience of this remarkable phenomenon. Then you have to imagine how a bunch of people on speed would try to watch these movies. Or even to film a building that, well, can't move. This kind of a sharp wit (sharp, actually, because it's so banal), I find in Duchamp as well. For me, it was metal dogs that look alive when painted because the real dogs they refer to don't have any fur (*Xoloitzcuintles*, 2005), or a giant motor that's a completely immobile object itself but is made to put things into motion. And because of the medium of painting, of course, it has to be rendered immobile again (*Motor, 2007). The characteristics of the medium are performed, so to speak, as an elegant gesture, which makes me think of Duchamp's 1916 semi readymade* With Hidden Noise*—as a rich covering for an invisible content that only the viewer can generate. With me, it's all terribly serious—almost overdramatic—but at the same time very tongue-in-cheek as soon as it's about art. The mime staging herself as a statue is the opposite of the lifeless stone that allegedly possesses vital energy (*Rare Desert Stone [No School Today], *2005).

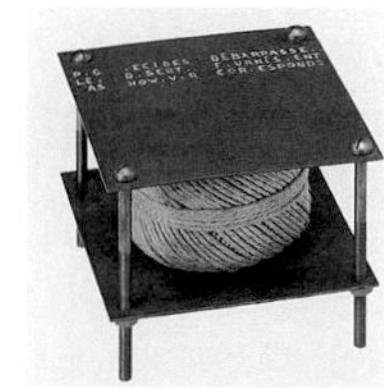

TW: That also makes me think about Agamben's writing on gesture, which he describes as a space of potentiality but also as a figure of transference, as a performance of communicability. Quoting Mallarmé, he discusses pantomime in this regard as that which renders the most familiar gestures alien in their performance. As such they remain "suspended ... between desire and fulfillment, perpetration and its recollection." [3] This pantomimic quality seems to me to show up in your later films as well. What stands out here, too, is the combination of the everyday and the familiar with the purposeless, brought together and represented by means of an extraordinary action. I have to think about the movements in *No School Today* (2005), which are between "potentiality and act," something like a combination of play, everyday activity, dance, and martial arts. Of course, what I'm calling dance, because of the unbelievably slow and sluggish movement seems more like the performance of the body's potential, as a dimming as well as an experiment with new possibilities. What does this speechless theatricality mean to you?

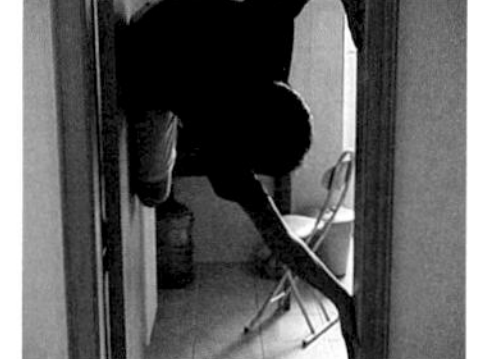

AM: Agamben's formulation is as precise as you can be when you want to describe something that's impossible to describe. The problem is that it would implode just in the moment at which it could become communicable in the sense of codification, signification, or narration. Because of this, pantomime that signifies the everyday but without the objects we're used to using is totally uninteresting to me. That mime I worked with was the only one I ever noticed on the street, because she was so absurdly good in her performance that represented nothing. I'm interested in dance that spins a kind of precise ecstasy using pantomimic elements, like early breakdance, krumping, or M'balax. And of course in parkour.

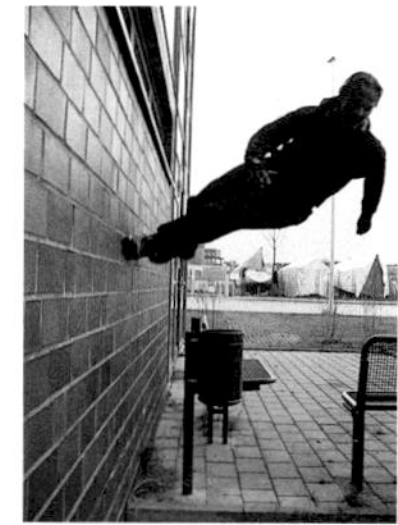

It's worth noting that the pictures themselves are not ecstatic, but rather perform ecstasy, just like these dancers, only through the development of grand precision and mastery of movement, are able to create ecstasy. And they achieve this mastery through unbelievable amounts of work and energy invested in something that produces no goods whatsoever, not even cultural value. I don't know anything in modern dance that looks in that direction. Maybe Wayne McGregor. I'm bored incredibly quickly if I notice that someone is trying, with all these movements and gestures, to get something across to me that I've already known for a long time.

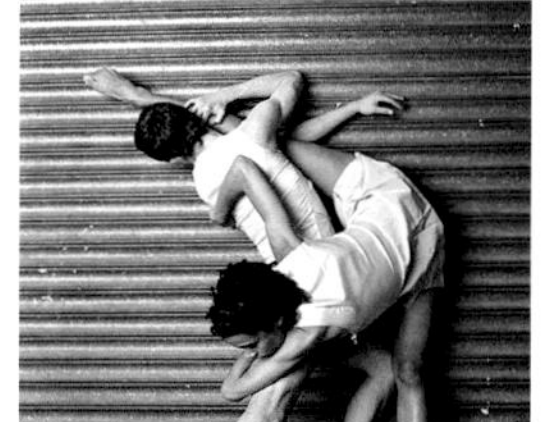

In my films, the first step is simply to do something in a different way. This something different can't have a purpose or a goal, or it would be just more of the same. And it has to take place in specific surroundings.

[3] Giorgio Agamben, "Notes on Gesture," in *Means without End: Notes on Politics*, trans. Vincenzo Binetti and Cesare Casarino (Minneapolis: University of Minnesota Press, 2000), 58.

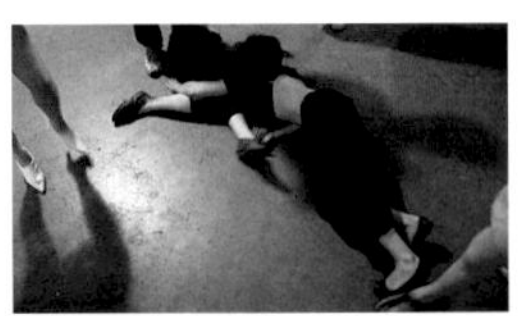

It is only in Tanz RGBCMYK *(2007–2008) that the dancers "perform" elementary colors on a dark, empty stage, but I'd like to show the paintings with* Rausch *(2008), a film showing ecstatic dancing in the very real Club Basso in Berlin's Kreuzberg district.*

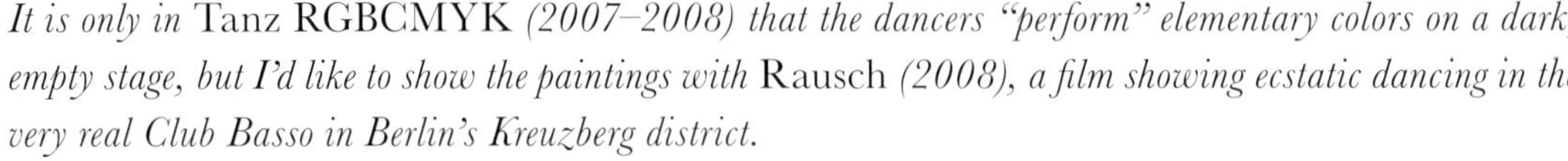

The pictures and films are couriers or vehicles—like in Vodoun where people are ridden by gods. For me, there are no gods and nothing to pray to them for. Nonetheless, I have the feeling that I'm evoking a space in which I don't find myself alone. The representation through actors is like calling out a name without knowing what entity, what being it summons. This invocation has to happen in some corner of the living room, or out on the street, not in a church. And it has to obey certain laws. Actually, though, it knows it's aiming into the void, because there isn't anything there. Only what we create for ourselves. Maybe that's where your feeling of alienation comes from, since actually there just aren't any promises.

TW: This as-if leads me to a somewhat differently directed question. What makes the photo-realistic tradition of painting possible for you? By referring to the concept of photorealism, I'm trying to bring several things together: that you've subscribed to a certain realism in painting and, at the same time, photos have often had an important significance for you as the basis, the reference point. What's interesting to me is this double layer. The photo you use is already a staged gaze, fixed on a potential constellation of elements. These elements, if dissembled, could also be reassembled in a new way before returning to the painting with specific difference. Just the same, this layer of the photographic is embedded to a certain extent within the painting.

At the same time, it also allows the elements of the real to break through in a certain sense—leading to a kind of disruption. Here we might also need to reformulate this notion of realism in more precise terms. Hal Foster, for example, attempts to apply this concept of the real to Lacan's seminars on the traumatic.[4] Using this reference as a point of departure, he ultimately also understands super-realism in relation to surrealism and the inclusion of photographic elements in Appropriation art, differentiates their diverging relationships to the real. In doing so something like the decision to celebrate and/or question or exhibit illusionism would be important, but also questions of de-realization, the attraction of surfaces, etc. How would you understand this idea of realism in the context of your work?

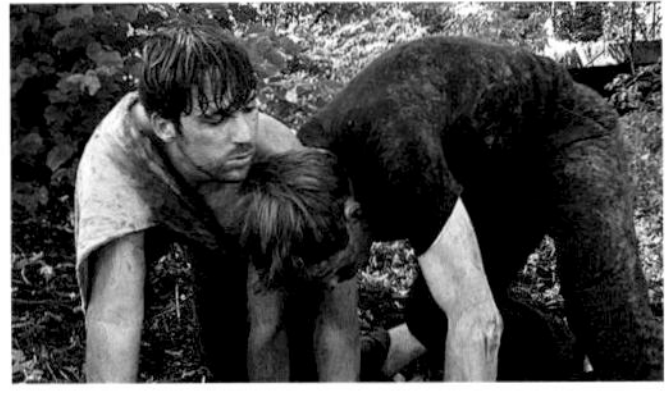

AM: For the paintings and in the films, I work together with people to whom I leave a lot of freedom. I usually have images in my head, but they change as I work on them with others. It goes so far that for Dekonditionierung *(2007–08), I just asked the actors to follow my directions to act out a different rule of communication each day, but otherwise they were left to improvise freely. Afterwards come really long periods of time in the editing or painting process, however, where I bring out what happened with my actors, on the one hand, but also what I want to see. Because these are people I'm interested in, it seems pointless to me to alienate them in my images. As with culture at large, my view is naturally influenced by films and photography. On top of that, I believe that the kind of painting from which I borrow certain allusions, was already determined by the use of optical media. In the last few years I've also started to be interested in shifted perspectives and in the application of a certain hand that leaves the picture to pulsate a little. That doesn't mean, though, that I think of this as a more "natural" view than the view through a lens. I gave* Mal de ojo *(2005) that title because I meant both the sinister look and pain in the eyes. The pictures have a traditional effect. They are actually disturbed, though, in a painterly way and because of their content,*

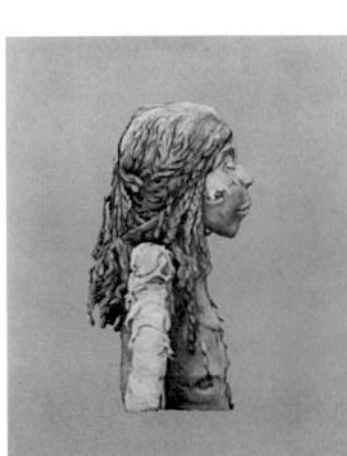

[4]See Hal Foster, "The Return of the Real," in *The Return of the Real. The Avant-Garde at the End of the Century.* (Cambridge, MA: MIT Press, 1996), 127–168.

which makes me really happy. In this series, like in The Royal Mummies *(2006), it's a lot about the question of timelessness, about the strange possibility that through the artworks you might create a vehicle that can allow something to time-travel over vast eras, which the viewer might encounter as living even if it's clearly only dead matter.*

I have always called myself a "realist," but I would use the word as Pier Paolo Pasolini did, as divorced from "naturalism." For him, film is a system of signs in which reality signifies itself. A tree "plays" a tree. Through being placed in a context it becomes a "kinem," it becomes possible to see it as if reality (or God, according to Pasolini) were to "speak" through it.

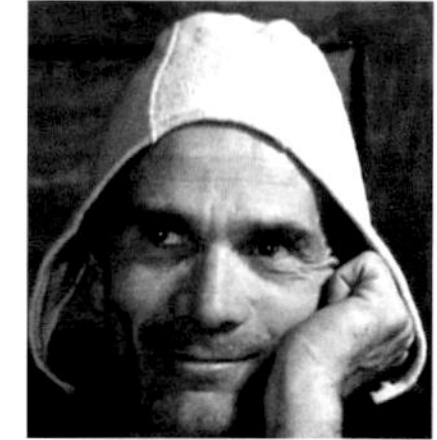

Pasolini's tremendous grief over the passing of old cultures could be called traditional; it also seems inconsistent with his Marxism. Subconsciously he might have been yearning for the "age of similarity" (Foucault), in which every object had a potentially sacred significance. This longing comes from the amazement over the existence of all these things, animals and people, and despair over the fact that they will all very soon be gone. If all these things could be brought to a process of signification—in a way that they signify "themselves"—then the process of transience might be forestalled. I see something similar with Hubert Fichte or in another way with Yasushi Inoue: the search for a possible, complex language that speaks not "about" reality, but "through" it. This gives rise to a certain obsession with detail, because without the details, nothing can be said.

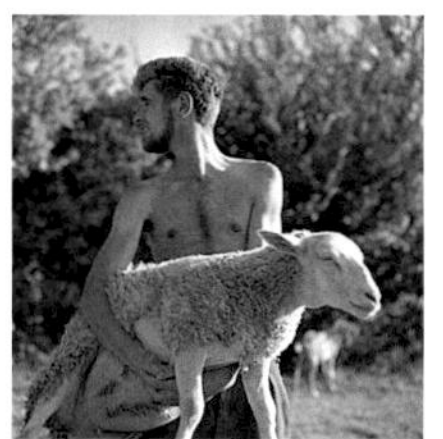

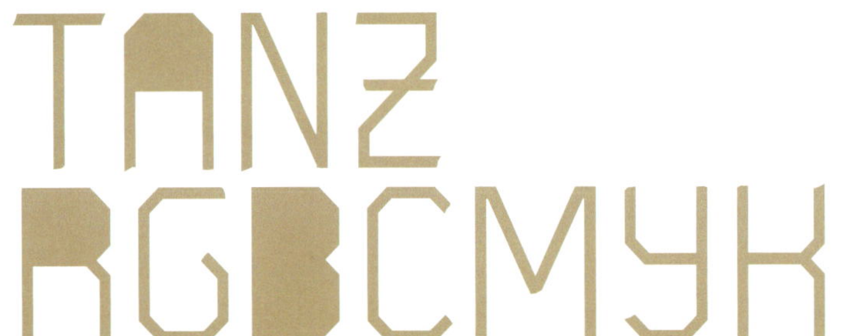
TANZ
RGB CMYK

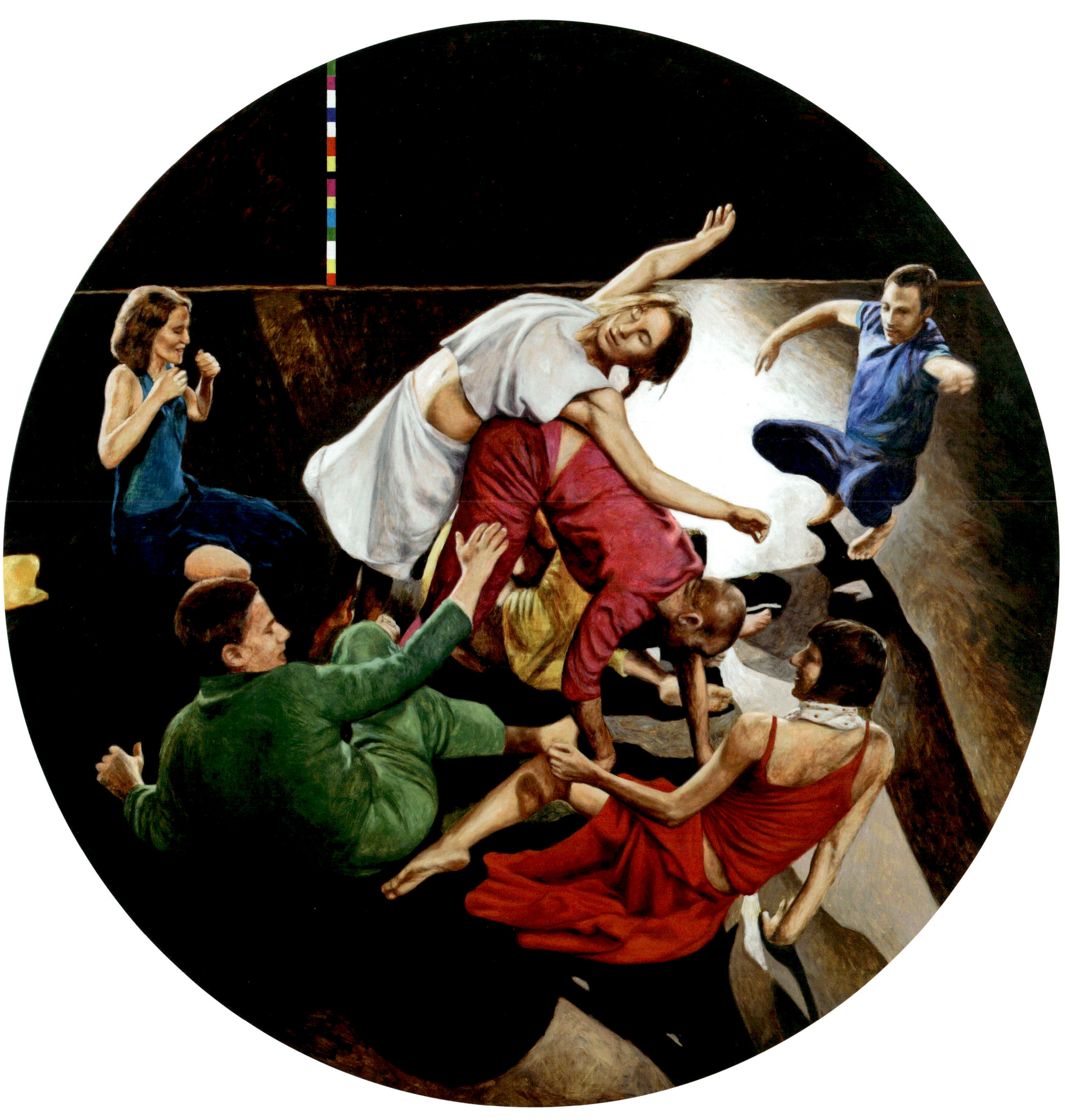

Tanz RGBCMYK 1
Oil and tempera on wood
200 cm diameter, 2007–08

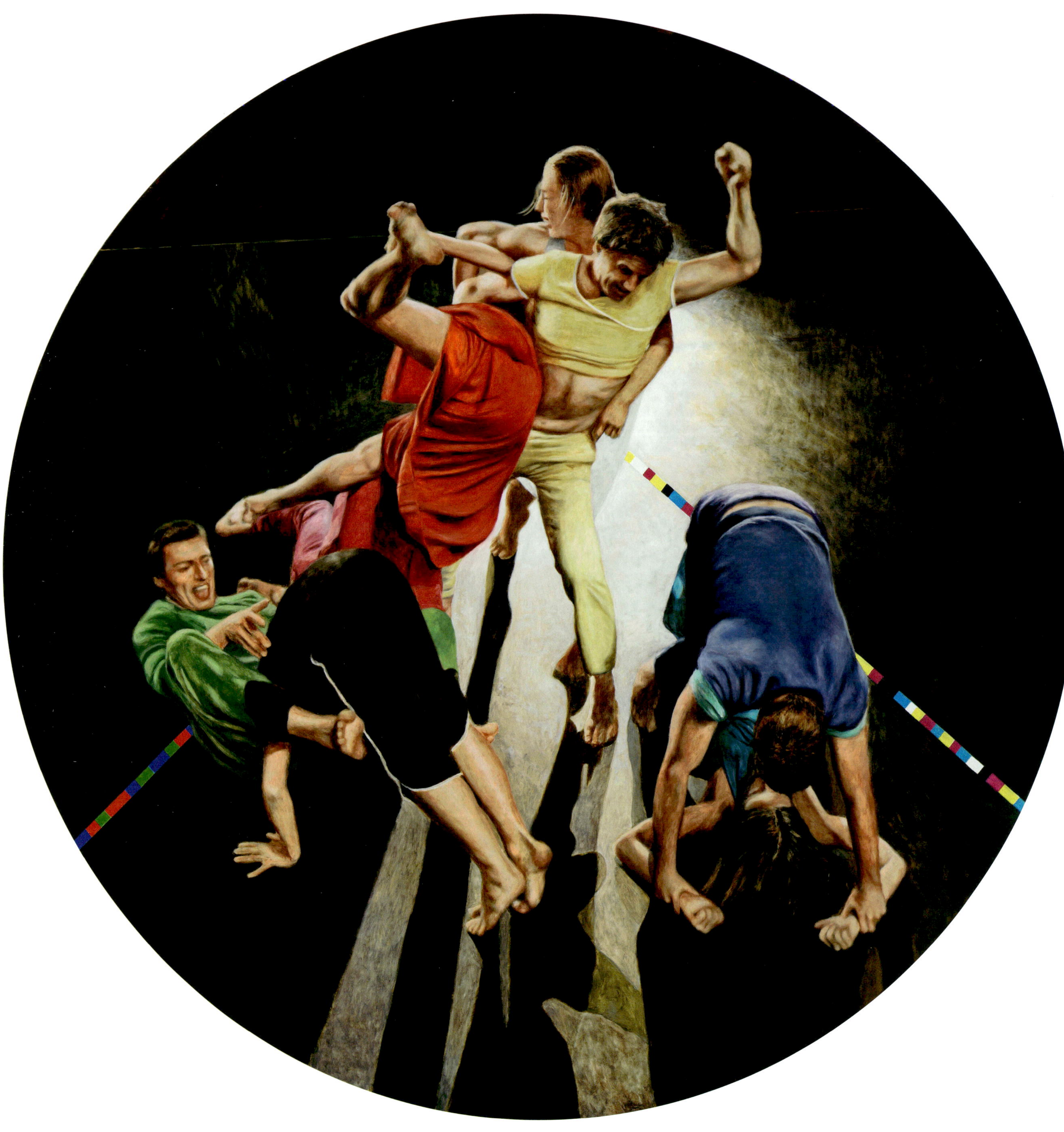

Tanz RGBCMYK 2
Oil and tempera on wood
200 cm diameter, 2007–08

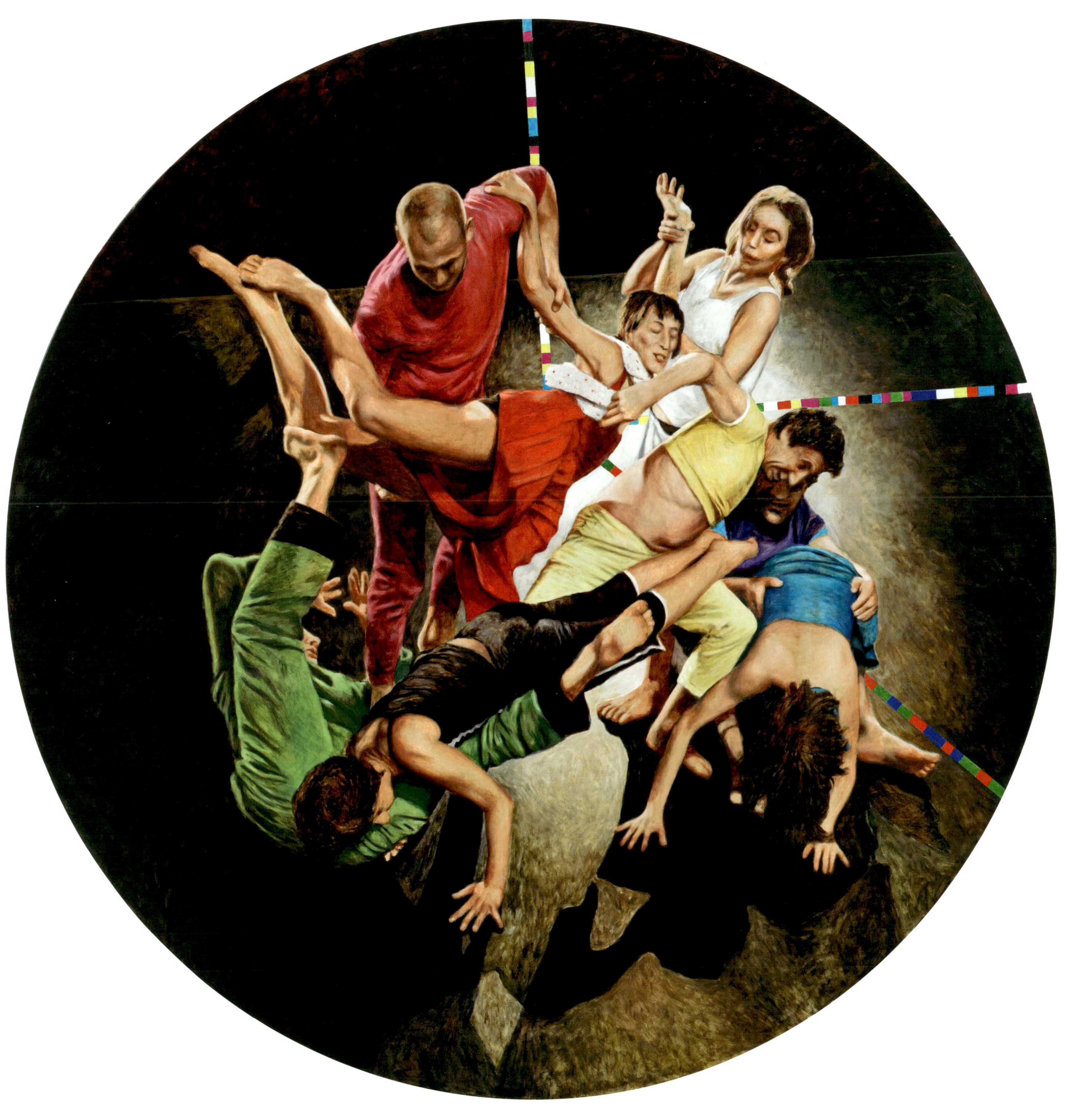

Tanz RGBCMYK 3
Oil and tempera on wood
200 cm diameter, 2007–08

95

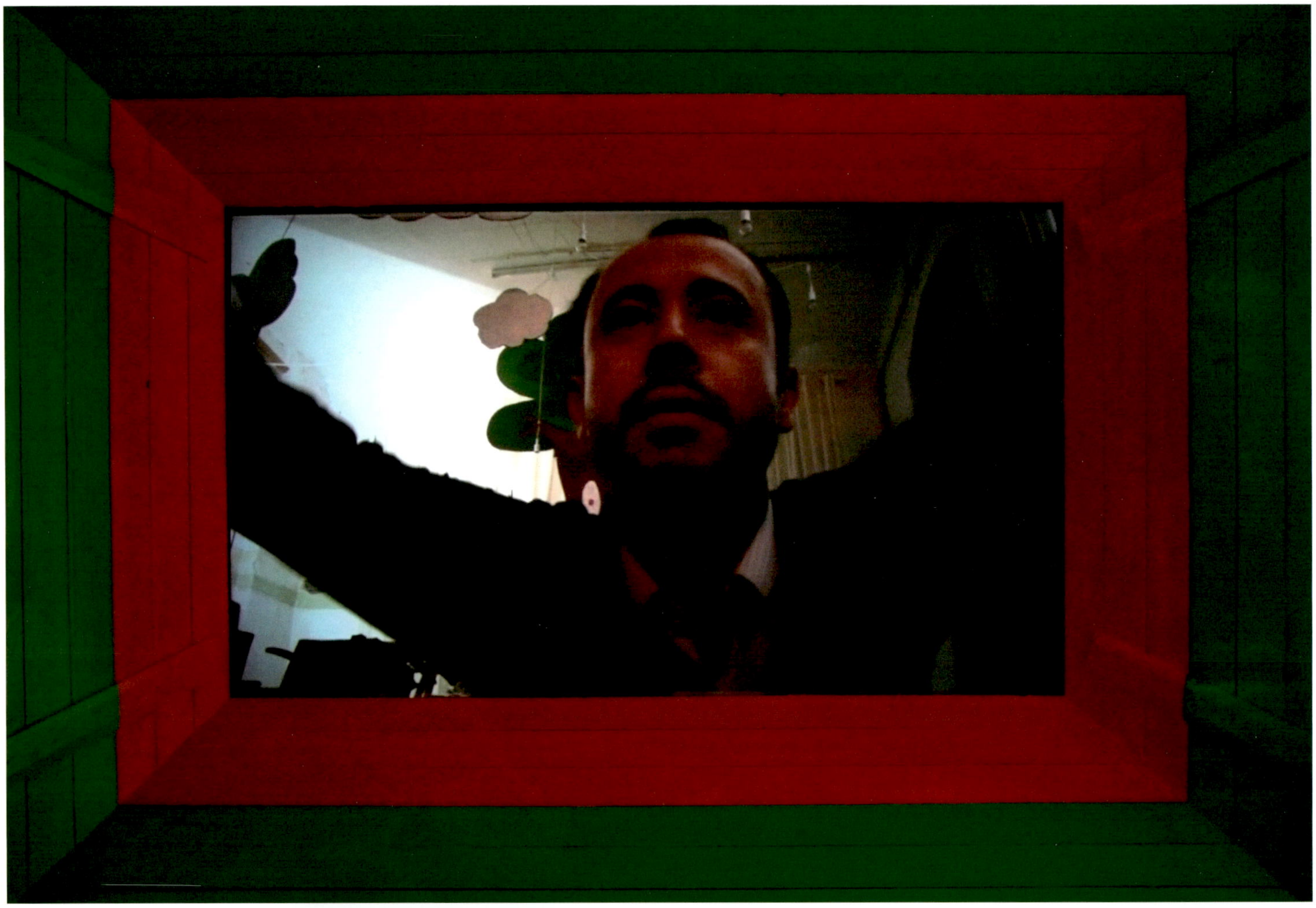

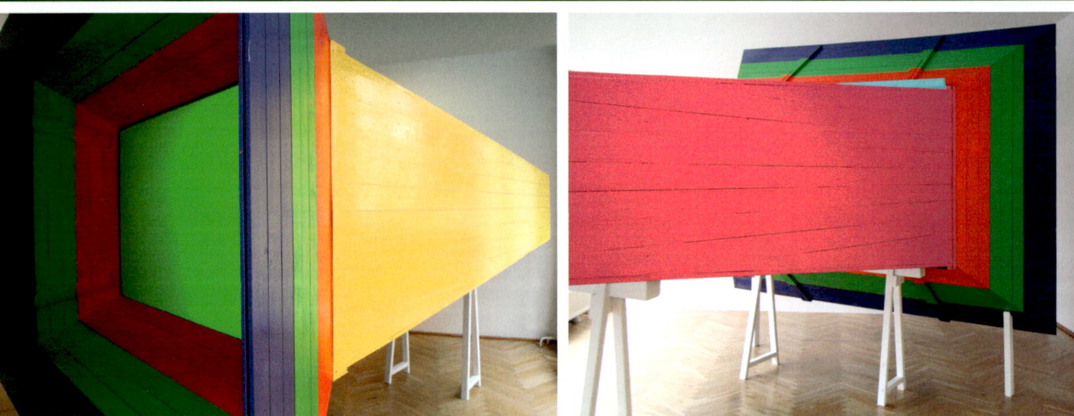

RAUSCH

Under Influence
Installation views
Kunsthaus Dresden, 2008

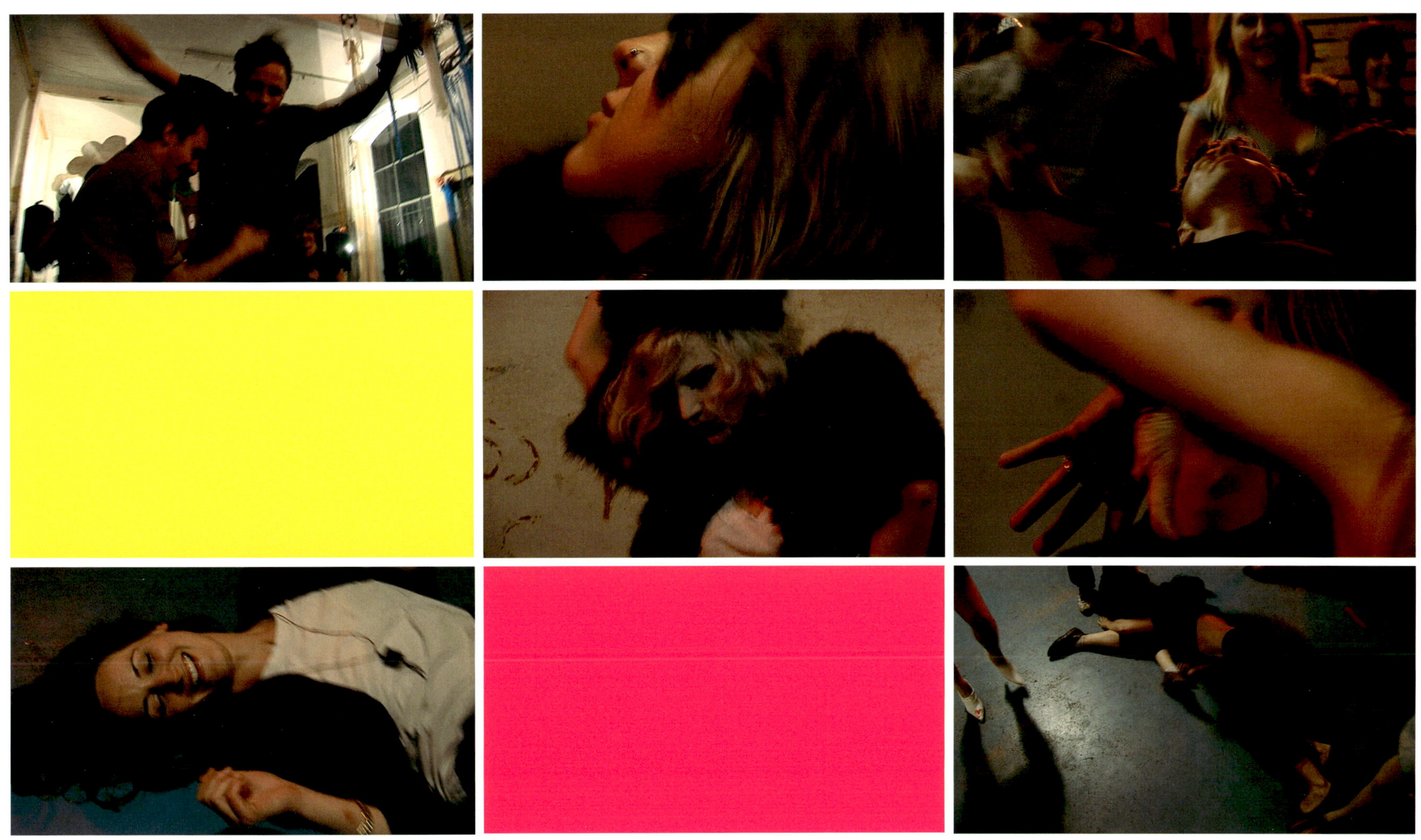

In *Rausch*, artists and their friends gather at Basso, Yusuf Etiman's club in Berlin Kreuzberg's district,
to dance as wildly as possible. This develops into a shared form of expression for a few hours before everyone
returns to his or her own specialized work, which is often carried out in isolation. What is not clear is
whether the frenzy is brought on by consuming intoxicants or dancing to the music, a post-rave piece specially
composed by Arises. In every culture, there are opportunities for people to come together and dance
frenetically, often to the point of ecstasy. Usually, additional intoxicants are consumed, from beer to peyote.
In our culture, the music, the place, and the dancers' clothing are, in themselves, a cultural occasion for ecstasy.
The film is shown in a wooden construction resembling a megaphone, painted in the primary colors RGB
and CMYK.   *A.M.*

Rausch
HD video, color, sound, 7 min, 2008
Single channel back projection in wooden construction

Director	Antje Majewski
Dancers	Ingo Niermann, Katrin Vellrath, Petr S. Kisur, Trevor Lee Larson, Juliane Solmsdorf, Heji Shin, Bettina Schoeller, Miguel Morcuende Gonzalez, Eduardo Raccah, Sabrina Fidalgo, Maja Björk, Andres Villareal, Darryl Natale, Monique Dorniak, Matthieu Malouf, Dan Bodan, Anita Leib, Veronika Schunk, Titus von Lilien, and others...
Cameras, lighting	Patricia Lewandowska, Kaspar Köpke, Nana Rebhan
Music	Arises (featuring Trevor Lee Larson)
Production	Kunsthaus Dresden

Antje Majewski

*Marl/Westphalia, Germany, 1968
Lives in Berlin

Solo Shows

2008   *My Very Gestures*, Salzburger Kunstverein, Salzburg, A
        (cat.)
        Tanz RGBCMYK, neugerriemschneider, Berlin, D
2007   *Dekonditionierung*, Ballhaus Ost, Berlin, D
        Erde Asphalt Wedding (with Juliane Solmsdorf), Institut
        im Glaspavillon der Volksbühne am Rosa-Luxemburg-
        Platz, Berlin, D
        Mal de ojo and other works, Darat al-Funun, Amman,
        Jordan
2006   *Mal de ojo and other works*, Goethe Institute, Damaskus,
        Syria
        The Royal Mummies, neugerriemschneider, Berlin, D
2005   *Mal de ojo*, neugerriemschneider, Berlin, D
        Skarbek, dance theater performance, directed by Antje
        Majewski / Ingo Niermann; stage and costume design:
        Antje Majewski; choreography: Tomasz Wygoda;
        music: Katrin Vellrath; Bytomskie Centrum Kultury,
        Bytom, PL, and Volksbühne am Rosa-Luxemburg-
        Platz, Berlin, D (cat.)
2003   *Nell'aqua nell'aria*, Galeria Monica de Cardenas, Milano, I
        Crystal Palace and the Dinosaurs, Asprey Jacques, London,
        GB
2001   *Twigs*, Goethe Institute, London, GB
        Video. Featuring Sarah Mucaria and Krylon Superstar,
        neugerriemschneider, Berlin, D
        Einer zu viel, Kunstverein Ulm, Ulm, D (cat.)
        L'invitation au voyage, Kunsthalle Basel, Basel, CH (cat.)
1999   *Invitation to a Voyage, Part I: Friends and Lovers*, Asprey
        Jacques, London, GB
1998   *Die Bergsteiger*, neugerriemschneider, Berlin, D
        Antje Majewski, Kunstverein Lingen, Lingen, D (cat.)
1997   *Spiegel*, neugerriemschneider, Berlin, D
1993   *Murphy Excellent Gas Superfine Chaos*, Lukas & Hoff-
        mann, Cologne, D
1991   *Una vita di campagna*, Galleria Communale, Ostuni, I

Group Shows

2008   *Helsinki Biennale*, Helsinki, FI
        Under Influence, Kunsthaus Dresden, Dresden, D
        Vertrautes Terrain, ZKM, Karlsruhe, D (cat.)
        *The 5th International Bangkok Experimental Film Festival
        (BEFF 5)*, Bangkok, Thailand and Kino Arsenal,
        Berlin, D
        Warsaw Does Not Exist, Galeria Kronika, Bytom, PL
        (cat.)
2007   *Kronacher Videopreis 2007*, Kunstverein Kronach,
        Fürstenbau der Festung Rosenberg, Kronach, D
2006   *Maskharat*, Künstlerhaus Stuttgart, Stuttgart, D
        Totalstadt, ZKM, Karlsruhe, D (cat.)
        Emergency Room, Galerie Olaf Stüber, Berlin, D
        Architektura intymna architektura porzucona, Galleria
        Kronika, Bytom, PL
        Soleil Noir: Depression und Gesellschaft, Salzburger
        Kunstverein, A
        A Home for Lost Ideas, General Public, Berlin, D
        Schauwerkarchiv, Kantonsbibliothek Appenzell
        Ausserhoden, CH
        Zurück zur Figur: Malerei der Gegenwart, Kunsthalle der
        Hypo-Kulturstiftung, Munich, D (cat.)
2005   *Convergence at E116°/N40° Beijing 2005*, Beijing, China
        (cat.)
2004   *6. Werkleitz-Biennale*, Volkspark Halle, Halle (Saale), D
        (cat.)
        Atomkrieg, curated by Antje Majewski and Ingo
        Niermann, Kunsthaus Dresden, D (cat.)
        *Daß die Körper sprechen, auch das wissen wir seit langem**,
        Generali Foundation, Vienna, A (cat.)
2003   *Berlin/Moskau*, Martin-Gropius-Bau, Berlin, D (cat.)
        Splendor Geometrik, curated by Anke Kempkes and Antje
        Majewski, Galerie Gisela Capitain, Cologne, D
        Help, Els Hanappe Underground, Athens, GR
        Windstöße, Kunsthaus Dresden, Dresden
        deutschemalereizweitausendunddrei, Frankfurter Kunst-
        verein, Frankfurt am Main (cat.)
2002   *Pleasant Thoughts*, griedervonputtkammer, Berlin
        Nach der Wirklichkeit—Realismus und aktuelle Malerei,
        Kunsthalle Basel, CH (cat.)
        layered histories, Staatsbank, Verein Berliner Künstler,
        Berlin, D (cat.)
        *Christian Flamm, Thilo Heinzmann, Michel Majerus, Antje
        Majewski, Nader*, aspreyjacques, London, GB
2001   *Abbild*, Landesmuseum Johanneum, Graz, A (cat.)

The Contemporary Face—Von Pablo Picasso bis Alex Katz, Deichtorhallen, Hamburg, D

Brown, The Approach, London, GB

2000   *Salon*, Delfina Project Space, London, GB

Malkunst, Fondazione Mudima, Milan, I (cat.)

Rocaille, Shedhalle, Zurich, CH

Drawings, Sommer Contemporary Fine Art, Tel Aviv, Israel

1999   *Bleibe*, Akademie der Künste, Berlin, D (cat.)

Nach-Bild, Kunsthalle Basel, Basel, CH (cat.)

Made in Berlin, House of Cyprus, Athen, GR (cat.)

1998   *El Niño*, Städtisches Museum Abteiberg, Mönchengladbach, D (cat.)

Made in Berlin, Rethymnon Centre for Contemporary Art, Crete, GR (cat.)

Beautiful World, Goethe Institute, Manchester; Goethe Institute Gallery, London, GB

Träume, curated by Antje Majewski and Ingo Niermann, ~Laden/Schillerstraße, Berlin, D

1997   *Schöne Welt*, Neuer Berliner Kunstverein, Berlin, D (cat.)

A Summer Group Show, neugerriemschneider, Berlin, D

1995   *Campo '95*, Corderie dell'Arsenale, Venice, I; Fondazione Sandretto Re Rebaudengo per l'Arte, Torino, I; Malmö Konstmuseet, Malmö, S (cat.)

45 Minuten später, Wiensowski + Harbord, Berlin, D

1994   *Group show*, Lukas & Hoffmann, Cologne, D

1993   *Futura Art Book Collection*, Air de Paris, Nice, F

Books and Catalogues

Gregor Jansen, ed. *Vertrautes Terrain*. ZKM, Karlsruhe, 2008.

Ingo Niermann. *Ich allein*. Illustration by Antje Majewski, Berlin: SuKuLTur, 2008.

Sebastian Cichocki, ed. *Warsaw Does Not Exist*. Exhibition as a book. Fundacja Bec Zmiana, Warsaw, 2008.

Ingo Niermann. *China ruft dich*. With 48 photos by Antje Majewski. Berlin: Rogner & Bernhard, 2008.

Christian Lange and Florian Matzner. *Malerei der Gegenwart. Zurück zur Figur*. Munich: Prestel, 2006.

Christoph Tannert. *New German Painting*, Munich: Prestel, 2006.

Maurizio Cattelan, Massimiliano Gioni, and Ali Subotnik, eds. *Checkpoint Charley*. Project for the 4th Berlin Biennial for Contemporary Art, Berlin, 2006.

Ingo Niermann and Antje Majewski. *Eins*. Beijing, 2005.

Irene von Hardenberg and Reto Güntli. *Künstlerinnen*. Hildesheim: Gerstenberg Verlag, 2005.

Feng Boyi, *Convergence at E116°/N40° Beijing 2005*. Beijing, 2005.

Antje Majewski and Ingo Niermann, eds. *Atomkrieg*, New York: Lukas & Sternberg, 2004.

Hemma Schmutz and Tanja Widmann, eds. *Daß die Körper sprechen, auch das wissen wir seit langem**. Vienna: Generali Foundation; Cologne: Verlag der Buchhandlung Walther König, 2004.

6. Werkleitz-Biennale, Volkspark Halle, Halle (Saale), 2004.

Pawel Choroschilow, et al., eds. *Berlin—Moskau/Moskau—Berlin*, 1950–2000, Berlin: Nicolai Verlag, 2003.

Nicolaus Schafhausen, ed. *deutschemalereizweitausenddrei*. New York: Lukas & Sternberg, 2003.

Antje Majewski and Ulrike Majewski. *Teenage Pantomime*. aspreyjacques, London, 2002.

Bernhard Mendes Bürgi and Peter Pakesch, eds. *Painting on the Move*. Basel: Schwabe Verlag, 2002.

Ulrike Kremeier. *layered histories*. Staatsbank; Berlin: Verein Berliner Künstler, 2002.

Peter Pakesch, ed. *Keine Kleinigkeit*, Christie's and Kunsthalle Basel; Basel: Schwabe Verlag, 2002.

Antje Majewski and Ingo Niermann. *Einer zu viel*. Kunstverein Ulm, 2001.

Peter Pakesch, ed. Antje Majewski: *L'invitation au voyage*. Kunsthalle Basel; Basel: Schwabe Verlag, 2001.

Peter Pakesch, ed. *Abbild*. Landesmuseum Johanneum; Vienna/New York: Springer Verlag, 2001.

Elke Naters and Sven Lager. *The Buch*. Cologne: Kiepenheuer & Witsch, 2001.

Birgit Hoffmeister. *Malkunst*. Milan: Fondazione Mudima, 2000.

Z2000, Positionen junger Kunst und Kultur. Akademie der Künste, Berlin, 2000.

Peter Pakesch, ed. *Nach-Bild*. Kunsthalle Basel; Basel: Schwabe Verlag, 1999.

Birgit Hoffmeister, ed. *Made in Berlin*. House of Cyprus, Rethymon Center of Contemporary Art, Athens, 1999.

Antje Majewski. Kunstverein Lingen; Lingen: Buxus Verlag, 1998.

Veit Loers, ed. *El Niño*. Städtisches Museum Abteiberg, Mönchengladbach, 1998.

Friedrich Meschede, ed. *Schöne Welt*. Neuer Berliner Kunstverein, Berlin, 1997.

Francesco Bonami, ed. *Echoes: Contemporary Art at the Age of Endless Conclusions*. New York: Monacelli Press, Inc., 1996.

L.A.S.T., L.E.A.K.
Sebastian Cichocki

Glasgow in den 40er Jahren des 20. Jahrhunderts. Das Haus von Allan H. Duncan, einem Liebhaber paranormaler Erscheinungen, Eingeweihten bekannt als der „subtile Jäger des Ektoplasmas". Er gilt nicht nur als vorzüglicher Kenner dieser ätherischen Substanz, dieser aufregenden *prima materia* des Jenseits, sondern wird auch gerühmt als talentiertes Medium, das bei den Reisen des Ektoplasmas in das Diesseits behilflich ist. Jeden letzten Freitag des Monats füllt sich der Salon des Herrn Duncan mit Gästen, einer sorgfältig ausgesuchten Gruppe Eingeweihter, die nach Kontakt mit dem Unbekannten dürsten.

Das enge, gewundene Treppenhaus in dem anonymen Mietshaus führt zu der massiven Tür auf dem Dachboden, die mit eisernen Riegeln und zahlreichen Schlössern versehen ist. Auf der Tür prangt ein silbernes Täfelchen mit der eingravierten Schrift „Les Magiciens de la Terre". Die Eingangstür führt unmittelbar in den Salon, den einzigen Raum, zu dem die Gäste Zutritt haben. In den anderen Räumen befindet sich, vor neugierigen Blicken sorgsam geschützt, die Sammlung von *Dingen*, die der Hausherr angehäuft hat.

Allan H. Duncan liebt Gegenstände. Diese Liebe ist ebenso unersättlich wie besitzergreifend und diszipliniert. Lange und widerstrebend überlegt er, welcher Gegenstand unter welchen Umständen ans Tageslicht geholt und unmittelbar den Blicken Fremder dargeboten werden soll. Er ist dabei launisch und störrisch. Seine Wahl lässt sich nie voraussehen.

Die junge Frau, die neben Herrn Duncan steht und die Gäste an der Tür begrüßt, heißt Stanisława P. Sie kommt aus Osteuropa, ist schüchtern, spricht wenig, errötet leicht und weint. Niemals verrät sie ihren vollen Namen. Sie assistiert Herrn Duncan seit drei Jahren. Immer trägt sie ein Heft bei sich, in dem sie interessante Aphorismen, Worträtsel, grammatische Ausnahmen und Sprichwörter notiert. Herr Duncan behauptet, das Mädchen habe eine ungewöhnliche Gabe, und die Sätze, die es in seinem Heft notiere, stammten nicht aus unserer Welt. Er nennt sie „Einflüsterungen der Zukunft".

Vor jeder Sitzung werden im Salon Gegenstände ausgelegt: Absonderlichkeiten der Natur, Kunstwerke, wertvolles Tischgedeck, medizinische Prothesen oder Proben der unterschiedlichsten Substanzen. Gegenstände hängen direkt an der Wand oder liegen auf speziellen Glasregalen und in Vitrinen. Die hauptsächlich aus der abgründigen Sammlung des Herrn Duncan stammenden oder von seinen Sammlerkollegen ausgeliehenen Objekte unterliegen ständiger Rotation. Schwer zu sagen, ob diese Kompositionen eher eine passende Atmosphäre zur „Jagd" auf die spirituelle Materie fördern oder die speziellen Fähigkeiten des Hausherren bezeugen sollen. Dieser selbst spricht bisweilen von *Intuitionen*, nie nennt er den Zweck, zu dem dieser oder jener Gegenstand in den Salon gelangt ist. Die Mehrzahl der Objekte hat der Besitzer mit kleinen Täfelchen versehen. Sie enthalten lakonische Beschreibungen, das Datum der Aufnahme in die Sammlung sowie den Namen des Eigentümers.

So auch diesmal, obwohl es nicht viele Gegenstände sind.

Eine Vase mit einem Mohnblumenstrauß auf einem Glasregal an der Wand.

Eine Bratschüssel mit halbflüssigem Fett auf dem Fensterbrett. Sie sondert einen unangenehmen Geruch ab.

Ein Glas Wasser. Der dazugehörige Text auf einem kleinen Zettel hängt hoch und ist unlesbar.

Eine mit peruanischem Sand gefüllte Sanduhr. Sie steht auf einem Bücherschrank.

Eine kleine Schachtel mit Deckel, mit der Aufschrift *Duncan, A. H., Mr., The Society for Psychical Research, 1939*. Sie steht auf dem Fußboden unter dem Kleiderständer. Die Schachtel ist halb geöffnet, ein weißes Stück Stoff ragt aus ihr heraus.

Und schließlich das Bild. Am zentralen Punkt des Salons positioniert, genau gegenüber der Eingangstür. Ziemlich groß, mehr als anderthalb Meter breit. Es ist nicht verpackt, lehnt jedoch mit der Leinwand an der Wand und liegt so eng an ihr an, dass man kein bisschen von dem sieht, was es darstellt.

Es ist neun Uhr abends. Ein frischer Abend am Frühlingsanfang. Die Gäste betreten pünktlich der Reihe nach den Raum. Die Gruppe ist diszipliniert, die Begrüßung beschränkt sich auf ein beiläufiges Nicken. Alle nehmen ihre Plätze auf den anspruchslosen Holzstühlen ein, die um den Tisch im Zentrum des Salons herumstehen.

Die Sitzung beginnt ohne überflüssige Einleitungen. Herr Duncan reckt sich schwungvoll, streckt den Hals und dehnt die Handflächen so sehr, dass die Knöchel im Gelenk knacken.

Stanisława P. greift nach dem Heft, das sie immer in ihrer abgrundtiefen Schürzentasche trägt. Sie blättert einen Augenblick in den Notizen, um dann an die Wandtafel zu gehen und mit Kreide zu schreiben: BOURGEOIS ART FREELY.

Herr Duncan schließt die Augen, hebt ein Bein an und erstarrt in völliger Bewegungslosigkeit. Sein Körper, reglos in dieser grotesken Pose, beginnt nach einer Weile gefährlich zu schwanken. Das Gesicht des Mannes läuft rot an. Endlich beugt er sich über den Tisch, röchelt, schlägt dann ein ums andere Mal mit der Stirn auf den Tisch. Das Gesicht, soeben noch rot vor Anstrengung, wird zur Abwechslung blau, und der steife Nacken streckt sich unnatürlich nach links. Kurz darauf schlüpft aus dem Mund des Mannes das Ende von etwas, das nach einer dicken Hanfschnur aussieht. Dieses Etwas bebt leicht und gleitet einige Zentimeter weit aus dem Mund. Herr Duncan, ungerührt, packt die Schnur zwischen Daumen und Zeigefinger, wickelt sie um seine Hand und zieht kräftig daran. Nach mehrmaligem Rucken präsentiert sich den Augen der Versammelten der Gegenstand in seiner ganzen Pracht – eine klebrige, speichelnasse, zuckende längliche Amöbe. Die Gäste sind begeistert. Das Ektoplasma! Beifall. Geschickt fasst der Mann das glitschige Geschöpf mit einer Silberzange und setzt das Fundstück in der Zuckerschale auf dem Tisch ab.

Kurze Pause, während der die Gäste Meinungen austauschen und die im Raum versammelten Gegenstände ansehen, nicht ohne von Zeit zu Zeit einen raschen Blick auf das überirdische Stück Auswurf in dem Gefäß zu werfen. Die Atmosphäre ist feierlich.

Der zweite Teil der Sitzung geht unerwartet rasch vonstatten.

Das Mädchen schlägt auf gut Glück eine Seite ihres Notizbuches auf und schreibt hastig an die Tafel: RADICALLY, DIALECTICALLY. Noch ehe die Gäste bequem auf den Stühlen Platz genommen haben, öffnet Herr Duncan weit den Mund, taucht mit seiner rechten Hand hinein und fördert mit schwungvoller Geste ein zerdrücktes Stoffknäuel zutage.

Dieses Stück Gewebe ist regsam, es beult sich aus und gibt ein leises Piepsen von sich. Mit feinem Lächeln reicht der Mann das Bündel der Assistentin. Diese wickelt den Stoff auf und präsentiert dem versammelten Publikum das Fundstück.

In dem Lappen befindet sich ein leise quiekendes Rattenjunges. Das Tier sieht sich um – wenn man die nervöse Bewegung des Kopfes so interpretieren kann, auf dessen Scheitel sich zwei schwarze, noch immer von einer Hautschicht bedeckte Punkte befinden –, springt auf die Erde und entwischt zum Erstaunen der Versammelten geschwind unter die Küchenkommode.

Applaus. Das Kunststück erntet Gelächter und Bewunderungsrufe.

In der Verwirrung achtet niemand auf die klebrige Spur, die die kleine Ratte hinterlässt. Vom Tisch bis zur Kommode zieht sich ein Streifen leicht phosphoreszierender Flüssigkeit.

Herr Duncan legt den Finger auf die Lippen und gebietet Stille. Er nimmt der Assistentin das verknäulte Stück Stoff ab, streicht es auf dem Tisch glatt, reibt mit der unteren Handfläche darüber und beleuchtet es zusätzlich mit einem Streichholz. Mit triumphalem Räuspern deutet er auf eine undeutliche, stark abgeriebene Aufschrift auf dem Stoff, die mit rotem Faden gestickt ist: „Passing places. Disturbed places. Unstable places. Windows disturbed by what happens behind them. Doors disturbed by those who open them. Corridors disturbed by those who walk along them."

Im selben Augenblick kichert jemand in der hinteren Reihe hysterisch und stürzt ohnmächtig zu Boden. Später stellt sich heraus, dass es sich bei dem Unglücklichen um Herrn Sazonow handelt, einen russischen Kunstsammler, den Eigentümer des Gemäldes, das mit der Rückseite zum Publikum steht.

Der Mann liegt die nächste Stunde auf dem Boden. Man lässt ihn unbehelligt. Wenn er sich erholt wieder erhebt, den Kopf voller exotischer Visionen, wird der Raum bereits völlig leer sein.

Der dritte Teil der Sitzung nimmt einen heftigen Verlauf, führt jedoch unerbittlich zur Enttäuschung.

Stanisława P. wischt sorgfältig die Tafel sauber und schaut in ihr Heft, gerät in Gedanken, lutscht an dem Kreidestummel, bis sie schließlich in Schönschrift an die Tafel schreibt: DESTRUCTION, EXISTENCE, FRAGMENT.

Die Lippen des Herrn Duncan zittern. Er sitzt in unnatürlicher Haltung auf dem Stuhl, den Rumpf an die Tischkante gelehnt, die Arme weit ausgebreitet, als schicke er sich zu fliegen an. Er murmelt Unverständliches. Keine fünf Minuten vergehen, da tritt eine klebrige Flüssigkeit aus dem Mund des Mannes, eine Art subtil schimmernden Pseudospeichels. Je mehr von dieser Substanz ihm über den Bart läuft, desto spastischere Zuckungen erfassen seine Innereien. Herr Duncan stößt Schreie aus und zappelt mit den Beinen, bis er krachend auf den Boden knallt. Er steht sogleich aus eigener Kraft wieder auf, klopft sich ab und schiebt sich an den Tisch. Mit der rechten Hand am Mund beugt er sich über die Zuckerdose. Angewidert, mit gnadenlos ver-

zerrtem Gesicht spuckt er eine kleine klebrige Kugel in den Zucker. Die Kugel rollt den Rand hoch und kullert langsam aus dem Gefäß heraus, hinterlässt auf dem Tisch eine kleistrige Schneckenspur mit Zuckerkristallen. Nach wenigen Sekunden willenloser, spiralförmiger Bewegung bleibt sie an einem auf dem Tisch stehenden Teller mit Wasser haften.

Erst jetzt fällt den Gästen auf, dass das Wasser in dem Gefäß eine eigenartige lachsrosa Färbung besitzt und am Boden die Buchstaben L.A.S.T., L.E.A.K. aufscheinen.

Stille tritt ein. Die nächsten Minuten ereignet sich nichts Bemerkenswertes. Auf dem Tisch ruht der kleine Auswurf, nichts weiter als ein von menschlichem Schleim bedecktes, zusammengeknülltes Blatt Papier. Herr Duncan massiert sich den Adamsapfel, greift nach dem Wasserglas, kippt es hinunter und spült sich laut gurgelnd den Mund. Er spuckt die Papierreste mit dem Wasser auf den Boden.

Vorsichtig nimmt er die Kugel und beginnt, sie auseinanderzufalten. Schon bald wird allen Versammelten klar, dass sich im Innern keine Nachricht befindet. Das Blatt, aus dem die Kugel geknetet war, erweist sich als völlig leer. Stanisława P. drückt ihr Heft mit den Notizen fest an die Brust und stößt einen langgezogenen, durchdringenden Schrei aus. Das ist das Zeichen, dass die Sitzung ihrem Ende zugeht.

Tee wird gereicht. Fragmente des zuvor gesammelten Ektoplasmas auf dem Boden der großen Zuckerdose aus Kristallglas pulsieren leicht. Die Gäste betrachten diese eigenartigen Überreste mit großer Aufmerksamkeit, schweigend – jeder Kommentar wäre fehl am Platz –, und kauen dabei süßen Zwieback. Aschenbecher werden hereingetragen. Zigarettenrauch und ein großes Rascheln füllen den Raum. Das Zucken der hautfarbenen Materie wird matter und matter.

Als die Gäste sich schon zum Gehen anschicken, zeigt Herr Duncan auf das an der Wand lehnende Gemälde, das während der ganzen Sitzung mit der Rückseite nach vorn dastand. Vorsichtig dreht er es den Versammelten zu, kniet dann nieder und erforscht behutsam, mit den Fingerspitzen, seine Oberfläche. Das Gemälde ist ansehnlich, farbig, illusionistisch. Aus der rechten oberen Ecke ragt eine Gestalt, die mehr als ein Viertel der Leinwand einnimmt. Diese Person, ob Frau oder Mann, ist schwer zu sagen, liegt auf der Erde, mit dem Gesicht eine schmutzige Pfütze berührend, die den größten Teil der unteren Hälfte des Bildes einnimmt. Eingehüllt ist diese Gestalt in einen Stoff, aus dem ausschließlich das Gesicht und eine Hand hervorragen, von unalltäglich blauer Hautfarbe. Über das Gesicht verlaufen farbige Streifen – rot, weiß und gelb. Die Lippen bleiben rosig. Die Gestalt schlürft von dem schlammigen Wasser, während ihr Antlitz sich undeutlich in der Pfütze spiegelt. Aus dem Mund ragt die Zunge, die bei näherem Hinsehen lebhaft an das Fragment der Substanz erinnert, das vor nicht ganz einer Viertelstunde aus dem Inneren des Herrn Duncan hervorgequollen ist.

Diese Koinzidenz ruft allerdings nicht die gewünschte Wirkung bei den Versammelten hervor.

Das Gemälde wird mit einer Decke verhängt, die Gäste gehen schweigend hinaus.

Der neue Eintrag in dem Heft von Stanisława P. lautet: THE HISTORY STILL TO BE MADE SHOWS ITSELF.

Crystal Palace and the Dinosaurs

Die Crystal Palace Grounds in London sind heute ein netter, etwas heruntergekommener Park, der vor allem von Familien mit eher niedrigem Einkommen besucht wird. Das gigantische Gebäude gibt es schon lange nicht mehr. Seine frühere Position wird nur noch von den ägyptischen Sphinxen markiert, die seinen imaginären Eingang bewachen.
Der Crystal Palace, im Wesentlichen ein vollkommen überdimensioniertes Gewächshaus aus Glas und Eisen, wurde von dem Landschaftsarchitekten Sir Joseph Paxton entworfen, um 1851 die Great Exhibition, die erste Weltausstellung, im Londoner Hyde Park zu beherbergen. Prinz Albert hatte die Ausstellung als eine eindrucksvolle Machtdemonstration auf dem Höhepunkt des britischen Kolonialismus und der erfolgreichen Industrialisierung des Landes entworfen. Nachdem die Weltausstellung beendet war, hatte Paxton die Idee, das Gebäude nach Penge Place Estate, Sydenham zu versetzen, als eine Art Winterpark und Garten unter Glas.
Der Palast und der Park wurden zum ersten Vergnügungspark der Welt. Er bot Bildung, Unterhaltung, eine Achterbahn und Kricketspiele und vieles mehr. Auch wenn der Palast viele Jahre ein Erfolg war und Millionen von Besuchern anzog, wurde er doch von finanziellen Problemen geplagt. Seine schiere Größe bedeutete, dass er unmöglich zu unterhalten war. 1911 wurde er für bankrott erklärt. Eine Stiftung wurde gegründet und Henry James Buckland als Manager des Crystal Palace engagiert. In der Nacht des 30. November 1936 gingen Buckland und seine Tochter Crystal, benannt nach seiner Liebe zum Kristallpalast, mit ihrem Hund spazieren, als sie ein kleines Feuer im Gebäude bemerkten. Es breitete sich schnell über das ganze Gebäude aus. Am Morgen war der größte Teil des Palasts zerstört.
Die Dinosaurier gehörten zum „Dinosaurierpark", ebenfalls eine Erfindung von Sir Joseph Paxton, der 1854 öffnete. Mit der Hilfe einiger Experten in Anatomie und Vorgeschichte waren die lebensgroßen Skulpturen, die ersten Versuche einer paläoontologischen Rekonstruktion, von Benjamin Waterhouse Hawkins geschaffen worden. Der Dinosaurierpark entstand sechs Jahre vor der Veröffentlichung von Darwins *Origin of Species*, dreißig Jahre nach dem Fund der ersten Dinosaurierknochen, die den Glauben an den Menschen als Zentrum des Universums erschüttern sollten, und steht so in gewisser Weise in Widerspruch zu dem Monument der (weißen, britischen, männlichen) Menschheit daneben.
Was die kleinen englischen Mädchen auf ihrem Ausflug aus alldem machen werden, wissen wir noch nicht. Sie scheinen ihre Umgebung kaum zu bemerken, denn sie sind in dem Alter, in dem das eigene Ich noch alle Aufmerksamkeit verdient. *A.M.*

Außergewöhnlich
Dominic Eichler

Manchmal wachen wir auf, und egal, was der neue Tag uns bringen mag: die Erscheinungen, die nachts oder frühmorgens zu uns gekommen sind, werfen Schatten in unseren Köpfen. Die Betrachtung von

Antje Majewskis vielfältigen Fotografien, Gemälden, Videos und Installationen der letzten ungefähr fünfzehn Jahre versetzt mich in genau diesen seltsamen geistigen Zwischenzustand. Ein Zustand, in dem die Gestalten der Träume und ihr fantastisches Reich uns ihre Anwesenheit spüren lassen und unsere Wahrnehmung der objektiven Welt einfärben. Vielleicht ist es dies, was wir in dem Selbstporträt der Künstlerin miterleben, das zu *My Very Gestures... Enchanted* (2001) gehört, einer Serie von Schwarzweißfotografien in Spiegelrahmen. Es zeigt Majewski, wie sie eine Hand auf die Stirn legt, die Augen halb nach hinten in den Kopf gerollt, als sei sie in dem Zustand (oder stellte ihn dar), in dem unser Realitätssinn von Visionen heimgesucht oder verbogen wird. Offenbar, und manchmal ist das schockierend, sind die außerweltlichen, glimmenden Protagonisten oder Wesen in diesen schnell schwindenden Träumen oder Visionen – ob Statuen oder Geister, und egal, wie seltsam, bunt oder sexuell aufgeladen sie auch sein mögen – immer Aspekte unserer selbst. Aber sie existieren auch außerhalb von uns, in unserer Beziehung zu allem, was wir jemals von dem Bereich erfahren, halb erinnert oder erdacht haben, der jenseits dessen liegt, was wir zu wissen und verstanden zu haben glauben.
Nehmen wir zum Beispiel den finsteren, unberechenbaren und mächtigen polnischen Geist der Bergwerke namens Skarbek aus dem von Majewski gemeinsam mit dem Autor Ingo Niermann verfassten gleichnamigen Tanztheaterstück, oder auch den Fake-Eingeborenenstamm von Gestalten mit Gesichtsbemalungen, Gewändern und Kapuzen in *Masken*, dem vierten Teil der Gemäldeserie *L'invitation au voyage* (1999–2001). Diese Arbeiten scheinen ein Auftauchen solcher Gestalten zwangsläufig mit sich zu bringen, ob nun ihr Schauplatz eine Art überhöhte Version von Normalität irgendwo in der Welt ist, mythisch, reine Fantasie oder eine Mischung aus alldem. In der ebenfalls *My Very Gestures* betitelten Ausstellung von 2008, die zwar keinesfalls eine umfassende Retrospektive, aber doch eine Art „Rückblick" oder eine überblickshafte Auswahl bietet, stehen diese Szenen und Szenarien nicht nur nebeneinander – sie koexistieren. Dies erreicht die Künstlerin bei einigen durch die Fixierung ihrer Umrisse, Konturen, Texturen und Tönungen auf der Oberfläche des gemalten Bildes. Woanders werden sie durch skulpturale Requisiten, Kostüme oder die Narration eines Videos lebendig. Es gibt weitere, ebenso wichtige Themenstränge in ihrem Werk, darunter eine Art von postmodernem sozialem Realismus, für den die Künstlerin oft Fernseh- und Reisebilder nutzt. Doch in der Ausstellung *My Very Gestures* und in diesem begleitenden Katalog ist es die Vorstellung, dass Kunst einen Ort bieten könnte, an dem die reale Welt sich mit der imaginierten mischt, die Majewskis verschiedene Arbeiten miteinander ins Gespräch bringt. Auf den Realismus anderer Bereiche ihrer künstlerischen Produktion hinweisend, würde Majewski wohl sagen, dass diese beiden Aspekte ihres Werks voneinander abhängig sind, dass sie ohne einander nicht existieren würden. Ihre Imagination bedeutet keine Flucht aus dem Erfahrbaren oder Beobachtbaren, vielmehr ist für die Künstlerin „das Imaginäre oder Visionäre in gewisser Weise in den Stoff des Wirklichen eingefaltet"[1]. Vielleicht das beste Beispiel dafür, wie das für Majewski funktioniert, ist Skarbek, der legendäre Geist, der seine sozialistischen Reformer

---

[1] Antje Majewski im Gespräch mit dem Autor, August 2008.

überlebt hat und noch immer die Bergbaustädte heimsucht, die ihn erschufen, auch wenn sich deren gesellschaftliche und ökonomische Bedingungen inzwischen immer mehr verschlechtern.

Davon ausgehend möchte ich gern eine der traumartigen Gestalten im Werk der Künstlerin genauer betrachten, beispielsweise den Geist, der auf dem fotorealistischen, figurativen Gemälde *Liebling* (1999) abgebildet ist – einem Werk, das nicht gealtert ist, so wie Ölbilder das nicht tun, wenn sie gut gemacht und richtig behandelt werden. (Die Künstlerin sagte mir im Gespräch, dass Ölgemälde sie unter anderem deshalb faszinieren, weil sie der Zeit widerstehen können, wenigstens der Zeit, die in Menschenleben gemessen werden kann.) Das Gemälde könnte ein heutiges Porträt des jungen Dorian Gray sein – wenn auch ohne die Zugabe teuflischer, den Tod bannender Magie. Aber auch so werden die Missetaten des echten Modells, die an die physische Welt gebunden sind, niemals seine unbefleckte Oberfläche beschmutzen. Die Arbeit zeigt einen nackten Jüngling, der in einem Spiegelkubus kauert, dessen Vorderseite zum Betrachter hin offen ist. Durch diese virtuelle Seite hindurch blickt auch die Figur aus ihrem zweidimensionalen Behälter oder Rahmen – in dem Raum eine durch Perspektive geschaffene Illusion ist – heraus in unsere vierdimensionale Welt. Der Körper des Jünglings wird in den Oberflächen um ihn herum in viele Richtungen reflektiert, eine Tatsache, die diesen friedlichen Exhibitionisten nicht zu beunruhigen scheint. (Sein Blick zum Betrachter hin deutet nicht auf narzisstische Selbstversenkung.) Eine lange Mähne und klassisch verdeckte Genitalien betonen eine gewisse Androgynität und machen ihn je nachdem verfügbar als: den Gegenstand einer pansexuellen Fantasie, Alter Ego oder kokette Muse, die als quälend-lockende Möglichkeit jenseits verfestigter oder verordneter Gender- oder Geschlechtercodes existiert. Er ist gemalt, und es ist dieses Medium, das der Erscheinung das Verweilen in immer wieder erneuerter Gegenwärtigkeit erlaubt, statt sie in der Einbildung verschwinden zu lassen, aus der sie kam. Möglicherweise stammt sie aus einem Traum und soll in unseren Träumen wiederkehren.

Wendet man sich nun der Außenwelt zu, dann kriechen dort Antje Majewski und die mit ihr zusammenarbeitende Künstlerin Juliane Solmsdorf durch die Straßen des Berliner Stadtviertels Wedding, auf bloßen Knien und in absurder Verkleidung. Majewski trägt dehnbare silberne Kleidung, Solmsdorf ein schwarzes Top und goldene Shorts mit Pailletten – als ob die beiden nach einem Zeitsprung aus einer Disco der 80er Jahre kämen. Teils ein verstörender Ausdauertest, der schon beim Zusehen schmerzt, ist es nicht klar, ob die Künstlerinnen irgendwie regrediert sind oder noch evolutionieren und ob ihr quälendes Vorwärtskriechen auf allen Vieren jenseits ihrer urtümlichen Bewegungen überhaupt irgendeinem bestimmten Zweck dient. Die rauen und trostlosen Straßen des Wedding werden im Video durch ihre Performance vollkommen verwandelt und erscheinen nun wie eine fremdartige Umgebung, unvertrautes städtisches Terrain. Das dazugehörige realistische Gemälde, *Säule Wedding* (2008), zeigt die beiden Künstlerinnen in einer Umarmung auf etwas stehen, das ein Trinkbrunnen sein könnte, wodurch sie zu einer Art provisorischem Wegweiser für den kreativen oder unorthodoxen Gebrauch des öffentlichen Raums werden. Das Gemälde konserviert und monumentalisiert ihre flüchtige performative Geste.

Ebenso waren es der heutige Zustand wie die kulturelle Geschichte eines spezifischen öffentlichen Raums, die das Interesse der Künstlerin an den Ruinen auf dem Gelände des Londoner Parks weckten, auf dem der Crystal Palace aus dem 19. Jahrhundert stand. Das Gemälde *Entrance to Crystal Palace* (2002), das von einem Wandbild mit historischen Postkarten begleitet wird, die die Kultur- und Sozialgeschichte des Crystal Palace aufscheinen lassen, und das Gemälde *Dinosaurs* (2002) lenken die kritische Aufmerksamkeit und Imagination des Betrachters gleichzeitig auf die Vergangenheit und die Gegenwart. In diesen Arbeiten sind die Protagonistinnen zwei anonyme junge Mädchen, die unterhalb einer Sphinx miteinander plaudern und deren Augen mit roter Farbe entstellt wurden. Später essen sie gemeinsam in einer Cafeteria vor einem Wandbild mit Dinosaurier-Modellen – den ältesten Attraktionen der Crystal Palace Grounds. Dargeboten werden hier alltägliche Szenen mit einer außergewöhnlichen Vergangenheit. Dadurch, dass sie sie malt, erreicht Majewski ein instabiles Zusammentreffen von Realität und Fiktion. In der Ausstellungsarchitektur und den Displays von *My Very Gestures* hallt die Idee eines Jahrmarktplatzes oder einer Weltausstellung nach. So erinnert zum Beispiel das Gehäuse für die Präsentation des Videos *Erde Asphalt Wedding* (2007) an einen frei stehenden Messestand. Das gilt auch für die gestreifte achteckige Plattform, die den Besuchern eine Insel bietet, um dort zusammenzukommen, auszuruhen, selbst Teil der Präsentation zu werden und die Kuriositäten um sie herum, wie die Skarbek-Marionette und die Masken, zu studieren.

Es ist hilfreich, zu den frühen Tagen ihrer künstlerischen Produktion zurückzugehen, um Majewskis künstlerische Intention im Verhältnis zu ihren unterschiedlichen Themen zu verorten und zu kontextualisieren. Mitte der 90er Jahre veröffentlichte die Künstlerin einen Text in einer der ersten Ausgaben von *Starship*, dem noch immer existierenden unabhängigen Berliner Magazin für Kunst, Kultur und Politik, der sich liest wie das ungezügelte Manifest eines Malers, genauer einer Malerin. In Wirklichkeit wurde der Text zur Gänze aus Zitaten der Malerinnen Rosa Bonheur, Marie Bashkirtseff, Louise-Catherine Breslau und Tamara de Lempicka zusammengesetzt. Der folgende Auszug kann davon eine Idee vermitteln:

Als junges Mädchen vergeudete ich meine Zeit mit exzessiven Fragen und exzentrischen Nichtigkeiten. Es gibt eine Zeit, wo man sich ganz naiv zu allem fähig fühlt. […] Ich rauche drei Schachteln Zigaretten pro Tag und schlucke nachts Unmengen von Schlaftabletten. Die Tage sind einfach zu kurz. Manchmal gehe ich abends aus, komme um zwei Uhr morgens nach Hause und arbeite bis sechs bei schlechtem Licht. […] Ich habe ein Ziel, und ich habe einen Plan. Nach jedem zweiten verkauften Bild werde ich ein Armband kaufen, bis die Diamanten und Juwelen vom Handgelenk bis zum Ellenbogen reichen. Man muss schon eine große Begeisterung für seine Kunst haben, um in diesem grässlichen Milieu und unter diesen plumpen Leuten leben zu können. Ich bin nur an den Besten interessiert.

Ich habe eine ganz schwarze Perücke auf und meine Augenbrauen sind ebenfalls geschwärzt. Ganze Nächte kann ich bei dem Gedanken an ein Bild oder eine Statue schlaflos verbringen; nie hat der Gedanke an einen hübschen Mann dasselbe bewirkt.

[…] Ich lebe hier glücklich, fern von der Welt, empfange den Besuch einiger intimer Freunde und arbeite, so gut es geht.

Wäre ich vollkommen glücklich, ich würde vielleicht nicht gearbeitet haben.[2]
Zwei Jahre zuvor hatte die Künstlerin den kunsthistorischen Text „Einige Realistinnen" veröffentlicht, in dem sie sich mit den Positionen realistischer Malerinnen der 70er Jahre, darunter Joan Semmel und Sylvia Sleigh, auseinandersetzte.[3] Ich erwähne diese frühen Texte, weil sie für mich zeigen, wie Majewski von Anfang an ihre Bezugspunkte, ihre Inspirationsquellen und ihre kritische Perspektive klargemacht hat. Was das Nachdenken über Fantasiefiguren, Performance, Rollenspiel und Kostüme in ihrem Werk angeht, so wird der theoretische Hintergrund von einer progressiven Form von Feminismus mitbestimmt. Man sollte insbesondere Judith Butlers These zur Bedeutung von Performanz und Performativität in der Geschlechterkonstruktion berücksichtigen. Wieder sind die lebendigen und geheimnisvollen *Masken*-Bilder vielleicht ein gutes Beispiel dafür, wie dieser Gedanke undogmatisch und forschend in vielen von Majewskis Arbeiten aufgenommen wurde. Die Serie zeigt eine Gruppe von FreundInnen und anderen KünstlerInnen, deren Gesichter wild mit geometrischen Mustern bemalt sind. Sie tragen geschmacklos gemusterte, nicht geschlechtsspezifische Gewänder, die die Künstlerin aus billigen Stoffen genäht hatte.

Masquerade (2006) wurde auf unbehandeltem Kupfer gemalt, was nahelegt, dass das Bild einen gewissen Anteil an Magie und Alchemie enthält. Gleichzeitig ist es die Feier einer potenziell befreienden Art von Performance.

Doch um zur jüngeren Vergangenheit zurückzukehren, ist es auch wichtig, sich daran zu erinnern, dass damals, in der Mitte der 90er Jahre, die Malerei – zumal die realistische oder figurative Malerei (für die Majewski dann vor allem in den späten 90er Jahren bekannt wurde) – in den künstlerischen Praktiken der jungen KünstlerInnen keine große Rolle spielte. Dabei sollte dieser inoffiziell verhängte Bann vonseiten der Kuratoren und in weniger starkem Ausmaß der Galerien schon bald in großem Stil aufgehoben werden, in Deutschland beispielsweise durch den kommerziell betriebenen Aufstieg der sogenannten Leipziger Schule. In scharfem Gegensatz dazu und Majewski weitaus näher waren da die ProtagonistInnen der in Entstehung begriffenen Berliner Szene, die im Vergleich zu heute noch relativ klein und selbstreferenziell war. Zu den KünstlerInnen, die für Majewskis speziellen Kontext besonders wichtig waren, zählten Lukas Duwenhögger, Ull Hohn, Michel Majerus und Katharina Wulff – die sich alle auf zugegeben höchst unterschiedliche Weise der Malerei mit diskursiver Energie und einer neuen Liebe für malerische Probleme näherten und den problematischen Status der Gegenständlichkeit direkt ansprachen. Damit soll nicht suggeriert werden, dass es da so etwas wie eine Berliner Schule oder Bewegung gegeben habe, aber es gab damals eine lebhafte Diskussion über etwas, das man verteidigen konnte, das nicht als kitschig, konservativ oder sonst wie rückschrittlich gesehen wurde. Es ist wichtig, Majewskis Werk in Bezug auf diesen Kontext und das intellektuelle Klima jener Jahre zu würdigen.

Der Ausstellungstitel *My Very Gestures* stammt aus dem Album *Welcome to the Pleasuredome* (1984) von Frankie Goes to Hollywood. Und zwar aus einigen Zeilen, die eine Passage aus Friedrich Nietzsches *Die Geburt der Tragödie* (1872) paraphrasieren, in der Nietzsche sagt: „Singend und tanzend äußert sich der Mensch als Mitglied einer höheren Gemeinsamkeit: er hat das Gehen und das Sprechen verlernt und ist auf dem Wege, tanzend in die Lüfte emporzufliegen. Aus seinen Gebärden spricht die Verzauberung. Wie jetzt die Thiere reden, und die Erde Milch und Honig giebt, so tönt auch aus ihm etwas Uebernatürliches: als Gott fühlt er sich, er selbst wandelt jetzt so verzückt und erhoben, wie er die Götter im Traume wandeln sah. Der Mensch ist nicht mehr Künstler, er ist Kunstwerk geworden." Die Künstlerin schrieb mir, dass dies vielleicht „mehr als irgendetwas anderes beschreibt, worum es mir geht". Für mich heißt das, dass im Herzen von Majewskis künstlerischer Praxis die Idee einer Feier liegt, das Arbeiten und Leben aus Freude. Die Gestalten und Personen ihrer Kunst entspringen dem Gewöhnlichen, um uns auf einen anderen, imaginären Gedankenflug mit auf die Reise zu nehmen.

The Royal Mummies

Diese Gemäldeserie versucht, die beeindruckenden Schwarzweißfotografien zu „remumifizieren", die sich in Grafton Elliot Smiths *Catalogue Général des Antiquités Égyptiennes du Musée du Caire* (1912) befinden und meist von dem Ägyptologen Emile Brugsch aufgenommen wurden. Die Ägypter hatten sich für die Ewigkeit konservieren wollen; indem sie sie wieder ans Tageslicht holten, setzten die Ägyptologen des späten 19. Jahrhunderts das Rad der Zerstörung wieder in Gang, das die Einbalsamierer hatten anhalten wollen. Sie wickelten die Mumien aus, manchmal auf sehr grobe Art; oft brachen äußere Gliedmaßen wie Finger, Ohren oder der Penis ab und gingen verloren, und die Feuchtigkeit im Museum färbte die Haut der Mumien dunkel.

Die Fotos von Emile Brugsch konservieren den Zustand, in dem sich die Mumien befanden, als sie zum ersten Mal nach Tausenden von Jahren wieder sichtbar wurden. Die Lebensdauer der Fotos selbst ist im Vergleich sehr kurz. Die Originalnegative, Vergrößerungen und Kataloge werden bald vergehen.

Die Aluminium-„Leinwände" wurden in der Hoffnung gewählt, dass sie besser als echte Leinwände überdauern werden. Für die Malerei wurden Bleiweiß, Rußschwarz und ein imitiertes „Mumienbraun" verwendet. „Mumia vera aegyptica" war ein Pigment, das aus im Mörser zerriebenen Mumienteilen bestand und unter Malern bis ins 19. Jahrhundert sehr populär blieb, unter anderem weil es natürlichen Asphalt (Bitumen) enthielt, was es sehr angenehm zu vermalen machte. Andere Zutaten wie Leinöl oder Dammar wurden bereits von den Ägyptern sowohl für das Konservieren von Körpern wie von Gemälden genutzt, und wir malen heute immer noch damit. Grafton Elliot Smith, der Begründer des „Hyperdiffusionismus", wäre wahrscheinlich entzückt bei dem Gedanken, dass nicht nur die Rezepte der Maler aus dem antiken Ägypten ins moderne Deutschland diffundierten, sondern auch der Realismus, den Echnaton/Akhenaton (oder seine Frau Nefertiti/Nofretete) erfand. Sein Schädel (die Zuschreibung ist umstritten) ist auf Seite 50 zu sehen.   *A.M.*

[2]Antje Majewski, „Pastiche", in: *Starship*, Nr. 3, Winter 2000, S. 124–125.
[3]Antje Majewski, „Einige Realistinnen", in: *Starship*, Nr. 1, Herbst 1998, S. 24–35.

Skarbek

Bytom ist eine polnische Stadt, in der jahrhundertelang Erze und zuletzt auch Kohle abgebaut wurden. Viele Häuser stehen schief und sind vom Einsturz bedroht, weil auch direkt unter der Stadt gegraben wurde. Mittlerweile mussten die meisten Minen schließen. Der Fortschritt hat die Bewohner der ehemals prosperierenden Bergwerkstadt zurückgelassen.

Die Menschen in dem Tanztheaterstück *Skarbek* (2005) wollen auf nichts mehr warten. Überstürzt steigen sie in eine verlassene Mine und versuchen, der Erde noch einmal einen Schatz oder ein Abenteuer abzutrotzen. Der Mangel an Luft und Reizen unter Tage versetzt sie in einen Schwindel, ihr Gefühl für räumliche und zeitliche Größenverhältnisse wird gestört. Sie bewegen sich an der Grenze zum Tod, und es scheint, als geriete durch ihr Eindringen auch die verlassene Mine in Bewegung. Skarbek und die Schätze der Erde – Gold, Silber und Kristall – treten auf.

Der Skarbek ist eine Figur der oberschlesischen Sagenwelt, ein Gnom, der in verlassenen Minen wohnt und die unterirdischen Schätze hütet. Als Erdgeist ist er den Toten und dem Tod verbunden. Er wacht über das Ethos der Bergleute und bestraft die, die den Berg nicht ernst nehmen. Er kann sich durch Geräusche bemerkbar machen und unterschiedliche Gestalten annehmen. Im Schauspiel zeigt er sich als Maus, als toter Bergmann und als drei Gestalten mit Masken: einer sehr großen, einer mittleren und einer sehr kleinen, die für den Kopf der Marionette benutzt wurde. Alle drei wurden in Mexiko gekauft. Ihre dramatischen gotischen Schnitzereien spiegeln den Stil der Zeit wider, in der die Spanier Mexiko und seine reichen Gold- und Silberminen eroberten. Auch in Real de Catorce mussten die Bergleute fürchten, El Jergas zu begegnen – Geschichten über Erdgeister gibt es überall, wo Menschen es wagten, ihrer natürlichen Angst entgegenzuhandeln, tief unten in der Erde zu sterben.

Skarbek spielt den Menschen harmlose Streiche und amüsiert sie, aber er kann auch rachsüchtig und gefährlich sein. Für die Menschen in diesem Schauspiel bleibt er unberechenbar. Der Welt des Anorganischen zugehörig, folgt er deren eigenen, den Menschen fremd bleibenden Gesetzen. *A.M.*

Atomkrieg

Silber auf Kupfer (Denkmal für Paul Rosbaud) war Teil der Gruppenausstellung *Atomkrieg*, die von Ingo Niermann und mir 2004 im Kunsthaus Dresden kuratiert wurde. Dieses Gemälde auf unbehandeltem Kupfer zeigt ein Schmuckstück, das von Frank Frink (geb. Fink), dem Protagonisten aus Philip K. Dicks Roman *The Man in the High Castle* (1962), hergestellt wurde und nun zu meiner Ehrenmedaille für den deutschen Spion Paul Rosbaud wird.

In meinem Text für den Ausstellungskatalog verbinde ich meine historische Recherche über die Geschichte von Paul Rosbaud, der gegen Ende des Zweiten Weltkriegs vergeblich versucht hat, die Geheimnisse um die Forschung an der deutschen Atombombe an die Amerikaner zu verraten – was den Einsatz der amerikanischen Atombomben unentschuldbar gemacht hätte, wäre es ihm geglückt –, mit dem Roman von Philip K. Dick. Er beschreibt das Szenario einer Welt, in der die Deutschen und die Japaner den Krieg gewonnen haben. Frink, einem amerikanischen Kunsthandwerker verheimlichter jüdischer Herkunft, gelingt es plötzlich, ein Schmuckstück herzustellen, in dem die Japaner *Wú* (oder chinesisch *Mu*) erkennen – die Leere des Geistes, das Nichts, das in der japanischen und chinesischen Philosophie als höchstes Ziel gilt und für die niedere Rasse der Amerikaner als unerreichbar angesehen wird. Dieses Schmuckstück erlaubt Frink einen Blick in die wirkliche Welt, in der die Japaner den Krieg verloren haben.

Da Frank Frink nicht existiert und ich nicht zu behaupten wagte, ich hätte etwas mit inhärentem *Wú* selbst erfunden, ist dieses Schmuckstück tatsächlich eine natürliche Silberstufe aus einem mineralogischen Museum. *A.M.*

Was ist mit den Menschen?
Ingo Niermann

Nicht nur der Mensch baut sich einen Unterschlupf. Gibt Laute von sich, um sich zu verständigen. Benutzt Geräte. Erkennt sich selbst im Spiegel. Lügt. Doch nur der Mensch hat den Willen, ein anderer zu sein, als er ist. Er bemalt sich, bekleidet sich, trainiert, begeht Suizid. Auch vom Körper losgelöste Artefakte erfüllen eine magische und damit die Menschen nicht bloß befriedigende, sondern sie und andere Wesen manipulierende Funktion.

Je mehr die Menschen in der Welt schaffen, desto mehr begreifen sie sich selbst als ein Gerät, dessen Äußeres möglichst zweckgerecht zu gestalten ist: beweglich und sauber. Selbst an Festtagen schminken sie sich nur dezent. Der Kunst, die sie kaufen oder sich in Ausstellungen und Theatern anschauen, gönnen sie mehr Extravaganz, weil sie sie nicht ständig wahrzunehmen brauchen und als weitgehend irrelevant erachten.

Erst wenn Maschinen zunehmend im Verborgenen wirken und kaum mehr der menschlichen Hilfe bedürfen, sondern im Gegenteil auch die Menschen nicht mehr nur zu reparieren, sondern umzubauen vermögen, lösen sich der Mensch als Maschine und seine Erscheinung voneinander. Bis dahin können Schauspieler zwar so populär werden, dass jeder Aspekt ihres Privatlebens interessiert, doch dauernden Ruhm erlangen sie nur als Teil in der Regel von anderen entwickelter Inszenierungen. In der bildenden Kunst ist bei allen noch so radikalen Grenzüberschreitungen eines klar: Sie ist nichts, was man sich irgendwo hinsteckt, hinreibt oder überstülpt. Nicht etwa, weil es sich dann zu schnell abnutzte. Denn längst gibt es Kunst, die sich allmählich selbst zersetzt oder regelmäßig erneuert werden muss. Doch während bildende Kunst die Häuser schmückt, ist Körperschmuck, wenigstens sobald er getragen wird, immer nur Kunstgewerbe.

Antje Majewski lässt diese Grenze nicht gelten. Als Sammlerin verwahrt sie opulente Kleider und Tücher ebenso sorgfältig wie Fotos und Gemälde, sie werden aber auch von ihr und Freunden getragen. Als Künstlerin malt und filmt sie nicht nur, sondern entwirft auch das

Make-up und viele der in den zugrunde liegenden Inszenierungen verwandten Kleidungsstücke. Wenn sie die in ihren Videos erscheinenden Gemälde später verkauft, ihre Kleider aber nicht, dann nicht, weil Letztere für sie weniger Kunst wären, sondern weil sie als Teil ihrer eigenen Sammlung weiterhin getragen werden. Von gewöhnlichen Kunstsammlern lässt sich das höchstens konzeptuell erzwingen.

Ob Antje Majewski Menschen in ihrer alltäglichen Erscheinung oder einer Inszenierung malt, sie ordnet sich unter. Was zu sehen ist, bleibt bei den Menschen. Sie sind die eigentlichen Bilder, die sich real jedoch nur flüchtig präsentieren. Auch auf den als Vorlage für die Gemälde dienenden Fotos sind sie bloß ein Schnappschuss. Von Majewski gemalt, wirkt das zu Sehende plastisch und gewollt. Die Bergbesteigung am Wochenende, der Museumsbesuch im Pelzmantel, der Karneval, der provisorisch sesshaft gewordene Landstreicher – das Streben der Menschen nach Selbstgestaltung ist überall. Die zeitgenössische Kunst ist dagegen ein Ewigkeit beanspruchendes Epiphänomen.

In der Ausstellung *Mal de ojo* (2005) und dem Tanztheaterstück *Skarbek* (2005) treten erstmals Gegenstände in den Vordergrund: Die Schätze der Erde werden lebendig, und auch Plastikhocker, Vorhang und Lampe werden, gemalt auf einer glatten, rutschigen Holzfaserplatte, verwischt und zerkratzt, zu unerbittlich harrenden Untoten. Andererseits gleichen die Xoloitzcuintles, mexikanische Nackthunde, bereits verwitterten Skulpturen, und der Schauspieler Kaveh Parmas stellt einen Toten dar. Wie im Animismus gibt es hier keinen grundsätzlichen Unterschied zwischen dem Lebenden und den Dingen. Diesem Irrsinn können auch Tiere anheimfallen (Katzen verlieben sich in Katzenminze), doch seine Systematisierung zum „bösen Blick" bereitete der Kunst ihren Weg und vermittelt sich den Ungläubigen nur noch als Kunst. Majewski vollzieht einen möglichen Anfang an sich selbst nach und sticht ein Ohrloch aus der Teenagerzeit wieder auf.

Das Gemälde *Entrance to Crystal Palace* (2002) zeigt eine ehemals den Eingang des Londoner Crystal Palace schmückende Sphinx, der ein Unbekannter die Augen rot angemalt hat. Der in *Venus* (1997) zu sehende Velázquez *Venus vor dem Spiegel* wurde 1914 von einer Suffragette zerschnitten. Die ägyptischen Mumien in Majewskis *The Royal Mummies* (2006) sollten für immer verborgen bleiben, aber die Tücher, in die sie gewickelt waren, wurden von Forschern zerschnitten. Nicht nur sich selbst, die Menschen maskieren und enthüllen auch Artefakte und entwickeln zu ihnen ein neues Verhältnis. Was früher Ehrfurcht erregte, daran lehnt man sich heute lässig an – oder auch umgekehrt.

In dem Video *No School Today* (2005) lässt ein Kind einen Erwachsenen sich nach neuen Regeln durch seine Hochhauswohnung bewegen. In *Dekonditionierung* (2008) absolutieren fünf Schauspieler und Laien grundsätzliche menschliche Verhaltensweisen wie Macht und Nähe. Majewskis Gemälde sind als Teil des Bühnenbilds wie im normalen Leben Dekor, dem sich die Akteure widmen oder das sie ignorieren können. In der Ausstellung stehen Film und Gemälde dann gleichberechtigt nebeneinander. Das Gemälde tritt vor beziehungsweise die Handlung tritt zurück als nun ebenfalls Kunst.

In *Säule Wedding* (2008) stehen Antje Majewski und Juliane Solmsdorf gemeinsam vor dem Eingang zur Berliner U-Bahnstation Pankstraße auf einer defekten Trinkwassersäule. Die Künstlerinnen setzen sich zu Lebzeiten ihr eigenes Denkmal. Doch auf der Säule auszuharren strengt schnell an, und auch jeder andere Passant kann sie für ein paar Minuten besteigen. Oder sich wie die beiden Künstlerinnen in dem Film *Erde Asphalt Wedding* (2007) nur noch robbend fortbewegen.

Immer wieder sollte es die Aufgabe der Kunst sein, absolut richtige Formen zu finden und damit den Menschen zurückzuwerfen auf sein sterbliches und endliches Maß. Der Glaube daran ist geschwunden. Was geblieben ist, sind staatliche Normen, wie breit ein Flugzeugsitz und wie hoch eine Wohnung zu sein hat oder wie hell eine Werbetafel leuchten darf. Doch das sind willkürliche Bestimmungen, denn jeder einzelne Mensch kann jederzeit neu entscheiden, was für ihn zu klein, zu groß, zu hell oder zu dunkel ist. Wie wandelbar dieses Maß ist, will Antje Majewski in einer Serie erkunden, in der sie ein Motiv immer wieder neu malt, unter dem Einfluss verschiedener Drogen.

Drogen sind die einzigen Dinge, die im Laufe der Menschheitsgeschichte, in der eine unfassbare Menge von Dingen angehäuft wurde, kaum an den Alltag transzendierender Wirkung verloren haben. Sie umgeben den Menschen nicht, sondern durchdringen ihn.

So ist auch Majewskis Ideal eine Kunst, die sich wie in der Kurzgeschichte *The Winter Market* von William Gibson direkt von einem Gehirn ins andere überträgt. Als eine nach innen gestülpte Maske wäre sie nicht mehr sinnlich wahrnehmbar und könnte die anderen Reize im Extrem komplett verdecken, der Mensch käme sich in seiner Wandelbarkeit selbst abhanden.

Doch was Majewski an einer direkt übertragbaren Kunst interessiert, ist weniger die Totalität als die Präzision. Am Beginn ihrer Karriere spielte sie noch mit dem Gedanken, die Ausstellungsbesucher überraschend einzuschließen, um sich der Bedeutungslosigkeit der zeitgenössischen Kunst zu widersetzen. Schnell hat sie gemerkt, dass sie mehr will. Ihr soll nicht weniger gelingen als eine Pracht, die sich an Velázquez oder Vermeer genauso messen kann wie an den Spektakeln eines Waldspaziergangs.

No School Today

Aufzuwachsen bedeutet, die Regeln der jeweiligen Zivilisation zu erlernen. Ein Teil davon ist es, mögliche Bewegungen zu reduzieren. Ein kleines Kind kann noch Mauern hinaufklettern, springen und öffentlich auf den Boden fallen; wenn ein Erwachsener das täte, würden die Leute ihn anstarren. Der Prozess der Zivilisation stellt sicher, dass ein Erwachsener nicht einmal dann daran denkt, seltsame Bewegungen zu machen, wenn er allein ist; mit Ausnahme des Sports, der wiederum eigenen Regeln gehorcht.

Die Routinen des Alltags verändern sich schnell in Beijing. Verändert werden sie nicht nur durch neue Arbeitsbedingungen, sondern auch durch die neuen Grundrisse der Privatwohnungen. In *No School Today* wollte ich ausprobieren, was passiert, wenn die Regeln für Bewegungen im begrenzten Raum einer der neuen, anonymen Wohnungen in Beijing verändert werden, so dass sie auf eine Art genutzt wird, die nicht vorgesehen war.

Ein Mann und ein Kind leben in einem der neuen Apartments. Die

Wohnung ist im „internationalen Stil" eingerichtet und verrät keinen besonderen Geschmack. Die einzige Ausnahme bildet das Ölgemälde eines *Gongshi*, das an der Wand hängt.[1] Die beiden beginnen ein Spiel, bei dem der Mann das Kind fangen muss. Er darf sich dabei nur mit dem ganzen Körper an Boden und Möbeln entlang bewegen, das Kind dagegen darf akrobatische Sprünge machen.

No School Today war ein Experiment, das auf Improvisationen basierte. Ich habe dabei mit Cui Tao von der Beijing Modern Dance Company zusammengearbeitet sowie mit dem 10-jährigen Zheng Chenggong, der auf der Dongcheng-Sportschule in Beijing Kampfsport lernt.

A.M.

[1] „Gongshi" (seltene Steine) oder „guaishi" (eigenartige oder fantastische Steine) sind kleine Steine, die wegen ihrer Form gesammelt und auf einem flachen Tablett präsentiert werden, das mit Sand, feinem Kies oder Wasser gefüllt ist; seit der Song-Dynastie (960–1279) wurden sie auf wunderschön geschnitzte hölzerne Sockel gesetzt, die Wurzeln ähnelten. Diese Mode verbreitete sich in ganz Asien; in Japan werden sie „suiseki" genannt, in Korea „suseok", auf Deutsch heißen sie Gelehrtensteine. Berge wurden in China wie in vielen anderen Ländern der Welt als heilig verehrt, Felsen sah man als die Knochen der Erde, vielleicht die Knochen prähistorischer Drachen. Als sich der Gartenbau zu einer Kunstform entwickelte, musste jeder Garten einen seltsam geformten Gartenstein haben. Die Steine galten als das Rückgrat des Gartens, dessen Erde als seine Haut. Steine mit Löchern wurden besonders geschätzt, weil sie es der kosmischen Energie erlaubten, durch sie zu zirkulieren.

Die Gelehrten benutzten dann noch kleinere Steine, um über den Kosmos zu meditieren, und stellten sie neben Landschaftsgemälde oder Kalligrafien. Durch diese Abstraktionen konnte sich die Einbildungskraft konzentrieren und reinigen. Im Jahr 1131 schrieb der Gelehrte Du Wan den *Stein-Katalog des Wolkenwaldes* und führte darin 116 verschiedene Arten von Felsformen auf, die von Connaisseuren unterschieden wurden.

Für mich ist der Stein, den ich gemalt habe, die westliche Adaption einer chinesischen Tradition, die auf einer tiefen Verbindung zur Natur beruht. Beijing ist auf den ersten Blick das extreme Gegenteil der chinesischen Liebe zur Natur; ich kenne keine andere Stadt, die so grau, so aus Beton gebaut ist und im Smog verschwindet. Aber bei näherem Hinsehen sind die neuen Häuserblocks um extrem manikürte Gärten herum angelegt; selbst junge Leute lieben riesige Aquarien mit Felslandschaften.

Die Bewegungen des Manns und des Jungen in meinem Film erinnern an die von Tieren; und sie bewegen sich ganz selbstverständlich so, denn schließlich sind Menschen Tiere. Der Stein des chinesischen Gelehrten ist eine extrem kultivierte Art, die Natur zu betrachten, eine Natur, die nicht als Gegner gesehen wird, sondern als etwas, von dem auch die Menschen einen winzigen Teil bilden. Obwohl die Steine sehr klein sind und zahm auf ihren hübschen Sockeln, sind sie nicht klein in den Gedanken des Gelehrten. Die Menschen sind es, die klein sind, so winzig wie auf den Landschaftsgemälden.

Heute wird man über das Verhältnis von Mensch und Natur in China noch einmal nachdenken müssen, da die Natur dort inzwischen auf extreme Art genutzt wird.

Antje Majewski & Juliane Solmsdorf
Erde Asphalt Wedding / Säule Wedding / Nichtstun

Zwei seltsame Kreaturen kommen aus dem Kanal am Westhafen im Wedding, einem der heruntergekommensten Viertel von Berlin. Ihre glänzenden Kostüme funkeln im frühen Morgenlicht. Der Straßenlärm nimmt langsam zu, während sie auf dem Boden vorankriechen: auf die Straße hinauf, über eine Brücke, über Kreuzungen und an Autos vorbei, bis sie schließlich hinter einer Betonrampe verschwinden.

Die Barstühle stehen auf dem Gehsteig, sie sollen zu einem Ort transportiert werden, an dem man zahlen muss, um sich daraufzusetzen.

Aber im Moment erfüllen sie noch keinen Zweck, haben nur angenehme Formen. Die schönen weißen Schaumgummibänder der Verpackung flattern im Wind. Darf ich sie benutzen, solange sie im öffentlichen Raum stehen?

Wir stellen uns in diesen Raum hinein, werden für die anderen Bewohner der Stadt zur Bildsäule. Die Größe der Gebäude hinter uns misst sich an uns, die Breite der Straße.

Valie Export hat in ihren Fotoserien von 1976 mit ihrem Körper Ecken, Linien und Kurven in der Stadt nachgebildet. Es sind zweideutige Fotos: es könnte auch sie sein, nach deren Vorbild die Stadt gebaut wurde, so dass sich die Stadt an sie anschmiegen würde statt umgekehrt. *A.M.*

À bruit secret
Tanja Widmann im Gespräch mit Antje Majewski

Tanja Widmann: Ich möchte bei dem Bild *Masken* (2001) ansetzen, das gewissermaßen zum Grund unserer Begegnung wurde. Ich würde es gerne ein weiteres Mal als Ausgangspunkt nehmen, jetzt für dieses Gespräch hier, und sehen, wohin wir im Blick darauf und im Reden darüber gelangen und inwieweit sich über diesen Fokus auch andere Arbeiten von dir mit einbeziehen lassen. Im neuerlichen Blick auf dieses Bild gibt es für mich mehrere Bezugspunkte. Einerseits erinnert es noch mal Watteau für mich – die Setzung einer Theatralik, die die Bühne aufruft, ohne dass sich die gezeigten Figuren auf ihr befinden oder bewegen würden. Diese Theatralik reicht vom Moment der Kostümierung über die Gesten bis hin zu den Masken. Wie bei Watteau gibt es auch hier eine Freisetzung der Zeichen – wären die Kostüme, wie die Gesten und Masken im Theater, eingebunden in ein Stück, eine Erzählung, würden sie mit spezifischer Bedeutung aufgeladen. Hier jedoch sind sie kräftig gesetzte Zeichen, die Bedeutungshaftigkeit zwar aufrufen, zugleich aber in der Schwebe bleiben. Sie erwirken unsere Aufmerksamkeit als unlesbare, gleichsam ausgehöhlte Zeichen, deren Verweis für mich als Betrachterin nur auf Abwesendes zielen kann.

Die vor mir erscheinende Gruppe trägt ein Versprechen von unverwirklichter Utopie in sich, sie evoziert freie Theatergruppen und sozialkritische Formierungen in den 1960er und 1970er Jahren, ebenso wie sie doch zeitgenössisch wirkt durch diese Gesichter, in manchen Stoffen, im Stil. Als Betrachterin werde ich adressiert und aufgerufen, und doch werden zugleich mehrfach Grenzen gezogen. Gerade die Theatralik der Szene, der Gruppe, des Ortes lässt den Ausstellungsraum und meine Bewegungen darin völlig undramatisch, alltäglich und nüchtern aufscheinen, auch die Gemeinsamkeit der Gruppe bleibt mir, die ich vereinzelt vor dem Bild stehe, gleichermaßen fremd, fern. In dieser Unentschiedenheit zwischen Adressierung und Unnahbarkeit, Alltäglichkeit und Außerordentlichkeit liegt ein unabschließbarer Sog, der auch in anderen Arbeiten von dir wiederkehrt. Welche Konstellationen von Gruppen, von Beziehungen rufst du auf?

Antje Majewski: Ich finde deine Beschreibung sehr interessant. Tatsächlich habe ich erst in den letzten Jahren gemerkt, dass meine Kindheit in den frühen 1970er

Jahren mich sehr geprägt hat. Ich bin ja 1968 geboren und ging in antiautoritäre Kindergärten, in denen wir mit Schlamm spielen, Wände bemalen und nackt durch den Wald laufen durften. Meine Eltern haben sehr bewusst darüber nachgedacht und mit anderen diskutiert, wie sie unsere Erziehung angehen wollten, und ein Ziel war auf jeden Fall, uns zu freien Menschen zu machen, die in der Lage sind, gewaltfrei miteinander umzugehen. Die Frage nach einer idealen Gesellschaft stand selbst in unseren Kinderbüchern im Raum, etwa bei F. K. Waechter oder A. S. Neill. Außerdem haben wir uns viel verkleidet, meine Mutter drehte Super-8-Filme mit uns, und wir inszenierten kleine Theaterstücke und Fotogeschichten. Als ich über Masken *nachdachte, fielen mir diese Fotos wieder ein, und daraus ist dann das Buch* Teenage Pantomime *(2002) entstanden.*

Als wir später umzogen, vom Land in die Vorstadt, wurde ich sehr plötzlich zur grüblerischen Einzelgängerin, und erst beim Ausgehen und in den Freundschaften über zwanzig habe ich dieses Gemeinschaftsgefühl der Kindheit wiedergefunden. Nun sind aber die Freundschaften und die Liebe als junger Erwachsener eine komplizierte Angelegenheit. Dazu kam, dass ich damals Nietzsche, Barthes, Elias, Wittgenstein gelesen und mich viel mit Sozial- und Mentalitätsgeschichtsschreibung beschäftigt habe, die davon ausgeht, dass es eine objektive Beschreibung nicht geben kann, aber trotzdem auf dem mühsamen Sammeln von Belegen für die eigene Version besteht.[1] Daraus ergab sich für mich der Wunsch, nicht Kunst über die Unmöglichkeit einer Wahrheit (in der Darstellung von Wirklichkeit oder den Gesetzen des Mediums) zu machen, sondern selbst Wirklichkeiten zu schaffen, indem ich erst in Fotocollagen Szenen konstruierte, die sehr überzeugend wirkten, aber räumlich oder zeitlich verwirrend waren, dann innere Bilder mit Akteuren inszenierte und Fotos machte, die als Grundlage meiner gemalten Bilder dienten.

Der Zyklus L'invitation au voyage *(1999–2001) versucht, innere Zustände nicht symbolisch darzustellen, sondern zu evozieren. Ich merkte nach dem ersten Teil,* Freunde und Liebende *(1999), dass es mir nicht reichte, die Menschen nur von außen abzubilden. Die Gefühle wurden dann in den folgenden Bildern weniger verkörpert als „aufgeführt" oder „performt". Denn es sollte nicht um meine Gefühle der Welt gegenüber gehen, wie man sie durch die malerische Handschrift übermitteln kann, sondern um die Darstellung von etwas, das in der Welt und den anderen Menschen ist und das vor allem zwischen ihnen stattfindet.*

TW Lass uns doch bei dieser Frage der Aufführung ansetzen. Wie würdest du dieses Aufführen genau beschreiben, und welche Bedeutung hat es für dich, dass das in den Bildern Umgesetzte, seien es nun Gefühle oder bestimmte Konstellationen, ein an spezifisch historische, gesellschaftliche Entwürfe gerichtetes Begehren zwar evoziert und zugleich ins Jetzt wendet, von den dargestellten Personen aber gerade nicht verkörpert wird? Denn weder Verkörperung im Sinne einer restlos aufgehenden Identifikation noch (Selbst-)Verwirklichung scheinen mir in deinen Arbeiten aufgerufen zu werden. Vielmehr ist es gerade diese Schicht der Distanz, Entleerung, Aushöhlung und gleichzeitigen Neuaufladung, die für mich das Spannungsverhältnis in der Erfahrung der Arbeiten ausmacht.

Performen, das heißt für mich auch immer Übernahme, Übertragung etc., das macht eine Möglichkeit zur Verschiebung auf. Als Setzung einer nicht-identifikatorischen Geste gedacht, verlinkt sich dies mit einer Infragestellung von Selbstverwirklichung, wie dies in den Konzepten der 1960er Jahre mitunter gar zu idealistisch aufscheint. Mich interessiert demnach eine Position, wie sie Judith Butler entwirft, die in dieser Frage nach einer möglichen „Praxis der Freiheit" die Konstituierung eines Selbst durch Codes, Regeln, Normen etc., die uns vorausgehen und die uns mitbestimmen, nicht aus dem Blick verliert. Auch wenn die Formung des Selbst nie gänzlich durch dieses Feld der Normen bestimmt ist, diese reflektiert und befragt werden können. Butler spricht in diesem Zusammenhang mit Bezug auf Foucault von „so etwas wie einer ‚ursprünglichen Freiheit' [...]. Etwas Ähnliches, aber offensichtlich nicht ganz dasselbe"[2]. Gerade in diesem Sinne wird für mich auch das Nennen einer Verschiebung bei dir wichtig, im Rahmen einer Fiktion, einer Theatralik im anfangs angeführten Sinne usw. …

AM Das ist für mich sehr schwer zu formulieren, denn hier fragst du nach etwas, was sich gerade der Beschreibung, der festgelegten Bedeutung entziehen muss, was in einem anderen Gebiet stattfindet. Aber ich versuche es mal so: Für mich sehr wichtige Begriffe wie Freiheit und Glück können nicht zur Darstellung gebracht werden. Die Bilder mit ihren Akteuren können deshalb nur etwas aufführen. Ich kann es nur über das „Als-ob" erreichen, dass etwas für mich Undarstellbares zur Anschauung kommt. Das Undarstellbare hat mit dem „Außer-sich-Sein" zu tun, einem Zustand, der mich sehr interessiert. Das Eingesperrtsein im eigenen Körper, im einzelnen Kopf, in der Sterblichkeit finde ich schrecklich. Aber auch das in kulturellen Vereinbarungen, in einer Regelhaftigkeit, die immer vergisst, dass sie historisch veränderlich ist, in Identitätszuschreibungen. Indem ich Personen male, oder mit ihnen an einem Film arbeite, gerate ich selbst ein wenig „außer mir" – in das Kunstwerk hinein, in das sich wiederum die Betrachter „außer sich" begeben können. Und das geht am besten mit der Hilfe von Akteuren, die sich selbst „außer sich" setzen wollen. Das kann der Drag-Tänzer sein, aber auch ein Landstreicher, der sich selbst außerhalb der Gesellschaft setzt. Deshalb haben alle diejenigen meine Sympathie, die sich neue Personae zulegen, gerade auch in Bereichen, die niemals zur Hochkultur gehören werden, wie die Straßenmimin aus Video *(2001) und* My Very Gestures… Enchanted *(2001), die ihre Kunst so perfektioniert hat, dass sie ihre Augen minutenlang offenhalten kann. Am Anfang weint sie mit offenen Augen, dann „bleiben sie feucht". Das ist pathetisch, aber nur dieses Pathos scheint mir geeignet.*

TW Deine Ausführungen zur Straßenmimin finde ich interessant. Denn dieses Nichts, das hier aufgeführt wird – das Vermögen, die Augen offen zu lassen –, das zugleich jedoch den Körper bewegt, Affekte aufruft, als Pathos(-formel) erscheint, führt mich geradewegs zu Warhols frühen Filmarbeiten, und den *Screen Tests* (1964–66). Auch da wurde nichts dargestellt, sondern Potenzialität vorgeführt, etwa eines Antlitzes, einer Oberfläche, einer Maschine, aber auch von Gruppenverhältnissen. Über das Verhältnis der Elemente wie der Kräfte und der gleichzeitigen maximalen Reduktion zeigte sich dann

---

[1] *Anfangs interessierte mich die Geschichte der langen Zeiträume (die longue durées von Fernand Braudel und die Mentalitätsgeschichte von Philippe Ariès). Meinen Magister habe ich dann bei einem soliden deutschen Sozialgeschichtler gemacht, Jürgen Kocka.*

[2] Judith Butler, „Was ist Kritik? Ein Essay über Foucaults Tugend", http://eipcp.net/transversal/0806/butler/de.

größte Komplexität, gerade auch durch das Aufeinandertreffen der reinen Oberflächen und der querenden Affekte in der Zeit. Zudem wird bei Warhol die Gruppenkonstellation zu einem zentralen Produktionsfaktor. So entwarf sich die Möglichkeit, das Regelwerk Hollywoods ebenso zu reflektieren wie zeitgenössische künstlerische Setzungen, im Blick auf die Gruppe und Einzelne die Zirkulation des Begehrens und die Formierungen des Selbst in der kapitalistischen Maschine ebenso voranzutreiben wie aufzuzeichnen. Siehst du in Warhol auch einen möglichen Bezugspunkt?

*AM Ich habe gerade noch mal Warhols Bücher gelesen. Ich finde die Filme auch sehr lustig, es sind fast Slapstick-Ideen. Wenn zum Beispiel das Gesicht eines Mannes gefilmt wird, dem unsichtbar einer geblasen wird (*Blow Job*, 1964), dann gibt es eine Versuchsanordnung, die aber kein anderes Ziel hat, als dass man das sehen kann, was man gern sehen will. Oder* Sleep *(1963), bei dem er selbst erklärt, es hätte einfach niemand mehr geschlafen und deshalb habe er dieses merkwürdige Phänomen festhalten wollen. Man stellt sich dann vor, wie ein Haufen von Menschen auf Speed versucht, sich diesen Film anzuschauen. Oder eben ein Gebäude zu filmen, das sich ja nicht bewegen kann. Diese Art von scharfem Witz – scharf, weil er eigentlich ganz banal ist – finde ich auch bei Duchamp. Bei mir wären das Metallhunde, die durchs Gemaltwerden lebendig aussehen, weil die echten Hunde kein Fell haben (*Xoloitzcuintles*, 2005), oder ein riesiger Motor, der ein unbeweglicher Gegenstand ist, aber gemacht wurde, um Dinge in Bewegung zu setzen. Und auf dem Bild natürlich schon vom Medium her unbeweglich sein muss (*Motor*, 2007). Die Eigenschaften meines Mediums werden hier sozusagen in einer eleganten Geste vorgeführt, wie bei Duchamps Readymade Aidé* À bruit secret *von 1916 – als reiche Hülle für einen unsichtbaren, nur vom Betrachter zu erzeugenden Inhalt. Bei mir ist alles gleichzeitig ernst, fast pathetisch, was aber die Kunst angeht, auch sehr tongue-in-cheek. Dabei ist die Mimin, die sich als Statue inszeniert, die Umkehrung des toten Steins, der angeblich lebendige Energie enthält (*Rare Desert Stone, 2005).*

TW Ich denke im Blick auf deine Arbeit aber auch an Agambens Passagen zur Geste, die er als Raum der Potenzialität, aber auch als eine Figur der Übernahme beschreibt, als ein Vorführen der Mittelbarkeit. Er spricht in diesem Zusammenhang Mallarmé zitierend von der Pantomime als dem, was die vertrautesten Gesten in der Vorführung fremd werden lässt und so in der Schwebe bleibt zwischen „dem Wunsch und der Erfüllung, der Ausübung und der Erinnerung daran"[3]. Diese pantomimische Qualität scheint mir auch in deinen späteren Filmen aufzuscheinen. Auch hier fällt das Zueinandertreten des Alltäglichen, Vertrauten mit dem zwecklosen und zugleich in einer außerordentlichen Bewegung Dargebrachten auf. So etwa die Bewegungen in *No School Today* (2005), die zwischen „Potenz und Akt" und irgendwo zwischen Alltagsverrichtung, Spiel, Tanz und Kampfsport liegen. Wobei das, was ich hier Tanz nenne, durch die unglaubliche Verlangsamung und die kriechende Bewegung eher als Potenzial des Körpers erscheint, als Eindämmung ebenso wie als Experimentieren mit neuen Möglichkeiten. Was meint diese sprachlose Theatralität für dich?

[3]Giorgio Agamben, „Noten zur Geste", in ders., *Mittel ohne Zweck. Noten zur Politik*, Freiburg/Berlin 2001, S. 53–62, hier S. 61.

AM Die Formulierung von Agamben ist so präzise, wie sie sein kann, wenn man etwas Unbeschreibbares beschreiben möchte. Das Problem ist ja, dass es in dem Moment in sich zusammenfallen würde, in dem es mittelbar wird im Sinn einer Festschreibung, eines Signifikanten oder einer Narration. Deshalb ist auch Pantomime, die Alltag bedeutet – nur ohne die benutzten Gegenstände –, für mich völlig uninteressant. Die Mimin, mit der ich gearbeitet habe, war die Einzige, die mir je auf der Straße aufgefallen ist, weil sie so absurd gut war in ihrer nichts darstellenden Darbietung. Ich interessiere mich für Tänze, die pantomimische Elemente verwenden und in so eine Art präzise Ekstase drehen, wie frühen Breakdance oder Krumping oder M'Balax. Aber natürlich auch für Parkour. Es ist notwendig, dass die Bilder selbst nicht ekstatisch sind, sondern die Ekstase vorführen, so wie auch diese Tänzer erst mit einer großen Präzision und Meisterschaft in den Bewegungen dahin kommen, außer sich zu geraten. Und diese große Meisterschaft erlangen sie, indem sie unglaublich viel Arbeit und Energie in etwas stecken, das keine Ware, nicht einmal einen kulturellen Mehrwert produziert. Im modernen Tanz kenne ich nur sehr wenig, was in die Richtung geht, vielleicht Wayne McGregor. Ich bin sehr schnell gelangweilt, wenn ich merke, dass man mir mit all den Bewegungen und Gesten nur etwas mitteilen will, was ich längst kenne.
In meinen Filmen wird zunächst einfach nur etwas anders gemacht. Dieses Andere kann keinen Zweck oder ein Ziel haben, sonst wäre es doch wieder nur dasselbe. Und es muss in ganz spezifischen Umgebungen stattfinden. Nur in Tanz RGBCMYK *(2007–08) werden einfach die Elementarfarben durch Tänzer auf einer leeren dunklen Bühne zur Aufführung gebracht, ich möchte die Bilder aber mit* Rausch *(2008) zeigen, einem Film, in dem in dem sehr realen Club Basso in Berlin-Kreuzberg ekstatisch getanzt wird.*
Die Bilder und Filme sind Träger oder Fahrzeuge, ähnlich wie im Vodoun Menschen von den Göttern geritten werden. Für mich gibt es keine Götter und nichts, was man von ihnen erbitten kann. Trotzdem habe ich das Gefühl, einen Bereich aufzurufen, in dem ich mich nicht allein befinde. Die Darstellung durch Akteure ist wie das Anrufen eines Namens, von dem man nicht weiß, welches Wesen er benennt. Und die Anrufung muss in einer Ecke des Wohnzimmers stattfinden oder auf der Straße, nicht in einer Kirche. Sie muss auch gewissen Gesetzen gehorchen. Sie weiß aber eigentlich, dass sie ins Leere zielt, denn da ist nichts weiter. Nur das, was wir uns schaffen. Vielleicht kommt daher dein Gefühl der Fremdheit, denn eigentlich gibt es keinerlei Versprechen.

TW Dieses Als-ob führt mich nun zu einer etwas anders ausgerichteten Frage. Was ermöglicht die fotorealistische Tradition in der Malerei für dich? Mit diesem Begriff des Fotorealismus versuche ich Folgendes zusammenzubringen: dass du dich einerseits einem gewissen Realismus in der Malerei verschrieben hast und zugleich wiederholt ein Foto als Grundlage, Referenz einen wichtigen Stellenwert einnimmt. Dabei interessiert mich die Doppelung – das vorausgehende Foto ist immer auch schon ein entworfener Blick, Festhalten einer möglichen Konstellation von Elementen, die jedoch auch noch mal demontiert und neu zusammengestellt werden können, bevor sie dann in spezifischer Differenz in der Malerei wiederkehren. Zugleich legt sich diese Schicht des Fotografischen in die Malerei gewissermaßen hinein, die wiederum die Elemente des Realen quasi durchbrechen lässt, so zu einer Art Riss führt.
Ich denke, da wäre es auch nötig, diesen Begriff des Realismus nochmal genauer zu fassen. Hal Foster etwa versucht, den Begriff des Realen

an Lacans Ausführungen zum Traumatischen anzulegen.[4] Von dieser Bezugnahme ausgehend, versteht er Superrealismus letztlich auch in Bezug zum Surrealismus und zu einer Aufnahme photographischer Elemente in der Appropriation Art und differenziert deren divergierende Verhältnisse zum Realen aus. Dabei wird etwa die Entscheidung für ein Feiern und/oder Befragen bzw. Ausstellen von Illusionismus wichtig, Fragen von Derealisierung, die Attraktion von Oberflächen etc. Wie würdest du diesen Begriff des Realismus im Rahmen deiner Arbeit verstehen?

AM Ich arbeite sowohl bei den Bildern wie bei den Filmen mit Menschen zusammen, denen ich viel Freiheit lasse. Ich habe zwar oft Bilder im Kopf, aber sie verändern sich, während andere daran mitwirken. Das geht so weit, dass ich in Dekonditionierung *(2007–08) die Darsteller gebeten habe, jeden Tag nur einer Verhaltensvorgabe zu folgen, sonst völlig frei zu improvisieren. Es folgen aber sehr lange Zeiten des Schnitts oder der Malerei, in denen ich das zum Vorschein bringe, was einerseits bei meinen Darstellern passiert ist, was ich aber auch sehen will. Da mich diese Menschen interessieren, scheint es mir sinnlos, sie zusätzlich zu verfremden.*

Mein Blick ist natürlich wie in unserer Kultur allgemein von Filmen, von Fotos geprägt. Ich glaube zudem, dass auch die Malerei, der ich bestimmte Anspielungen entlehne, bereits vom Blick durch optische Medien bestimmt war. In den letzten Jahren habe ich aber begonnen, mich in der Malerei auch für verschobene Perspektiven und für eine bestimmte Art von Handschrift zu interessieren, die das Bild etwas pulsieren lässt. Das heißt aber nicht, dass mir das „natürlicher" vorkommt als der Blick durch die Linse. Mal de ojo *(2005) habe ich deshalb so genannt, weil ich den bösen Blick wie das Augenweh meinte. Die Bilder wirken traditionalistisch, sind aber malerisch wie inhaltlich eigentlich auf eine Art verstört, die mich sehr freut. In dieser Serie wie auch in* The Royal Mummies *(2006) geht es auch sehr um die Frage der Zeitlosigkeit, um die merkwürdige Möglichkeit, mit Kunstwerken Vehikel zu schaffen, die über lange Zeiträume hinweg etwas transportieren können, das die Betrachter als lebendig empfinden, obwohl es selbstverständlich nur tote Materie ist.*

Ich habe mich immer als „Realistin" bezeichnet, würde aber das Wort verwenden wie Pier Paolo Pasolini, der es gegen „Naturalismus" absetzt. Für ihn ist der Film ein Zeichensystem, in dem die Wirklichkeit sich selbst bedeutet. Ein Baum „spielt" einen Baum. Dadurch, dass er das in einem Zusammenhang tut, dass er ein „Kinem" wird, wird es möglich, ihn so zu sehen, als „spräche" die Wirklichkeit (oder nach Pasolini Gott) durch ihn.

Pasolinis große Trauer über das Vergehen der alten Kulturen kann man traditionalistisch nennen, sie scheint auch im Widerspruch zu seinem Marxismus zu stehen. Möglicherweise sehnte er sich eigentlich nach dem „Zeitalter der Ähnlichkeit" (Foucault), in dem jeder Gegenstand eine heilige Bedeutung haben konnte. Diese Sehnsucht entspringt dem Erstaunen, dem Erschrecken über die Existenz all dieser Dinge und Menschen, und die Trauer darüber, dass sie gleich wieder vergangen sein werden. Könnten sie alle zu Bedeutung gebracht werden – so, dass sie „sich selbst" bedeuten – könnte der Prozess der Vergänglichkeit gestoppt werden. Ähnliches sehe ich bei Hubert Fichte oder anders bei Yasushi Inoue: die Suche nach einer möglichen komplexen Sprache nicht „über" die Wirklichkeit, sondern „durch" sie. Daraus entspringt eine gewisse Detailbesessenheit, denn ohne die Details kann nicht gesprochen werden.

---

[4] Siehe Hal Foster, „The Return of the Real", in ders., *The Return of the Real. The Avant-Garde at the End of the Century*. Massachusetts 1996, S. 127–168.

Rausch

In *Rausch* finden sich KünstlerInnen und ihre FreundInnen im Basso, einem von Yusuf Etiman geleiteten Club in Berlin-Kreuzberg, zusammen, um möglichst wild zu tanzen. So bildet sich für ein paar Stunden eine gemeinsame Ausdrucksform, bevor alle wieder zu ihrer spezialisierten und oft allein verrichteten Arbeit zurückkehren. Unklar bleibt, ob der Rausch durch konsumierte Rauschmittel oder durch das Tanzen zu der von Arises für den Abend komponierten Musik, einem Post-Rave-Stück, entsteht. In allen Kulturen gibt es Gelegenheiten für Menschen, zusammenzukommen und gemeinsam zu tanzen, oft bis zum Rausch. Meist werden zusätzlich Rauschmittel konsumiert, vom Bier bis zum Peyotekaktus. In unserer Kultur bilden die Musik, der Ort und die Kleidung der Tanzenden selbst den kulturellen Anlass für den Rausch.

Der Film wird in einer Holzkonstruktion gezeigt, die einem Megafon ähnelt und in den Primärfarben RGB und CMYK gestrichen ist.

A.M.

I would like to thank all of the actors, models, dancers, and team members that have participated in my paintings, films, and dance theater pieces; as well as Charles Asprey, Judith Banham, Elke aus dem Moore, Monica de Cardenas, Sebastian Cichocki, Dominic Eichler, Yusuf Etiman, Heike Föll, Sarah Gläsner, Tatjana Günthner, Melvyn Harrison and the Crystal Palace Foundation, Dani Jakob, Gregor Jansen, Stefan Joachim, Ingo Keller, Jan Kern, John Kutolowski, Ulrike Kuschel, Michaela Lederer, Patricia Lewandowska, Helga Liebe, Martine Maffetti, Brigitte Majewski, Ulrike Majewski, Christiane Mennicke, Tim Neuger, Peter Pakesch, Nana A. T. Rebhan, Joachim Reck, Burkhard Riemschneider, Bettina Schoeller, Tanja Widmann, Katrin Vellrath (Arises), Elmar Vestner, Elfrid Wimmer-Repp, Claire Rose, Susanne Weiß, Tomasz Wygoda, Amy Patton, Stefanie Peters, Florian Seedorf, Hemma Schmutz, Heji Shin, Simona Thalheimer, Ma Yingli, Jens Ziehe; especially Juliane Solmsdorf; and always, Ingo Niermann.   *A.M.*

This publication was made possible by the generous support of neugerriemschneider and **i f a** Institut für Auslandsbeziehungen e. V.

Photo Credits

Plates
p 18/19 photo: Andrew Phelps, p 35 postcards: Crystal Palace Foundation, p 38/39 photo: Andrew Phelps, p 53-55 photo: Sebastian Bolesch, p 56/57 photo: Andrew Phelps, p 73 photo: David Brandt, p 78 photo: Andrew Phelps, p 81, 83, 84/85 photo: Andrew Phelps, p 96 photo: Antje Majewski

Small Images
Dominic Eichler: Out of the Ordinary
My Very Gestures... Enchanted (2001); *Skarbek* (2005), photo: Sebastian Bolesch; *Liebling* (2000); *Erde Asphalt Wedding* (2007), still image; installation view of *Crystal Palace and the Dinosaurs* at Asprey Jacques Gallery (2003); *Pastiche* (2000); Marie Bashkirtseff, author unknown, wikimedia; Rosa Bonheur, c. 1880, © Pierson—Hulton Archive/Getty Images; Sylvia Sleigh, photo: Antje Majewski; *Masquerade* (2006); *Rausch* (2008), still image; *Dekonditionierung* (2008), still image

Ingo Niermann: What Is with the People?
Video. Antje's Photos (2001); Antje Majewski & Juliane Solmsdorf: *Bridge* (2006); *Bergsteiger 1* (1998); *Venus* (1997); *Dekonditionierung* (2008), still image; *Säule Wedding* (2008) photo: Andrew Phelps

À bruit secret: Tanja Widmann in Conversation with Antje Majewski
Masken (2001); *Huckepack* (2000); cover of *Teenage Pantomime* (2002); *Im Wasserfall* (1995–97); *Ute und Doreen* (1999); *Streife* (1999); *Landstreicher* (1999); *My Very Gestures… Enchanted* (2001); Andy Warhol, *Screen Test: Ingrid Superstar* (1966), photo: The Andy Warhol Museum, Pittsburgh, PA, a Carnegie Institute museum; Andy Warhol, *Blowjob* (1963), photo: The Andy Warhol Museum, Pittsburgh, PA, a Carnegie Institute museum; Marcel Duchamp, *À bruit secret*, © 2001 Succession Marcel Duchamp, ARS, N.Y. / ADAGP, Paris; *No School Today* (2005), still image; *Parkour*, photo: Marco Marenco; Random Dance Company Members in press photos for AtaXia, photo: Ravi Deepres; *Rausch* (2008), still image; *Vodoun*, source unknown; *Dekonditionierung* (2008), still image; *Queen Notmit* (2006); Pier Paolo Pasolini, acting in *Canterbury Tales* (1972); 7.8.1960: *Hubert Fichte in Montjustin*, photo: Christian von Alvensleben

This page: Antje und Ulrike als Mexikanerin und Zauberin, photo: Brigitte Majewski; The Masquerade Palace, flyer, Mexico

Unless otherwise indicated, photos by Jens Ziehe

Antje Majewski
My Very Gestures

Publisher: Sternberg Press

This catalogue was published on the occasion of the exhibition Antje Majewski. *My Very Gestures*
at the Salzburger Kunstverein, September 25 – November 30, 2008.

Exhibition
Curator: Hemma Schmutz
Communication Manager: Michaela Lederer
Exhibition Production: Simona Thalhamer
Exhibition Installation: Jon Kutolowski
Front Office: Susanne Knauseder

Catalogue
Editors: Hemma Schmutz, Caroline Schneider
Editorial work: Tatjana Günthner
Translation: Olaf Kühl (Sebastian Cichocki, Polish-German),
Antje Majewski (Dominic Eichler, English-German), Amy Patton (Ingo Niermann, Tanja Widmann,
and short texts, German-English), Marcin Wawrzynczak (Sebastian Cichocki, Polish-English)
Proofreading: Signe Bergstrom, Sabine Grimm
Graphic design: Judith Banham / Middlecott
Typeface: Adhesive Black, Baskerville
Paper: ProfiSilk 170 g/m²
Reproductions: bildpunkt GmbH, Berlin
Printing and binding: Medialis Offsetdruck GmbH, Berlin

ISBN 978-1-933128-56-6 (Sternberg Press)
ISBN 978-3-901264-39-9 (Salzburger Kunstverein)

Salzburger Kunstverein
Hellbrunner Straße 3
A-5020 Salzburg
www.salzburger-kunstverein.at

Sternberg Press
Caroline Schneider
Karl-Marx-Allee 78, D-10243 Berlin
1182 Broadway #1602, New York NY 10001
www.sternberg-press.com